Creating Value in a Regulated World

Creating Value in a Regulated World

CFO Perspectives

CEDRIC READ

John Wiley & Sons, Ltd

Published by John Wiley & Sons Ltd, The Atrium, Southern Gate, Chichester, West Sussex PO19 8SQ, England
Telephone (+44) 1243 779777

Email (for orders and customer service enquiries): cs-books@wiley.co.uk
Visit our Home Page on www.wiley.com

Other Wiley Editorial Offices
John Wiley & Sons Inc., 111 River Street, Hoboken, NJ 07030, USA
Jossey-Bass, 989 Market Street, San Francisco, CA 94103-1741, USA
Wiley-VCH Verlag GmbH, Boschstr. 12, D-69469 Weinheim, Germany
John Wiley & Sons Australia Ltd, 42 McDougall Street, Milton, Queensland 4064, Australia
John Wiley & Sons (Asia) Pte Ltd, 2 Clementi Loop #02-01, Jin Xing Distripark, Singapore 129809
John Wiley & Sons Canada Ltd, 22 Worcester Road, Etobicoke, Ontario, Canada M9W 1L1
Wiley also publishes its books in a variety of electronic formats. Some content that appears in print may
not be available in electronic books.

Library of Congress Cataloging-in-Publication Data

Read, Cedric.
  Creating Value in a Regulated World: CFO Perspectives / Cedric Read.
    p. cm.
  Includes index.
  ISBN-13: 978-0-470-01353-3
  ISBN-10: 0-470-01353-2
  1. Corporations—Finance. 2. Corporations—Finance—Law and legislation.
  3. Corporate governance. I. Title.
  HG4011.R35 2006
  658.15'5—dc22

                                                                                2006020353

British Library Cataloguing in Publication Data

A catalogue record for this book is available from the British Library

ISBN-13: 978-0-470-01353-3
ISBN-10: 0-470-01353-2

Typeset in 11/13pt Rotis by Sparks, Oxford – www.sparks.co.uk
Printed and bound in Spain by Grafos SA, Barcelona
This book is printed on acid-free paper responsibly manufactured from sustainable forestry in which at
least two trees are planted for each one used for paper production.

Preface

This book is appearing at a time when two factors are reshaping the CFO's role. On the one hand, it is being written against a backdrop of vigorous expansion: companies have survived the dot-com bust and weathered major reputational scandals; today, they are enjoying strong profits, investing heavily in innovation, and looking outward to vibrant new markets like India and China. And on the other hand, regulatory burdens, both in-country and international, have increased exponentially. The intensity of these two converging forces is unprecedented. At a time when business horizons are broadening, regulatory pressures threaten to seriously impede – or even stifle – corporate growth.

One CFO referred to this dual challenge as riding a "two-headed monster." The image seems apt. It raises a question at the heart of this book: How can CFOs simultaneously help their companies grow and innovate while effectively managing the regulatory pressures they face? How can they pursue the tremendous opportunities for expansion currently on the horizon while keeping a handle on complexity?

The search for answers to these questions led to a two-and-a-half year independent research program. During this period, more than 200 CFO dinners were held in virtually every major city in the United States, Europe, Canada, South America, and Asia. In all, more than 1400 CFOs and senior finance executives attended these events. The goal of these discussions has been to share ideas and experiences while also creating productive cross-industry exchanges.

Out of this program, a more focused forum emerged: the Value Network Initiative (VNI). The VNI was initiated when a small group of executives from leading companies like Unilever, GlaxoSmithKline, and Diageo decided to meet together on a regular basis to discuss specific projects and initiatives centered on the issues raised in this book. The

VNI brought many of the companies featured in its pages together in New York, London, and Frankfurt several times a year to track their progress and compare notes. In one sense, *Creating Value in a Regulated World* is a frontline report on the issues raised and the results generated by members of the VNI.

As discussions and research for *Creating Value in a Regulated World* progressed, it became clear that CFOs today are becoming more and more central to their companies' broader economic agendas for promoting growth and innovation. Companies are beginning to appreciate as never before the role of finance in understanding and pulling the levers of value creation. The role of the CFO, not just in finance support but also in business strategy and partnering, is seen as increasingly critical to corporate profitability.

At the same time, spirited exchanges by members of the VNI and other senior finance executives highlighted a number of issues that CFOs around the world are grappling with. At the top of their agendas are:

Meeting the twin challenge: coping with increasing regulation while pursuing growth and innovation. Throughout this book, we address this central theme from many perspectives, exploring the creative ways in which the CFOs of leading companies are leveraging regulations to actually enhance performance while nurturing business innovation and expansion.

Identifying new structural models: managing the increased emphasis on control and regulation. We examine the steps that outstanding CFOs are taking to ensure enterprise-wide accountability while optimizing processes and reducing complexity. We also look at the vital part that CFOs are playing as change agents, whatever their companies' starting points are on the road to transformation.

Managing the drivers of value creation: pulling value levers in a regulated world. Key chapters focus on the pivotal role of the CFO in releasing intangible value, fostering innovation, harnessing new, forward-looking financial disciplines, and fostering a business partnering culture.

Focusing on the future: reshaping the ways that world-class companies conduct their businesses. Here, we explore the impact of global connectivity, evolving approaches to risk management, and the emerging link between shareholder value and corporate responsibility.

Creating Value in a Regulated World delivers exactly what its title suggests. The book is built around richly informative interviews with senior finance executives at more than 35 of the world's best-run companies, from GE and Procter & Gamble to BP and Philips. Through their detailed descriptions of their strategies and best practices, you'll gain first-hand insight into how global leaders are responding to the biggest, most challenging issues on the finance agenda. The goal is to motivate you to manage regulatory and reporting demands successfully, while energetically pulling all the value creation levers at your command.

Acknowledgments

This book has been two years in the making. It was inspired, in large part, by the insights and support of the Value Network Initiative – and many of its talented members are interviewed in its pages. I am deeply appreciative of the time and thought that these outstanding executives contributed. I also wish to thank the scores of executives who offered ideas and war stories at our globe-circling CFO dinners:

Chapter 1

- Bjorn Bergabo of GE, Hannu Ryopponen of Ahold, Dudley Eustace of Aegon, Jan Hommen of Philips, Nick Rose of Diageo, Jos Nijhuis of PwC Netherlands.

Chapter 2

- Maurice Oostendorp of ABN, Iain Macdonald of BP, Wolfgang Reichenberger of Nestlé, Philip Yea of 3i.

Chapter 3

- Paolo Fietta of Parmalat, Mark Hunter of Axon, Sir Peter Gershon of Premier Farnell, Stephen Jones of HMRC, Thomas Buess of Zurich Financial Services.

Chapter 4

- Dr Kurt Bock of BASF, Rolf-Dieter Schwalb of Beiersdorf, Simon Richards of E.ON, Margherita Della Valle of Vodafone, Juan Carlos Stotz of Siemens, Martin Scholich, and Jutta Menninger of PwC Germany.

Chapter 5

- Thorsten Knopp of Diageo, Clayton Daley and Wade Miquelon of P&G.

Chapter 6

- Jeff Baxter and Paul Fry of GlaxoSmithKline, Michael Coveney and Donna De Winter, Doug Norton-Bilsby of Extensity.

Chapter 7

- John Ripley, Paul Baumann and David Calle of Unilever.

Chapter 8

- Thierry Moulonguet of Renault, Colin Sampson and Peter David of SAP, Ray Joy of Diageo, Paul Hart and Alan Broomhead of Microsoft.

Chapter 9

- Santiago Fernandez-Valbuena of Telefonica, Helen Weir of LloydsTSB, Philip Broadley of Prudential, Michael Sproule of New York Life, Jesus Diaz de la Hoz of PwC Spain.

Chapter 10

- Angus Russell of Shire Pharmaceuticals, Mads Ovlisen of Novo Nordisk, Per Mansson of Novozymes, Thorlief Krarup of TDC, Helle Bank Jorgensen of PwC Denmark and the Good Business Ethics and Non-Financial Reporting Initiative (NVIR), Leo Martin of GoodCorporation.

I also wish to give special acknowledgment to our external advisors and contributors and to the team that helped put this publication together. Special thanks go to Christy Kirkpatrick, who produced the diagrams; to Emily Hayes, who took most of the workload in typing the manuscript; and to the entire team at CCR Partners, who worked tirelessly over many weekends on this project. This book would not have been completed without their help. Finally, thanks also go to our editor Karin Abarbanel, and the team at John Wiley, especially Rachael Wilkie and Chris Swain.

– Cedric Read

Contents

CHAPTER 1

Today's Challenges, Tomorrow's Aspirations

What a difference a few years makes! After tremendous upheaval and uncertainty, the corporate world has restored its reputation and is eager once again to take advantage of the opportunities presented by changing global dynamics. World markets are opening up as never before. India and China are having a massive impact. And major players in every industry sector are moving aggressively to reap the benefits of brand and scale.

It's now more than three years since a series of major financial scandals rocked the capital markets. Companies in the US such as Enron, WorldCom, Tyco, and even Arthur Andersen, started the ball rolling. In Europe, problems at Ahold, Parmalat, and Shell continued the trend. The world's regulators responded; some would say they overreacted. But on mature reflection, the prevailing view coming through from leaders of the world's top corporations is surprisingly positive!

What's the feedback from CFOs on the front line? Smaller companies may view the regulatory burden as intolerable. Others may believe that many well-run and responsible companies are being penalized for the mistakes of the few. And in many respects, the regulation and standards are too detailed, too complicated, and often confusing. Nevertheless, some larger companies believe that the new regulations have actually done them some good; secretly they may even feel that they strengthen their dominant positions and reinforce their barriers to entry.

Undeniably, the fresh emphasis on corporate governance has been beneficial – and proven to be a much needed shot in the corporate arm. Despite all the controversy surrounding the new regulations and accounting standards, there is now a far greater awareness of both an individual's responsibilities and a corporation's liabilities. And this is all to the good: it's brought new rigor and more transparency to businesses worldwide.

How are leading companies responding? And how are the roles of the CFO and the finance function changing as a result? Even with their preoccupation with regulation, transparency, and accountability, we are seeing a greater appreciation among CFOs of their vital role in value creation.

In the corporation as a whole, in fact, the roles of the CFO and Controller have undergone a step-change in importance. Chairmen, senior non-executive directors (NEDs), and CEOs of leading companies are more involved than ever before in the CFO's world: corporate governance, control, and risk are all very high on their agendas. So, too, are the escalating demands of investors and regulators who are setting higher standards, changing accounting rules, and requiring more and more information. Underpinning all this change is the need for "business as usual" – to meet the needs of the customer, to beat the competition, to grow shareholder value, and to innovate.

Every CFO we've interviewed aspires to similar goals. What differentiates them is their starting point. In this first chapter, we provide an overview of key issues addressed throughout this book. First, we look at how GE's finance function is supporting its innovation edge. Then we explore how senior finance executives at companies such as Ahold and Parmalat have assisted in the recovery from accounting scandals. We offer the views of a leading chairman on the impact of changes in governance and regulation. We go on to show how the CFOs of companies such as Philips and Diageo are making change happen from a position of maturity and leadership in their sectors. The chapter concludes with an introduction to the remainder of the book – the value creation agenda for the future.

We start with an in-depth interview on how GE tackles the twin-challenges, the "*two-headed monster*": regulation and innovation.

RIDING THE TWO-HEADED MONSTER

GE is among a select group of companies widely recognized as best-practice leaders in finance. It's also one of the most admired corporations in the world. How does the finance function help GE sustain its financial performance, maintain its world-class reputation, cope with never-ending regulation, and keep tight control over what is arguably the largest, most diverse global industrial enterprise? We begin with an interview with Bjorn Bergabo, a CFO in the GE Commercial Finance division.

BALANCING GROWTH WITH CONTROL
Bjorn Bergabo, CFO GE Commercial Finance, Corporate Financial Services Europe, General Electric Company (and extracts from the GE 2004 Annual Report)

GE is one of the largest, most respected and sustainable companies in the world. Revenues in 2004 exceeded $150 billion, earnings grew to $17 billion, and the company remained one of only six "Triple A" rated US industrials. Our shares trade at a premium, as an industrial multinational because GE inspires investor confidence – in terms of growth, high return on equity, and low overall risk.

Marketing and Innovation
GE recently launched a process for innovation called "Imagination Breakthroughs" (IBs), designed to apply GE rigor to the creation of products and services. Each IB project has the potential for at least $100 million in incremental growth. Today, the company has 80 IBs; some may happen soon, others make take ten years to reach full maturity, and still others may not fly at all.

While delivering a total shareholder return of 21%, GE was still able to invest $13 billion in further strengthening its intellectual foundation. We've also announced a new company-wide initiative called "ecomagination." GE has committed itself to reducing greenhouse gases and to making the environmental consequences of its work more transparent. As a company, we're focusing on inventing green technology and on doubling green research spending to develop new products and services.

Over the last few years, GE has undergone a transformation – reinventing itself in order to stay aligned with customers and markets as they've evolved. We have eleven key businesses, including Healthcare, NBC Universal, Infrastructure, Consumer and Industrial, Consumer Finance, and Commercial Finance. In each business, GE provides sufficient information to ensure transparency externally and convey internally its relationship to growth, returns, and investment.

GE's value proposition for business partners and customers is based on the following principles:

- *Best practice sharing: access to proven game-changing tools for leadership development, acquisition integration, and organizational change acceleration.*
- *Six Sigma and Lean Six Sigma: the opportunity to learn and own the Six Sigma methodology used for statistical process analysis, methodology training, and project support.*
- *Business solutions: partners and customers can leverage GE's industry breadth and balance sheet in a variety of sectors, ranging from healthcare and aviation to transportation and automotive.*
- *GE as a channel: GE can be sold to (as a customer) and through (as a channel).*

Role of the CFO

When Jeff Immelt, Chairman and CEO, recently discussed the "role of today's CFO," he emphasized:

- *Ensuring the foundation of integrity: this requires rigorous oversight and sustainable controllership.*
- *Building the systems of accountability: a constant drive to identify and manage both risks and opportunities requiring strong capabilities in financial planning and analysis.*
- *Helping to create a new future: developing business leaders and promoting winning business models.*

Keith Sherin, GE's Group CFO, set out the challenge recently for the finance function: "To remain good business partners, given the increasing focus on controllership." It's the dichotomy between these two roles that companies like GE must reconcile.

Finance as business partners

Finance at GE's Corporate Financial Services division has a dual role – business partnership and controllership. As business partners, they have to bring finance knowledge to complement the expertise of other players. As team players in finance, they meet commitments of the business.

We're involved in leading business initiatives to grow the business and champion quality. As controllers, we need to ensure compliance.

At GE Commercial Finance, we pride ourselves on being one of the world's leading corporate lending businesses – and one of the largest growth engines of GE. Our five major business units focus on customers in areas ranging from fleet to real estate to equipment financing and corporate financial services.

In Corporate Financial Services Europe, we have to stay close to our CEOs to support them. At the same time, we have to provide even better controllership, even more rigor, and even better systems. My role is to support our infrastructure, while also looking forward to see where the business is headed. It's also my job to understand our options and to ensure that we have the right value propositions for the future.

Connectivity with reality of operations

We believe that finance occupies a unique position in the organization: no other function has the same deep involvement across all business issues. All operational activities are ultimately expressed in financial terms. We leverage our organizational positioning to improve results by:

- *Knowing how the individual moving parts translate into results.*
- *Knowing how each moving part affects the others.*
- *Changing operational behaviors to improve performance.*

Generally speaking, CFOs at GE act as operating managers. As a result, we're in a strong position to connect strategy and operations. Finance is a language for expressing performance. Consequently, finance has a lot of power.

Consistency in delivery and execution is a constant mantra. Looking backwards and evaluating performance is vital in keeping the business under control. This is essentially tactical. However, there is a strong emphasis in finance at GE on strategy – focusing not just on the next quarter, but on the next two to three years. Understanding strategic choices from a financial perspective is essential.

How do I spend my time as a CFO in GE's Corporate Financial Services team?

- *1/3 on the past (compliance and controllership);*
- *1/3 on the future (business partnership and global mindset);*
- *1/3 on our people (personal performance and career development).*

The approach to finance at GE is summarized in Figure 1.1.

What binds all this together is a distinctive set of shared values, such as having an external focus, being a clear thinker and inclusive leader – we can achieve better results when everyone is pulling in the same direction. We can combine domain expertise – for example industry specialization – with cross-functional capability. This is where the finance function plays a vital role. Corporate Financial Services provides a wide spectrum of business activities and uniformity is key – there is a strong cultural unity among the people and strong processes, which go right across the company.

Operating rhythm

The GE operating rhythm is the glue across the group and it supports a set of standardized GE business processes. The reviews that occur throughout the year drive GE's success. These reviews range from our three-year strategic outlook to our annual operating plan, from our quarterly short-range outlook to monthly CEO reports and weekly CFO evaluations of operations and cash.

In GE's Corporate Financial Services business, finance executives are constantly "managing" the future. The finance function does not just produce forecasts – it is also held accountable for them. I own the numbers. Although I cannot guarantee certainties, when I produce a forecast, I have to live with it! I need to plan for contingencies: what could happen and what my actions would be. I don't wait until the end

Figure 1.1   *Finance in GE*

of the quarter to report on deviation from plan – I have weekly updates. I work with management in the short term to decide what we need to do to follow our strategic intent.

Corporate audit and controls
There have always been strong reporting lines and accountability for results within the finance function at GE. We're involved in technical and operational controls, as well as financial. Corporate audit, with a staff of 400, is a prominent management presence across GE. Most of our senior finance executives have been through the corporate audit function. We spend more time auditing our financials than ever before to make sure that our controls are even better than they were before. We divide controls into three categories:

- *Technical controls – a focus on integrity; ensuring we comply with policies, maximize returns on invested capital, and safeguard assets.*
- *Operations controls – ensuring quality processes; integrating, standardizing, and taking advantage of our Lean Six Sigma approach to process streamlining.*
- *Disclosure controls – creating credible communications; basing our external and internal reporting on reliable metrics, forecasts, reporting, and analysis.*

We take a very process-driven approach to external compliance requirements: converting and merging them with GE standards; implementing rigorously; and disclosing to external stakeholders consistent, accurate information. As illustrated in Figure 1.2, we have what we call a "controllership value chain."

All accounting requirements – US GAAP, local country GAAPs, and our management results – are managed through one set of systems. As a result, they are fully integrated and consistent – and there is no need for additional adjustments.

The future
Looking forwards, Jeff Immelt, Chairman and CEO, speaks in his 2004 Annual report about a generation of growth leaders: "We've studied great growth businesses at GE and across the world – and our leaders are being trained and evaluated against five capabilities. They must:

- *Create an external focus that defines success in market terms.*

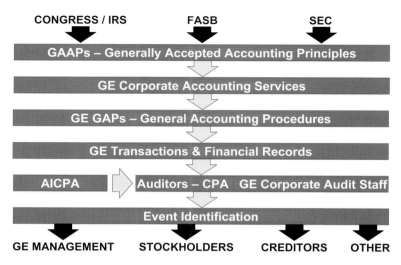

Figure 1.2 *GE controllership value chain*

- *Be clear thinkers who can simplify strategy into specific actions.*
- *Have the imagination and courage to take risks on people and ideas.*
- *Energize teams through inclusiveness and connection with people, building both loyalty and commitment.*
- *Develop expertise in a function or domain using depth as a source of confidence to drive change."*

Jeff goes on to comment in GE's annual report on Sarbanes-Oxley: "None of us likes more regulation, but I actually think SOX 404 is helpful. It takes the process control discipline we use in our factories and applies it to our financial statements. At GE, we embed governance and integrity in the operating culture. High standards facilitate growth. They are not a burden."

Undoubtedly GE's emphasis on the twin challenges of innovation and control is part of its secret of long-term success. Like GE, most companies are focused on sustainable growth. What's different about GE is that it has built a high-tech services and financial enterprise that endures. And its finance function is heavily involved in the business, is sustainable in its own right, and has a distinctive set of shared values that binds finance executives across the company together.

Not all companies have the benefit of GE's corporate reputation and successful track record. Next, we interview two senior finance executives who have a very different starting point from GE – *recovery from scandal*.

GETTING "BACK IN THE SADDLE"

Royal Ahold was one of the major success stories of the 1990s but, unfortunately, it suffered a major meltdown in 2003! Until this point, Europe had not suffered accounting scandals on the scale of America's massive ones, such as Enron and WorldCom. Coming after fraud was discovered at ABB, a widely admired Swedish company, and after the debt crisis at Vivendi, a giant French conglomerate, the Ahold scandal has called into question the belief among some Europeans that their style of corporate governance and ownership is adequate.

Ahold is a Dutch-based international group of local food retail and food service operators. The company operates principally through subsidiaries and joint ventures in the US, Europe, and Central and South America. In 2004, Ahold owned, or had interest in, about 9,000 supermarkets in some 25 countries, as well as a food service business. Ahold owns (in the United States) the Stop & Shop, Giant, Bruno's, and Bi-Lo supermarket chains, as well as Dutch supermarket leader Albert Heijn. As the world's largest food distributor, it has worldwide consolidated net sales of €52 billion and over 200,000 employees/associates. It had grown by acquisition and was very keen on preserving the individual quality of its retail "thoroughbred" brands.

In early 2003, as Ahold was gathering its 2002 results, the world's third biggest retailer announced unexpectedly that it had overstated profits by at least half a billion dollars at its US food distribution service. It also announced that its CEO and CFO were quitting! Ahold postponed its 2002 results indefinitely. Subsequently, an independent evaluation revealed that its profit overstatement was nearer US$880 million.

Until this time, the company had been on a worldwide acquisition spree, acquiring operations from Chile to Thailand and running up net debts of around €13 billion. Its shares had fallen sharply, apparently due to worries about the reliability of its accounts and disappointment at missed forecasts. In response, the group embarked on a program of divestments, jettisoning some of its Latin American and several Asian operations.

Investigation into Ahold's US operations showed that promotional rebates from suppliers were booked fraudulently to meet aggregate revenue targets. Even worse, it was later revealed that promotional payments from suppliers were booked before they were received – stretching the rules, and the credibility of Ahold's accounting methods, beyond the breaking point. It was against this backdrop that Hannu Ryopponen was invited to join the board as CFO to spearhead recovery, refinance the business, and install a new CFO.

REGAINING CONTROL
Hannu Ryopponen, former CFO, Royal Ahold

When I arrived at Ahold, things could not have been any worse! Organizationally, we were set up on a decentralized basis. We had 22 operating companies around the world. The management style was heavily operating-company oriented and we had only a thin layer of regional geographic management at the top.

The bubble bursts!
As our situation was unfolding, the bubble burst around the world! Enron, of course, had happened much earlier, but now we had the high-profile failure of Andersen to contend with. The whole attitude in society towards corporate management and governance changed. For better or worse, controls over business tightened. Sarbanes-Oxley hardened attitudes and expectations: standards of corporate behavior became much higher. In many countries, new codes of conduct – for example, the Higgs report in the UK – were part of this growing trend towards improving corporate integrity.

Suddenly, we moved from the environment of the 1990s to more formal, rigid controls. This was a shock to our system! Not only did senior corporate managers have to respond, others must respond as well – for example, the accounting and legal professions.

When frauds of the nature of Ahold's are disclosed, there are two implications:

1 *People lose their jobs. Some of these people should have known better and there were questions about their integrity. Of course, the finance department was affected dramatically. So we really had no one minding the shop.*

2 *People are paralyzed. It's a bit like a corporate tsunami. People are in shock. They ask the question: "How can I survive this?" Some almost feel guilty; they think they could have done something to prevent the disaster. Others feel personally vulnerable: "Was I too close to the situation? Am I also at risk?" So people become defensive and the organization becomes immobilized.*

Recovering from crisis

When I first started at Ahold, it was only a few months after the disclosure of the accounting problem. I remember my first meeting: it was like talking to ghosts. We had to find new top management: The company was a bit like a body without a head. The supervisory board put a new management in place to provide leadership, energize the company, and resuscitate the share price.

The first challenge, for me, was to close the 2002 annual accounts, which were still unresolved. At least we all felt a measure of relief that things were starting to get back on track. At the same time, we were heavily preparing to raise capital through a share issue, which was successfully completed. We found the necessary financing – €3 billion – in the bank. This was an important step in stabilizing the business.

During 2003, our first priority was reporting – to close the previous year's books, which we only finalized towards the end of that year. Meanwhile, we had not closed a single quarter in 2003! We had a lot of catching up to do. Eventually we closed both 2002 and quarter three 2003. Gradually, we moved towards a normal reporting sequence. Our closing cycle is still slower and more cumbersome than I would like, but we are improving and gaining confidence. We can now show the world that we can close our books accurately and track our progress.

In the short term, we had to bring in consultants to fill the empty jobs. Meanwhile, the forensic activity also required an external accounting firm's involvement. But business as normal had to carry on. We had to restructure for recovery and for the longer term.

If you have forensic investigations, accountants are bound to find problems. In a company like ours, these will always run into the hundreds, all of which need to be acted upon. The accountants found 780 different issues! None of these in them-

selves were ultra important, but they still needed correction. In 2004, we also had to renew our focus on internal controls to comply with SOX 404. Beyond all this, we had to handle the IFRS conversion, which had lain dormant during the crisis year.

Regaining control

First and foremost, we wanted to regain control without the help of outsiders. Second, we wanted to put in the right processes and controls to ensure that they complied with regulations. Unlike other organizations that weren't responding to a crisis, we did not get much resistance to SOX 404 from management and staff.

If I look back at the two years I spent at Ahold, I feel a sense of accomplishment. Given where we were, I do not think we could have done things much differently. We had the whole world watching us. Regulators, investors, the media – everyone was checking up on what was going on at Ahold. They were asking: "How bad was it?" So not only was the organization in shock internally, but we had external pressures to deal with as well. You have to raise quality immediately because the auditors are all over you. There is a lot of checking and double-checking. All your weaknesses are exposed for everyone to see.

Rebalancing the decentralized model

Under the previous regime, we had invested in a series of "thoroughbred" retail brands – these thoroughbreds were raced as if they were individual horses! We needed to herd the brands together while maintaining their individualism. Unfortunately, we had 22 concepts based on the 22 operating companies. We had to decide which ones to keep and which to abandon.

We changed strategy: the decentralized mode of operating wasn't working. The food retail business is low margin and high volume. We needed to go for economies of scale. If you look at the other big supermarket retailers – Wal-Mart, Carrefour, Tesco – they all try to streamline their operations by largely focusing on one operating concept.

We had different accounting and different reporting systems. We needed a "one-stream" reporting approach. We needed one worldwide standard chart of accounts and common definitions – for example, how to define shrinkage, or "like-for-like" sales. We had as many ways of doing things as we had operating companies!

We carried out an analysis to decide how to create economies of scale. For the food service business (which supplies wholesale to hotels, hospitals, and schools) we had to build a new platform and a new operating model to secure a sound base and to prevent fraud from occurring again. We were still making good profits at the time and had every reason to be confident about the future.

At headquarters, however, we didn't have the knowledge of the business we should have had. We needed to improve our business analytics – our understanding of what was going on at the front line. It was not enough for the central accounting function just to be bookkeepers, we had to better understand the business drivers underlying performance.

If we had three minutes with the CEO in the elevator, we had to be able to tell him where the business stood financially. But we needed to go beyond what I call the "elevator analysis." For example, if we knew that Stop & Shop sales had gone up by, say, 5% then that was the end of the analysis! We needed to know why they went up 5% and what the underlying drivers were.

The "one-company" approach

We reorganized the operating businesses into a more streamlined management structure – we call it the "one-company approach." Our retail operating companies are now structured into four geographic management regions – we call "arenas" – plus an arena for our Scandinavian joint venture.

We also appointed arena CFOs, each with a very clear reporting line to their arena CEO. They support the business, but they had a strong dotted-line reporting relationship through to me, the group CFO. Depending on the size of the arena, we have arena accounting departments, which have very solid-line reporting relationships to our central Accounting and Reporting function. We installed a new chief accounting officer to take responsibility for a revitalized Accounting and Reporting function – getting the numbers together accurately and on time. We also installed fresh internal audit reviews and controls on the closing processes.

Standardization and harmonization are the goals we strive for today! We are probably more than halfway there. We are standardizing our IT and centralizing our accounting. We are building shared services slowly but surely. We are implementing one center right now in Central Europe. We also have shared services for accounts payable in the Netherlands and in the US. However, we continue to wrestle with the issue of which activities should be located centrally, and which should be local.

We are reducing the variety of accounting systems across the business. Currently we just have four different systems with some variations. We have an agreement in principle across the business to migrate to one standard accounting system and one ERP architecture. IT outsourcing is also on the agenda.

Getting closer to the business

Today, we have a stronger business analytics capability and a better understanding of what is going on. Apart from financial controls, we now have a much better grip on the business. The local CFO's responsibility ends in practical terms at the EBITA level. We have a centralized treasury and tax function. We are getting the treasury staff more involved with the business internally. We are creating better cash management and a deeper understanding of where and how our foreign exchange exposures arise. We are getting everybody closer to the business!

What do I look for in my senior finance executives? High professional standards, and strong personal qualities in terms of leadership and experience. I look for a willingness to cooperate, to work across disciplines and as a member of a team. Strong personal balance is important; so is the willingness to share information happily. Most important, I want people who will be proactive when "something does not feel right." I encourage this proactivity at junior levels too.

In a year or so, I would like to see Ahold back where it deserves to be – a top player in the retailing world. I want the company to be seen by external investors, bankers, and professionals as being a quality share fit for any quality investment portfolio. And, like Philips, I want us to have built a world-class finance function that properly supports the business – and to operate as one company across the world.

Ahold had to reorganize, change its strategy, install a new central accounting and control function, and implement generally higher professional standards. One of the key issues it has grappled with is how much to centralize and standardize – a dilemma for most companies in today's much harsher regulatory and control regime, no matter what their starting point. No one wants to *throw the baby out with the bath water*! A degree of decentralization and local empowerment is still important for an innovative and responsive organization.

In the interests of control and objectivity, should divisional CFOs now have a direct, *firm black-line* reporting relationship to their group CFO?

Some multinationals are following this approach. However, many other companies continue to support the dotted-line relationship between their divisional CFOs and the group CFO, with a firm reporting line to their local CEO. This latter approach does have the advantage of creating a positive climate of business partnership.

Also, there is a growing appetite among investors for much broader, non-financial information to provide a clearer picture of how a company is doing – both in relation to its peer group competitors and in terms of future value creation. Quite often, the latest accounting standards are difficult to interpret and, in some cases, just confusing.

COPING WITH GOVERNANCE AND REPORTING

Is it the role of the CFO to be responsible for this published non-financial information? If so, what are the implications for quality assurance and enhanced control? Remember: the previous Chairman and CFO of Shell lost their jobs for overstating the value of oil reserves. These values were governed by SEC reporting standards but were not included in the balance sheet numbers, just in the supplementary notes, since they were deemed leading indicators of future value.

It's these types of external pressures for higher standards from investors and regulators, coupled with much better defined codes of conduct for corporate governance, that are influencing the role of the CFO and the future of the finance function.

It's now taken for granted in Europe that the roles of chairman and chief executive should be separate. Board committees are commonplace as vehicles for overseeing audit arrangements and senior management remuneration. In mainland Europe there is a two-tier board structure – one for non-executive supervision and one for executive management. In the UK and the US, the single-board approach prevails.

This brings us next to the perspective of senior non-executive directors (NEDs). When we interviewed Dudley Eustace for this book, he was chairman and senior non-executive of many prestigious European companies. However, earlier in his career, he had been Group CFO of Philips, and was appointed interim CFO of Ahold following the scandal. From a non-executive perspective, Dudley comments on the impact of recent changes in corporate governance and regulation – and what it means for a CFO.

A CHAIRMAN'S VIEW

Dudley Eustace, Chairman of Aegon, former Chairman of Smith & Nephew, Vice Chairman of KPN and Hagemeyer

What do I look for in the CFO of a major multinational? Integrity, judgment, and trust. Also, strong reputation and a past track record of success. Independence on the one hand and the ability to be a team player on the other – a real balancing act!

The CFO is the conscience of the corporation. For example, in my experience, growth has a cost: Growth for growth's sake is likely to destroy value. In such circumstances, it's difficult to say no to management. The CFO has to be independent, which can be very challenging. You can't just go on gut feel; you have to deal with realities based on facts.

It is also important for the CFO to have ambition, to want to grow as an individual. I always try to find people who are better than their predecessors – that way, the company can really grow too.

Bringing outsiders onto the board provides a fresh perspective and helps get things done.

Given recent accounting scandals, the Chairman has to be more concerned about what the CEO and the CFO are up to. On one company board, I was not confident in the CEO and his team. On another occasion, when I was appointed Chairman of Smith & Nephew, my priorities were twofold:

- *To have a top-class board representative of the company's industry sectors.*
- *To provide for succession for both myself and senior management.*

At Smith & Nephew, I now have a multinational board of directors that meets six times a year. It has strong American representation, and its members have relevant pharmaceutical and industrial experience. John Buchanan, my successor, is already on board. John, having been CFO of BP, brings experience from a very big company.

As retirements come up at Smith & Nephew, we shall also refresh the senior executive team. We are a good company, but we're constantly striving to be a great company. The only way you can become a great company is to replace people, including yourself! It is important to keep raising the bar. Part of my role is to help attract great people to a company which is ethically driven, proud of its products, and brings an ethos of high integrity to everything it does.

Corporate governance

The corporate governance model in the Netherlands is run on the two-tier board structure – a non-executive supervisory board that is clearly separated from the executive management team. The Dutch model, of course, applies to the boards of Aegon and KPN.

In the UK, where Smith & Nephew is based, we have a single board, but I still try to separate the non-executive and executive roles. The chairman has to give the CEO room to breathe and mustn't get involved in operations. For this reason, I don't believe the CEO of a company should ever become the chairman or non-exec in their company, since they're already too involved. It is appropriate for the chairman to advise on strategy and to act as a sounding board.

I'm Chairman of the Audit Committees at two leading Dutch companies: KPN and Hagemeyer. Prescribing what the Audit Committee should or should not do is a major issue. For example, one of the things to come out of Sarbanes-Oxley is the "whistle-blower" procedure. One of my companies had a much-publicized issue; we had to immediately set up an investigation, hire forensic accountants, bring in outside lawyers, review what went on, and then deal with the outcome. As Chairman of the Audit Committee, this created much additional work over a concentrated period of time. It also put us in direct conflict with management, which was defending itself.

If you are on the Audit Committee you are a delegated part of the board – jointly and severally responsible. You have to get at the truth. Potentially, this can damage the relationship between the non-executives and the executives. So it's important that any actions taken are consistent with company values, but also consistent with relevant international and, often competing, local regulations and jurisdictions. Undoubtedly, due to increasing regulations, the non-executive role is getting tougher!

The role of the CFO is crucial in the interface between non-executives and executives. The CFO now has to be ambidextrous – on the one hand reporting to the CEO, on the other, to the Audit Committee. The CFO has to have an open channel of communication to the Audit Committee on any matter. This is not disloyal to the CEO; it is good governance. It's in everybody's interest. It's also essential for transparency.

Inside the company – on the question of whether divisional CFOs should report to the group CFO – I believe that the group CFO should have the final say in the way in which the finance function is run across the company.

The impact of regulation and standards
What do you learn from scandals like Ahold's? As CFO, you have to trust, but you also have to verify! This was a wake-up call to manage cash: Ahold needed cash forecasts, cash control, and management needed to worry about where the cash was coming from to stay in business.

Turning to Sarbanes-Oxley, in well-run companies, the controls should already have been in place and further regulation shouldn't have been necessary. For example, when I was at Philips, we had what we called a Document of Representation – a sign-off by the CEO and CFO of each business unit of their results. But the CEO would typically rely upon his CFO. Under SOX, the CEO has to satisfy himself with documentary evidence.

What do I think of IFRS? It's the right way to go – it's setting a new benchmark for consistency. However, I do know that American companies would find it difficult to give up US GAAP. But if we can come close to bringing the two sets of standards together, then the reconciling items are less distorting – and we'll move much closer to one version of the truth!

As the effects of accounting volatility – bookkeeping rather than real cash – are introduced by the new accounting standards, they are likely to be discounted by investors. More and more investor attention will be on free cash flow per share. As a trend, you want to sustain your dividend stream based on your free cash flow rather than asset valuations. Cash, unlike profit, cannot be manipulated.

The group CFO is the one person in the company where everything comes together – for example, the annual report and accounts – thereby ensuring everything across the organization is in balance.

I really worry about attempts to value intangibles. For example, to gross-up a company balance sheet to value both organically grown brands and those acquired would inevitably be arbitrary, subjective, and open to criticism. We have to live with the inconsistencies of valuing intangibles – but it's imperative that a company publish a list of brands to inform readers about what they're investing in. This intangible value should be implicit in the share price.

You can always debate: What is fair value? What is market value? The standards are evolving. If we have to report more information than the existing standards require, then we have to keep open the possibility of publishing further regulated supplementary reports. This will help provide better transparency. Anything that helps put performance in perspective and make the results easier to read has to be encouraged! However, more information is not necessarily better.

Despite the negativity surrounding the cost and confusion of the new regulations and standards, one message comes out loud and clear from the chairmen and senior NEDs interviewed for this book: corporate governance is improving. And it needed to improve.

Nevertheless, there is generally a feeling that codes of corporate governance conduct should be combined across countries, initially across Europe and, ultimately, with the US. Companies are global, investors are increasingly global – so why not?

However, the CFOs we interviewed are not so supportive of what's happening with accounting standards. IFRS is seen as a confusing mixture of different accounting conventions – fair/market value in some respects, traditional historical cost accounting in others. There is also concern that individual countries will have their own interpretation of the standards, which are often difficult to apply in practice. Ultimately, most CFOs support the ideal of one global GAAP. However, the *principles-based* approach coming from Europe is generally preferred to the *rules-based* approach in the US.

As implementation of the new Sarbanes-Oxley regulations (SOX) and IFRS accounting standards settle down, more and more CFOs and their companies are likely to see beyond the initial one-off costs to the longer-term benefits. Experience will also grow in terms of what's important during implementation – for example, key controls – and what isn't.

As the stock markets recover, and as the world's economies become much stronger and more sustainable, CFOs are now turning their attention away from the scandals of the past and away from the negative aspects of the regulation. The fundamental issue that concerns them most today is how to play their part in creating value and growth.

CREATING VALUE AND GROWTH

Earlier CFO books[1] focused on the shift in finance functions from transaction processing to decision support. This comes through very strongly at GE. Finance functions are shrinking as a result of technology and the inexorable trend towards shared services, off-shoring and, in some cases, outsourcing. The emphasis continues to be on higher value-added decision support. Finance functions generally are investing heavily in developing their analytical and best-practice capabilities to support the business.

However, until recently, CFOs have been overtaken by events – the fallout from the spectacular accounting scandals, the resulting regulation, and a general tightening up in governance, control, and reporting. The changing shape of the finance function, from the late twentieth century to the present day, is illustrated in Figure 1.3. What's different is the increased attention being given to risk and regulation – and the emergence of an entirely new reporting function: sustainability, social responsibility, and corporate citizenship.

In Figure 1.3, the finance function of the 1980s is portrayed as a relatively fat pyramid, emphasizing transaction processing and lightly pro-

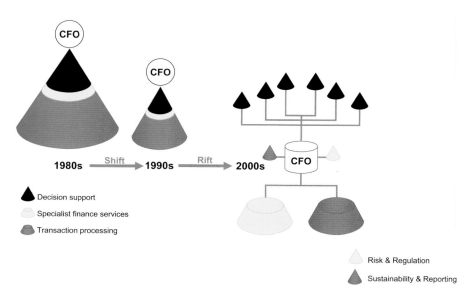

Figure 1.3   *The changing shape of finance*

moting decision support. In the 1990s, finance-leveraged ERP systems became more compact, with leaner transaction-processing operations and a greater focus on performance management. At the turn of the century, as explored in the book *eCFO: Sustaining Value in the New Corporation*,[2] the CFO became the center of a web of relationships managing the value of the extended enterprise.

Today, as we discuss throughout this book, the focus is not only on value creation but also on new dimensions of *"risk and regulation,"* and the new function for *"sustainability and reporting."* We devote our last chapter to this latter, much broader specialty, which is being driven by:

- Corporate governance: the personal sensitivity of board directors, be they non-executive or executive, to the need for absolute and total compliance – and their drive to be seen externally as good corporate citizens.

- Reporting and transparency: increasingly, either through legislation or investor pressures, companies are required to report on key non-financial information – the source of future value.

- Reputation and ethics: the growing awareness of the importance of a much broader group of stakeholders of the need for responsible corporate behavior, and for management practices that reflect the highest standards.

When polled over the last 12 months, the views of senior finance executives involved with the Value Network Initiative (summarized in Figure 1.4) show that two issues now rank very high on their agendas: the impact of regulation, and growth and sustainability.

The following trends have been identified, based on analysis of change programs in corporate finance:

- The importance of benchmarking shareholder value performance in better understanding value drivers – and the increasing reliance on key performance indicators (KPIs) for managing value.

- The growing proportion of a company's value tied up in its intangible assets – such as intellectual property, brands and R&D, customers and talent.

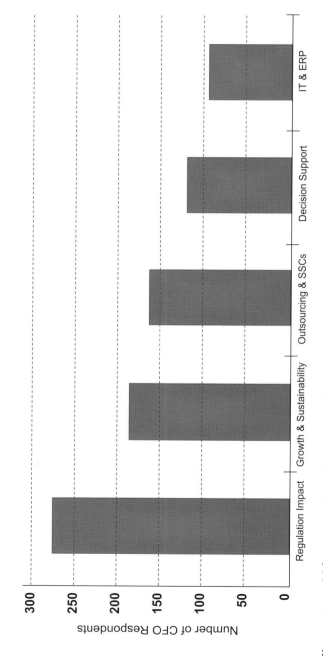

Figure 1.4 *Value network initiative: top CFO issues*

- The increasing importance of, and rigor behind, non-financial information – and the responsibility of the CFO and the finance function for its authenticity.

- Changes in financial management processes: looking forwards rather than backwards, coping with ever-increasing degrees of uncertainty, and extending risk analysis from a relatively narrow financially oriented discipline to enterprise-wide risk management.

- Increasing organizational and structural flexibility: taking advantage of the trend towards shared services, identifying which parts of the value chain should be insourced, which should be outsourced – and going either near-shore or off-shore to achieve lower costs and find new talent pools.

When individual members of the VNI ranked themselves against best-practice criteria on a scale of 0 to 5, all felt they had a lot to do in performance measurement, analytics, intangibles, and connecting strategy with operations. The results of this benchmarking are reproduced in Figure 1.5.

The finance functions of many of the companies surveyed are now developing their decision-support capabilities. This is a relatively new field of specialization and it raises many unanswered questions: How do you incorporate shareholder value thinking in your management and financial processes for planning, performance, and creating incentives? What is best practice in growing and managing the value of intangible assets? Management gurus gave us the *thinking* behind the value chain, but they didn't tell us how to *value* it in practice!

Consider next what Jan Hommen said just before he retired as CFO of Philips. Jan is currently very active in leading Dutch companies – as Chairman of the boards of Reed Elsevier and TNT, and of Ahold's audit committee, and as a board member of ING.

 ## VALUING THE VALUE CHAIN
Jan Hommen, former CFO of Philips

Philips has been transitioning from a multi-purpose structure to a more single-purpose organization. Its new strategic focus will be on "healthcare," with an overflow into "lifestyle" products supported by our strong technology capability. We've made

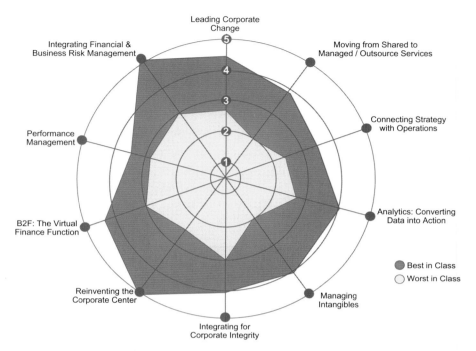

Figure 1.5 *Best practice implementation gap*

a number of acquisitions in healthcare already. These are now integrated and work-ing quite well.

Unfortunately, the market has not recognized the full value of our new strat-egy. So there should be significant upward potential, if we can execute this strategy well and convince the market of our capability and determination to do so. This will require:

- Finding the right acquisitions, integrating them quickly, and making the earn-ings accretive, along with organic growth.
- Liquefying financial assets on our books and using them to optimize share-holder value. Also, we still have a number of activities in Philips that are not highly cash generative – these either need to be disposed of or de-risked.

This strategy will make our earnings much more consistent and predictable, and will simplify our organization and ways of working. We are also improving our forecasting accuracy and reducing the volatility in our earnings by making costs variable.

Shareholder value analysis

When we take "the sum of the parts," as analysts do, it's greater than the current share price. We value each of our major business units by benchmarking their value drivers against those of their competitors – and then working out the business unit proportion of the group's total shareholder value.

Analysts punish us with a conglomerate discount of approximately 20%. The rationale for such a discount is not always clear. But the real question is how to convert this into a premium. That is the management challenge at the group level: to add value to these businesses, rather than destroying it!

How are we addressing this undervaluation? We need to make more of the "One Philips" idea – leveraging the benefits of being a large company with a strong brand, special distribution capabilities, and innovative technology applications. This needs to be reflected in better performance for the group as a whole.

Optimizing value in the value chain

We recognize that value is generated by being a successful technology company and through our investments in research, product creation, design, marketing and branding. Also there is significant advantage in having a low-cost, but high-quality supply chain and in strong channels to market.

Increasingly, however, we are finding that, in some areas, being in manufacturing is less and less attractive, especially as cut-throat cost competition from the East continues to bite into our value. We're constantly trying to maintain an optimal balance. Excellence in all areas is not always possible, so we need to find partners and alliances with special capabilities and the right cost structures.

In each business unit, we try to understand how the "value" in the value chain is built up. We define where the principal economic control points are in the chain. At these control points, we like to have strong competitive positions – where the value created is greatest. In some parts of our business, time-to-market is critical for competitive advantage. In others, the quality of customer insight can be more important than speed.

The medical business is a good illustration: we place a high value on our relation-ship with physicians. Since they are effectively our customers, we have to better understand how they work and what they need. By contrast, value created in the consumer electronics sector is moving either upstream to the design and intellectual property of semi-conductor chips or down the value chain to distribution, market-ing, and the retailer. Value in the middle – in manufacturing – is being squeezed.

R&D and finance
Finance is in a good position to help define the right measurements and perform-ance yardsticks for innovation management. We measure innovation as the propor-tion of our sales generated from new product introductions over the last two years. In the medical division, 62% of our sales are generated from products introduced in the last two years.

Finance staff in the R&D area need a good grasp of technology, but they also need to be savvy business people who can work with marketing and sales in appreciating what the marketplace will require tomorrow. The finance function helps make R&D economics visible to management, analyzing and presenting the value opportuni-ties going forward. Then it identifies the necessary investments required to exploit them. Not an easy task!

Finance and standardization
When I first arrived at Philips, finance was mostly an administrative and accounting function with little real decision-support capability. As a result, it was very difficult to see and predict the total financial picture. We had inadequate information on which to base reliable forecasts, since the focus was backward rather than forward, and there was very little in the way of risk management. The product divisions had a great deal of freedom to decide on strategy. There was hardly any coordination across the group on capital allocation, R&D investment, systems or marketing. It was every one of the thirteen divisions for themselves – with little or no synergy among them.

We have taken hold of this "monster" by simplifying the business and cutting back on our structural complexity.

We have rationalized our excessive number of business units from approximately 160 down to 40; the number of divisions from 13 down to 5; the number of ERP systems from 600 down to about 40; and the number of employees from 280,000 down to 160,000. Underneath all this, we changed from processes that were pre-dominantly organized into vertical functional silos to horizontal business processes that are now more integrated. We also standardized many of these processes across the company.

Today, we have a fundamentally different kind of company. Rationalization has delivered significant efficiency improvements. It's also meant much quicker decision making from the top to the bottom of the company – and a more forward-looking management supported by better planning.

Finance agenda for 2006

Finance has been a major catalyst for all these changes. In 2003, we started a "Best in Finance 2006" program. Using benchmark studies, we proved that we were too focused on low value-added processes. We designed a plan that was extremely well received by management: we were to be not just "best in class" in terms of our finance cost base, but in the processes and results we were to achieve for the busi-ness. In finance, we now see ourselves as the co-pilot of the CEO and the business partner for the rest of the company.

The highly successful Philips 2006 finance program focuses on five major initiatives:

- **Portfolio management** – supporting the strategy of the business in innovating and developing new products, making selective acquisi-tions and divestments, and generally maximizing value through value chain optimization.

- **Analytics** – increasing capability to better understand margins by products, and where and how profits are made.

- **New systems** – implementing enterprise-wide applications that are integrated with ERP and data warehouse resources for group financial consolidation, planning, and performance management.

- **Forecasting** – making improvements to the rolling forecast process, identifying value drivers in greater granularity on a monthly basis, and understanding the impact on the next quarter's performance.

- **Accounts close** – speeding up the time taken to close the monthly accounts and to produce detailed financial information.

Later in this book, we explore many of the issues raised by Philips – for example, how companies are optimizing the value of their R&D pipeline, how they are standardizing their finance operations, and how they are implementing best practices in financial management, such as rolling forecasts.

There is one company, however, that stands out from the many interviews we've conducted during our research: Diageo. Of particular interest are its decision-support function and global shared service center. We cover these aspects of Diageo's finance agenda in greater detail in subsequent chapters, but here, we interview Nick Rose, the CFO. He brings a number of the VNI themes together *as an action blueprint for others to follow!*

SHAPING THE NEW AGENDA

RAISING THE BAR
Nick Rose, CFO of Diageo

For Diageo, total shareholder return (TSR) – share price appreciation plus dividend – still remains the best and most fundamental financial indicator for measuring how we're creating value for shareholders.

What we've learned in the last five years is that it is very difficult to sustain your TSR performance in the top quartile of your industry peer group. If you take a three-year rolling view, then we've achieved a top quartile position on some occasions. But it's very difficult to sustain that performance as your share price adjusts to this new base performance level.

Your peers are always trying to raise the bar and share prices are often subject to market forces that you're not in a position to influence. So this is a very challenging benchmark, and we're never complacent. Although we're number one in size in the global alcoholic drinks market, we're always learning from other marketing-led companies with great performance track records, such as L'Oréal and Colgate Palmolive.

It's critical for finance to help Diageo to beat the competition! To improve our efficiency and effectiveness, we've had to be rigorous in defining our structure for the company as a whole and in how the financial processes should work to support it – at a global level, regionally, and in local markets. This has certainly influenced how we've organized the finance function.

Global business support
At Diageo, we now embrace the concept of global business support. We used to have a lot of overlapping effort among head-office functions. Today, we only have one integrated team, which supports the local market when required.

In fact, my own role as CFO – at executive committee and board levels – has also broadened: I'm now responsible for strategy, supply chain, and IS, as well as finance. We're seeing the benefits globally, as well as locally, of integrating these functions into one coordinated service.

We're clearer about where the finance function can add value to the "front-end" of our business, which is all about consumers, customers, sales and marketing. We've built a shared service center in Budapest to manage key processes globally. Our goal: to liberate the front-end of the business, including the finance people who support it.

We started with shared services in Europe and have extended this to include North America and Australia. All time zones are now covered. Having one global SAP platform helped and our migration to one global shared service center in Europe has not been as difficult as it might have been. But I'm not saying it's been easy!

Out of this organizational change has emerged a new support function that we call global business support (GBS). GBS has three core capabilities: decision support, strategic planning, and change management. Together, they help drive performance improvement for the front-end of the business and provide it with integrated support.

The upside of regulation
Against the background of accounting scandals and reporting mishaps elsewhere in the corporate world, we too – like companies such as BP and Shell – have reviewed our internal reporting lines and controls and made a few changes.

I always try to create a positive outcome in responding to, for example, SOX regulations and corporate governance changes. They can be demoralizing. But if these changes lead to a stronger company foundation, then you can create a positive environment. Today, for example, the general managers who run our markets don't have to worry about control glitches; they can concentrate on beating the external competition. Another chance to liberate the locals!

I chair the audit committee of another company, Scottish Power. Currently, we're focusing on what we can really do to add value to the company, as opposed to just what's required by law. The real challenge for audit committees – where the non-execs' personal reputations are at risk – is to avoid excessive demands for detail and bureaucratic control. You need to "see the wood for the trees" and strike the right balance between risk and reward.

There is no black and white answer to the question: how much centralization? It's a mixture. At Diageo, by centralizing what we see as global processes, we've put the pressure on business performance: We're encouraging local-market units to improve by putting them in a stronger competitive position.

After years of experience of dealing with this issue, it is vital to be clear on the dividing line between what should be central and what should be local. You want to focus the energy of your people, not on arguing about where to draw the line, but on how to create value for the organization as a whole.

Sustainability and social responsibility

Most CFOs have to focus on the sustainability of earnings, on growth over the longer term – ten years or more. They wrestle with balancing longer-term investment against the short-term pressures imposed by the market. However, stakeholders today are using a wider variety of measures – non-financial as well as financial.

The ability of a company to deal with governmental, environmental, social, and community issues – being a good corporate citizen – is under increasing scrutiny and regulation. These pressures and the risks they raise are real – not academic – and may affect whether or not a company will be around at all in ten years' time! For example, if you take company pensions, there are now many more stakeholders involved and there's much more today for the CFO to worry about than just the financial implications.

In our industry, alcoholic beverages, we have to recognize that alcohol abuse is a big and controversial issue: you only have to pick up the newspaper to see stories of irresponsible drinking. For Diageo to be sustainable, we have to be proactive in *promoting responsible alcoholic consumption. Consequently, there has to be a clear link between sustainability and long-term shareholder value.*

As far as performance reporting is concerned, I believe this will continue to develop along a more integrated route – bringing together more of the broader, non-financial information related to future sustainability together with the financials. The external stakeholders, including investors, are likely to want to cross-relate the non-financial to the financial information to ensure consistency.

We're working on how best to integrate the two different sets of data collection routines involved into our financial system for our year-end reporting. I can only see this going one way: By integrating sustainability information into our statutory financial planning process, putting it all through the filing assurance committee – our year-end clearance process – we can best assure the quality and consistency of the broader picture.

What's ahead?
As CFO of Diageo, what's on my agenda for the future?

- *Business performance: How do you beat your competition on a sustainable basis and beat the expectations of your shareholders?*
- *Business risk: How do you deal with the broader picture, from the sheer weight of governance and regulation to providing the best growth environment possible?*
- *Business process efficiency: How do you continue to take out cost, looking again at outsourcing and the role of the Far East in the entire business supply chain? What should be "in" and what should be "out"?*
- *Tracking our shareholders: Who will they be in five years? Hedge funds are having an impact on the ownership of major companies. What does this mean for investor communications and performance expectations?*

Not all CFOs have gone as far as Nick has with his finance function: Diageo's decision-support function is quite advanced and its global shared service center in Budapest is state-of-the-art. And Nick himself, in addition to leading finance, now has quite a broad role: he's also responsible for strategy and IT, as well as Diageo's supply chain.

In the chapters that follow, we cover in greater depth what CFOs and senior finance executives are doing to address their twofold challenge: coping with regulation driving while pursuing growth and innovation.

In Chapter 2, we review some of the structural models that are emerging in response to the increased emphasis on control and regulation – and offer choices for how far CFOs need to go. Chapter 3 sets out how to get there.

Subsequent chapters focus on the role of the CFO in managing the drivers of value creation in a regulated world. Those drivers are: intangible assets (Chapter 4) and innovation (Chapter 5). Next, we cover the new financial management disciplines, specifically forecasting (Chapter 6) and how one company, Unilever, brings these disciplines and tools together in a business-partnering culture (Chapter 7).

In the last section of the book, we focus on the future: how global connectivity and seamless support are reshaping the ways that companies around the world do business (Chapter 8); how companies in various industries are trying to benefit from a positive approach to risk and regulation and where this is all likely to lead (Chapter 9). Finally, we make the link between shareholder value, social responsibility, ethics, and sustainability (Chapter 10) – a new discipline for a new world!

STRAIGHT FROM THE CFO

Summarized below are the key insights emerging from the CFO research program on which this book is based. For ease of reference, these are arranged by chapter.

- **Reshaping finance**

  Centralization: make choices about how far to go. Strengthen reporting lines. Promote consistency and accountability across the enterprise. Standardize where possible. Optimize processes. Reduce complexity and streamline structure. Learn from private equity.

- **Making change happen**

  Know your starting point – it's unique! Lead from the front: you're the key sponsor and change agent. Pull *all* the change levers. Take *all* the stakeholders with you. Attract and nurture fresh finance talent. Move from CFO to COO!

- **Releasing intangible value**

  It's more about execution than valuation. Find the missing half of your balance sheet! Know how different intangible assets contribute value. Select the right valuation techniques. Move from the back office to the front.

- **Driving growth and innovation**

  Make innovation an "all-the-time," everywhere capability. Be honest: do you really encourage breakthrough ideas? Make it your job to transform the internal business model and align it with the broader innovation agenda. Develop an innovation scorecard. Become the "value architect." Work with external customers for a win-win.

- **Looking *forwards*, not backwards**

  Expect the unexpected. Close the strategy gap. Harness the value in the value chain. Connect the dots: integrate your processes for performance management. Roll those forecasts!

- **Innovative business partnering**

  Take the plunge and throw away the comfort blanket! Create a business-partnering culture. Go for best practice, not just good practice. Learn from the outside, not just the inside. Trade war stories and celebrate successes. Energize and share through a finance academy.

- **Promoting global connectivity**

  Flatten your world! Stretch the shared services envelope. Aspire to seamless support. Go near-shore or off-shore. Build a worldwide center: make it into a business in its own right. Develop global partnerships. Create value by outsourcing.

- **Leveraging risk and regulation**

  Look for the benefits in SOX. Consider what IFRS conversion means to your business. Where you can, integrate regulatory initiatives to avoid implementation overload. Weigh the possible benefits of dual accounting. Assess your risk appetite. Make the case for a separate enterprise-wide risk discipline. Appoint a CRO!

- **Becoming a "good corporation"**

  Link ethics to shareholder value. Lead the charge for corporate responsibility. Broaden your corporate reporting – test your indicators against industry benchmarks. Consider the triple bottom line. Spread the word. Do a sustainability health-check with stakeholders. Become the "good corporation!"

REFERENCES

1 PricewaterhouseCoopers Financial and Cost Management Team (1997/1999) *CFO: Architect of the Corporation's Future,* Wiley.

2 Cedric Read, Jacky Ross and John Dunleavy (2001) *eCFO: Sustaining Value in the New Corporation,* Wiley.

CHAPTER 2

Reshaping Finance

Most CFOs say that the additional work associated with regulatory compliance is taking us in the wrong direction – it's distracting, it's costly, and it's not adding value. But many of the world's leading companies are taking a different view. They don't see this regulatory hit as a one-off, but as an influential step in a large, ongoing transformation. They see the need to improve control and compliance – and they want to take advantage of the opportunity.

Companies such as ABN Amro, BP, and Nestlé are taking their operating models for finance, critiquing them, and then going on to address ever-increasing complexity with simplification and standardization.

But where do you start? How do you evaluate the effectiveness of today's finance operating model? And how do you shape the finance model of the future?

This chapter opens by examining the ways in which leading companies are confronting these challenges and then offers guidance on how to evaluate your present position, review the structural choices open to you, and redesign the finance function. Later in the chapter, we get down to the nitty-gritty – into processes such as reporting. We look at what large publicly quoted companies are actually doing to reduce complexity – and how one corporation is moving to a European one-company model. *Finally, we look at what's happening in the world of private equity – and the lessons it offers.*

CENTRALIZATION: *WHERE* TO DRAW THE LINE?

Take the case of ABN Amro. With its roots and headquarters in the Netherlands, ABN is an international bank with over 3,400 branches in more than 60 countries. The company has substantial overseas operations in

North America and Brazil. Most recently, it announced the acquisition of the Italian bank, Banca Antonveneta.

The challenge for ABN Amro: to be in the top five of its selected peer group of 20 banks in terms of total shareholder return (TSR) and to compete successfully on the global banking scene. Traditionally, the bank was run on a decentralized basis. Today, it is following a shared services agenda and pursuing a policy of global functional coordination where appropriate. Maurice Oostendorp, Head of Group Finance, talks about the organizational issues he faces.

ONE GROUP, ONE BANK
Maurice Oostendorp, Head of Group Finance, ABN Amro

Overall we're measuring our TSR against our peer group – the other major banks in the world. Traditionally, ABN Amro is number 10 in the rankings, measured on a four-year cycle basis, so we've some way to go! Next to that, our strategic ambition is to be in the top five European-based banks measured by market capitalization.

Some five years ago, we were organized on divisional lines – a mixture of geography, clients, and product-based businesses. And, traditionally, we've always had a strong focus on the Netherlands with only limited coordination between group functions and the businesses.

Recently, we announced a transformation into a business unit (BU) structure. BUs became responsible for their client-product business and our functional departments were even further decentralized. We needed to move to a "one-group, one-bank" approach while keeping the benefits of the increased focus on client-product business that the BU structure has created.

In the US we have a lot of experience in integrating acquisitions – we've acquired several banks over the last fifteen years. We have an experienced "integration machine" carving out more than 25% of costs. Consolidation of this nature can generate synergies relatively quickly, often within 18 months of acquisition. In Europe, however, you cannot yet achieve such synergies on a cross-border basis because of the country-based structure of the European banking market and regulations.

European acquisitions, such as the Italian Banca Antonveneta, however, do need to be integrated into the way that ABN Amro runs its business, especially the way we want to grow revenues in our consumer and commercial sectors.

Dual reporting

Our organizational change has gained momentum. Today, our bank services are organized globally into three business lines: Wholesale Clients, Consumer and Commercial Clients, and Private Clients and Asset Management.

We are trying to get the best of both worlds – global client segment, product development, and functional coordination – as well as local customer and product intimacy.

Functions such as finance are managed globally through a dual reporting structure: BU CFOs report both directly to the group Head of Finance and to their local BU CEO. We believe we've succeeded in avoiding unnecessary reporting overlaps by separating central and local functional responsibilities.

As head of group finance, I oversee the finance function of the global bank as a whole. I report to the group CFO and my responsibilities include not only financial accounting and management accounting, but also asset and liability management, tax and strategic decision support. These functions all operate on a dual reporting basis with the notable exception of group strategy decision support.

Integrating finance and risk

We see the need for greater alignment among the functions of finance, asset and liability management, and risk. Risk does report to the same management board member – the group CFO. We are starting an integrated group initiative called "capital management," covering finance, asset and liability management, and risk.

This initiative will not interfere with local risk management but will define group hurdle rates, pricing parameters, and hedging policies. The way we manage our risk-rated regulatory and economic capital will increasingly become a group function.

Regulatory fatigue

One thing's for certain – the regulatory workload is not going to decrease in the future! Most CFOs, no matter what industry they're in, are fatigued with the sheer volume of regulation we have to cope with. We're no exception in banking. IFRS, Basel II, SOX and the Dutch "version" of SOX (Tabaksblat), the client-based (AFM) banking regulation, and CAAML regulations (client acceptance, anti-money laundering, transaction monitoring) – all this means more and more internal initiatives.

After sustaining the costs of Sarbanes-Oxley, Europe's banks now face the costs of Basel II. Compliance is an integral part of both client service and quality proc-

esses. It cannot be seen as something on the side. It is part of the job: you have to make sure you can implement correctly.

I support the Basel II framework, which takes effect in 2007: it makes internal decisions about where you allocate capital easier. The speed of regulatory change, however, is stretching our legal, financial, and compliance staff.

While you can't avoid additional work, you can implement more efficiently – and secure benefits along the way. Central coordination certainly pays off! For example, our technology for transaction monitoring is now coordinated across the group; Basel II and SOX implementations and reporting are also consistent and optimized worldwide.

As head of group finance your team definitely needs technical accounting skills. What's more important, however, are other qualities: leadership (managing both group and local agendas) and understanding the business – being able to sit at the table with line management and add value.

Innovation

We're moving towards our market capitalization objective by making acquisitions in other countries, such as Italy. However, we want to drive innovation within the business too. We now have what we call "value area themes": centers of excellence where cross-functional teams come together on a project basis to promote out-of-the-box thinking.

New products sold to existing clients create more value than old products to new clients. We're looking for "breakout growth pockets." We want a business model where the bank's product owners – for example, of product development in transaction banking – are directly connected to customers.

Shared services and outsourcing

Our shared services agenda focuses on four objectives:

- Improved service quality – better supporting the front office in delivering products and increasing client satisfaction.
- Creating value through increased efficiencies – releasing funds to be reinvested in growth activities.
- Sharper management of operational risk – reducing capital tied up in operations.

- *Reducing time-to-market by adapting to fast-changing front-office needs and market dynamics.*

Our intention is to deliver at least €600 million a year in sustainable savings from 2007 onwards through our shared services initiatives. For example, we've developed a sourcing strategy to provide a global, bank-wide technology service. We recently decided to outsource; a major global contract has been announced for IT outsourcing of data centers.

Off-shoring is often seen as just a "lift-and-drop" exercise, predicated on the cost benefit of wage arbitrage. This gives you a quick win but, longer term, you need to rationalize your processes. We have a wholly owned subsidiary based in India called ACES and soon we will have around 5,000 jobs off-shore in India.

Through ACES, a wide variety of the bank's processes, including those related to HR, finance and IT services, are being optimized. So it's arbitrage first, optimization and standardization second! As we standardize processes, shared services ceases to be "shared" and becomes a purely global services organization. ACES is also becoming an insourcing hub for other financial institutions – a self-standing business.

Finance processes for improving performance

We're working on improving performance by "slicing 'n' dicing" information on customers, products, and distribution. We're bringing this information together across the group and relating it to our value chain – identifying value-creation opportunities, as well as cost improvements.

We don't want two versions of the truth, only one! We have a "top-down" approach to standardizing our management information. For example, we have an initiative called "transaction banking." Transaction banking includes product design, manufacturing, and specialized sales. It provides a standardized P&L format worldwide, so that we can make like-for-like performance comparisons between, say, Brazil and the Netherlands.

We've decided that a six-quarter rolling forecast should provide much earlier warnings of deviation from the four-year performance contract improvement trend. In the long run, we're hoping that this rolling forecast will enable us to overcome the disadvantages of fixed annual performance contracts, which can rapidly become out of date.

The future: cultural integration

Perhaps the most challenging barrier to change that we face is overcoming cultural differences across our company. While we're a Dutch-based bank, we have large operations all over the globe. These differences have to be openly discussed, under-stood, and translated into a shared understanding of how we want things done – not easy!

In the future, we in finance will be spending much less time on reporting "actuals" – by relying on better automated and integrated systems – and much more time on analyzing results and better understanding where the profits are made.

As highlighted by ABN Amro's experience, our research has identified four key pressures on the finance function:

- Cost – creating more value for less cost.
- Regulation – dealing with the impact of SOX and IFRS.
- Governance – identifying and evaluating business risks.
- Information – obtaining richer value-adding information.

More than half the CFOs we interviewed said that they needed more "business-savvy" finance executives working for them. They also said they needed to invest in building their finance team's knowledge of the business and the environment in which it operates. But fewer than 20% have programs in place to improve their teams' business analysis, com-munication, and problem-solving skills.

Change is often gradual and finance organizations typically pass through different stages of development as they evolve. Figure 2.1 shows how many companies see the level of their finance function's maturity – from a purely *functional orientation*, through *selective performance improvement*, all the way to *process integration* and, finally, to a *world-class* model.

Key questions every CFO should ask:

- At what stage of maturity is my finance organization?
- Do I understand the drivers of cost and service levels?
- What options are available to improve these drivers?

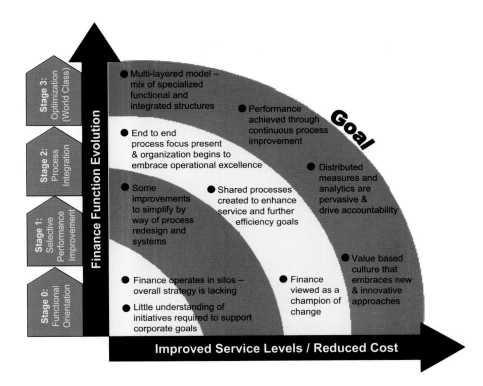

Figure 2.1 *Evolving the finance function: three stages of maturity*

- What are my plans to improve performance?
- Do I have the capabilities to implement them?

Low-cost, high-service finance organizations are typically advanced in applying strategies for improving organization, processes, and systems. In the table on the next page, we compare the characteristics of high-cost finance organizations with those of average and low-cost finance organizations. Until recently, companies with finance functions that were both low cost and high service tended to follow these development strategies:

- Adopting process orientation and simplification programs, rationalizing end-to-end processes – for example *purchase-to-pay and order-to-cash.*

Characteristics	Low cost	Average cost	High cost
	<1.0%*	1.0%–1.5%*	>1.5%*
Organization	Global shared services	Central processing	Decentralized
	Outsourced	Near/off-shore	On-shore
Processes	Lights out!	Re-engineered	Manual input
	World class	Standardized	Non-standard
Systems	One ERP	Multiple ERPs	Legacy
	Fully web-enabled: self-service	Best of breed point solutions	Spreadsheet proliferation

Finance cost as % of revenue

- Leveraging shared services to deliver routine, high-volume transaction processing with economies of scale – some companies consider outsourcing to extend value.

- Standardizing and integrating systems – migrating to a common ERP platform and extending this with best-of-breed, web-based planning and reporting applications.

Today, with all the additional pressures for regulation, control and transparency, the development agenda has been expanded:

- Reducing structural complexity and clarifying *line-of-sight*.

- Optimizing the control environment, identifying *redundant operations and controls*.

- Driving timely strategic decision making and *forward-looking insight*.

- Managing capitalization and investment across the enterprise, with a focus on *risk*.

- Developing specialized capabilities to improve productivity.

In reshaping their finance functions, companies must balance the often-conflicting corporate objectives of growth, efficiency, and control. And in pursuit of standardizing and simplifying their business processes they must also ensure that they don't "throw the baby out with the bathwater" by compromising good control and risk management. So the heart of the issue today is: how much to standardize? Next in this chapter, we see how BP is addressing this question.

THE QUEST FOR STANDARDIZATION

In the last two decades, BP has undergone several major transformations to become the largest UK-listed company. After streamlining its organizational footprint, the company gained a fresh performance edge. From the late 1990s, BP has built up a distinctive set of assets and market positions, and now has a formidable array of technologies at its disposal. After several mergers and acquisitions, its focus is on optimizing its footprint, controlling capital, increasing returns, and identifying sources of future growth.

BP has a highly successful track record in driving change. A recent survey ranked it as the UK's leading company for getting change right, citing as evidence: merger integration, structural reorganization, management of environmental issues, and transition to outsourcing. But the group has changed dramatically in recent years – and BP's past performance culture may not be the most appropriate for the next stage of its evolution.

Iain Macdonald, BP's Group Controller, talks about how he and his finance team are transitioning to a structural model for finance today while planning for the future.

MAKING CHOICES
Iain Macdonald, Group Controller, BP

BP's rapid expansion in the last ten years is largely the result of acquisition. It has strong legacy cultures with their attendant customs and practices. BP is making a determined attempt to create a "one enterprise" culture and reduce complexity.

Historically, BP had a disparate organization – this meant we were very successful in growing the company and in integrating acquisitions, but there was a relatively high degree of management autonomy. BP has outgrown its old governance models, but we want to retain our entrepreneurial culture.

New management framework

The public rightly demands ever-increasing corporate responsibility – be it in the form of regulation, wealth distribution or security of supply. Our challenge: growing organically and moving beyond our traditional geography and oil heritage.

As we develop in areas of the world where governance and risk are less well understood, we face significant people issues – development, motivation, and recruitment. So we've introduced a new "Management Framework."

Sponsored by our Chief Executive, this framework redefines roles, account-ability, and management control processes. The framework applies across the breadth and depth of the organization – from senior executive level down through the businesses.

BP's sheer size offers many opportunities for scale efficiencies. We've standard-ized and simplified our processes wherever possible. The dilemma we face, like all big multinational companies, is how far do you go with control and standardization? And how do you retain the goodwill of the people involved and empower them to continue making decisions?

Single-point accountability

We have a centralized Finance, Control and Accounting (FC&A) organization of 4,000 people that reports directly to me. We're responsible for the group finance infrastructure – our shared services organization, finance control processes, global reporting and management information.

Perhaps one of our biggest changes has been in the reporting lines. The senior finance executives in our largest businesses – called Segment Controllers – have a firm reporting line to me as group controller and a dotted line to segment execu-tive vice presidents. They are deeply involved in business management and sit on the segment executive teams. Strategic Performance Unit (SPU) Controllers report directly to the Segment Controllers – a firm black reporting line running all the way up to the group CFO.

We employ "single-point accountability": accountability no longer rests with committees but with individuals. For example, accountability in Exploration and Production (E&P) lies with the CEO of E&P, not his management committee. The SOX 302 attestation process has clarified responsibility and cascaded it down through the company. Issues are also driven up through the organization in a clearer way than in the pre-SOX 302 world.

So, the single-point accountability for effective financial controls, effective management information and external reporting ultimately, lies with me!

Control culture

FC&A is BP's newly defined function, responsible for all controls over financial reporting. It is centralized in reporting to me directly at headquarters, but parts of it are physically distributed throughout the organization. I do feel that we also influence the "control culture" of the entire company.

We've been running a SOX 404 project for more than three years, at a direct project cost run-rate of $50m annually. So it's a big, expensive project! But the benefits to BP have been twofold:

- *An overhaul of the control environment across the company – a **single** control function, a single way of defining processes, applying controls, and evaluating their effectiveness.*
- *A better "top-down" understanding of the risks to the business.*

If you have as many processes as BP does – one estimate has been as high as 15,000 different processes, of which about 3,000 we regard as material for SOX purposes – and you go through all these control evaluations, you're bound to discover opportunities for greater commonality.

We've also learned more about our risk appetite. Credit risk is relatively straightforward to define, but business risk is more complex. You can't aim for a zero-risk control environment in a thriving business – it's just not realistic. So the SOX exercise should lead us to a shared understanding and better management of our risk tolerance. In FC&A we look at risk in three categories:

- ***Operational risks** – our appetite for the risks which FC&A is responsible for.*
- ***Transformational risks** – risks associated with internal changes to our processes and systems.*
- ***Interface risks** – the impact of what's happening in the external environment – for example, politically or environmentally – on the business.*

It's not easy defining controls in a world that is constantly changing – our control framework has to be dynamic and flexible.

Process standardization

We're approaching process standardization in FC&A through a nominated Control Processes delivery team. Its task is to develop universal standards and work with local FC&A operating units in adopting these standards at the appropriate level. In FC&A, we look at processes from three viewpoints:

- *Business support – our business leadership teams, who are responsible for controls and management information.*
- *Centers of expertise – process-oriented, control-based, aggregators of information.*
- *Transactional accounting services – be they outsourced or insourced, built on standard processes.*

If all standards were implemented at all levels, they wouldn't work; they would just glue the organization up! The key is getting the right balance: the right tension between what should be prescribed centrally and what should be generated locally. This balance is crucial for us in having a fast, but robust, accounts closing and consolidation process.

Through SOX, we've prescribed and driven standard processes – what we call "white and green box" processes – which have had a material impact on the group. Such processes relate to balance-sheet integrity, inter-company reconciliations, provisioning, and journal adjustments.

For those processes outside FC&A's direct responsibility – for example, those which determine oil reserves or production reporting – control and reporting responsibilities are specifically defined. So for oil reserves, for example, where the central reserves organization is heavily involved, we have a defined part to play in FC&A.

Common systems

We now have a common agenda for systems and data. Currently, approximately 75% of the company uses SAP. However, we still have the remnants of legacy systems and software suppliers, and prior implementations. We're trying to build a common process and systems platform – using one technical and information architecture (a data warehouse concept) with integrated forecasting, management information and reporting systems.

Like most complex groups of companies, we have our fair share of spreadsheets. We had to introduce spreadsheet controls for reporting the "actuals." But we're moving away from spreadsheets to more sustainable system solutions. But whole-sale spreadsheet elimination is a step too far – they do have their rightful place!

Currently, we don't have the ability to drill down and capture the data we need. For statutory purposes and for joint ventures we still have to have a lot of different books of account. But we are developing the "group financial template" – our standard chart of accounts. Some data definitions can be standardized – for example, data related to vendors and employees – to provide cross-organizational leverage benefits. Others, such as customer data definitions, may be more local and less standardized.

We're rolling out the standard chart of accounts – extending it to all of Europe and all new implementations. This initiative should reduce inter-company reconciliations and provide us with the means to exploit the data in our systems, through data mining.

"One" function
When we set up FC&A, our first priority was to maintain connectivity with the businesses. Controllers in the business units could have been isolated by their local management colleagues as part of the new central, and potentially disenfranchised, FC&A organization. Fortunately, that didn't happen.

The segment and business unit controllers needed to gain a "seat" on their business leadership teams. They had to position themselves as having eyes into the business on the one hand – and providing local decision support on the other.

In FC&A, we've had to learn how to remain connected with the businesses, but also how to think, behave and act, when necessary, as one function. We've had to build this dual perspective into the organization. We've emphasized what we call "leadership alignment": having a common vision, sharing a definitive agenda, articulating it, and lining up our leadership behind its delivery.

We started building this alignment as a group of 10 or so FC&A leaders, and have expanded it to the next 150 managers. We've managed to engage the FC&A community as a whole in the change program. We started out not only with a series of project teams but also with the concept of the "virtual" finance university.

This university has a long heritage at BP but the FC&A faculty is relatively new. It's helped enormously with the dilemma so many of us face – being part of the FC&A function, as well as delivering service to the business unit – and gain-

ing relevant behavioral training. In its first year, this faculty delivered well over 100 courses – touching 2,000 people – over half the FC&A function!!

We live in the real world: not everything is under our total control. BP operates in more than a hundred countries. We celebrate diversity in our people – but not diversity for diversity's sake. We strive for homogeneity in our accounting and control.

Clearly, there is huge power in having a centralized finance organization equipped to deliver compliance in this changing world of regulation and ever-increasing standards of control. The learning process companies like BP go through en route to standardization is complex and takes time to introduce.

Go too fast, and you'll probably fall over. You have to find the right balance for centralization and decentralization. You have to earn credibility from business unit leaders first, before redefining process and control responsibility boundaries.

Having satisfied themselves that integrity and transparency are fully assured, companies that have been through the SOX processes successfully are, once again, considering the opportunities for further efficiency that have arisen.

After extracting the core control aspects of finance from each business segment, companies like BP still have to address how to structure the residual financial management responsibilities of their business units.

The finance function is under pressure to provide much greater transparency in reporting, while also coping with internal demands to reduce cost and maximize value. The cost and value trend has been disrupted by the compliance requirements of SOX and IFRS.

For many businesses, the cost of compliance is considerable: one estimate puts the average cost for listed companies at between $5 million and $8 million. Some of the largest companies, like BP, face costs of up to $50 million or more.

Squeezing sustainable improvements from the changes required by SOX – that's the challenge! Rigid best-practice methodologies and models won't work. The approach should be holistic, allowing for a wide range of models and behaviors.

To optimize standardization and centralization, consider the spectrum of choices, from laissez faire to ruthless standardization, on a number of change dimensions, ranging from control to behavior and systems. These choices are set out in the finance optimization model table on the next page.

Laissez faire	Collaborative	Ruthless standardization
Principles and values: High level, variable, self policed, sanctions rare	Control 5 – – – 0 – – – 5	Deep, rigid, comprehensive, policed, sanctions
Poor to non-existent standards, not maintained, no change control, not necessarily followed	Process 5 – – – 0 – – – 5	Common, detailed, documented, change controlled, rigidly followed
Uncontrolled invention, diversity tolerated, no group norms, no discernible underlying culture	Behavior 5 – – – 0 – – – 5	Compliant, defined roles, highly centralized, strong culture, limited diversity
Multiple, locally driven charts of accounts, no data definitions, multiple versions of the truth	Coding data 5 – – – 0 – – – 5	One detailed chart of accounts, data dictionary, single version of the truth
Multiple structures, highly matrixed, diffused accountability	Organization 5 – – – 0 – – – 5	Single structure, common grading, common roles, minimal matrix, prescribed accountability
Highly individualistic, generalists, little training	People 5 – – – 0 – – – 5	Clones, role specific, specialists, accredited
Multiple platforms, no architecture, multiple instances	Systems 5 – – – 0 – – – 5	Uniform systems, single instance, centrally hosted

The scale of 0–5 represents – at its extremes – degrees of flexibility and standardization. The mid-point of the optimization table implies a degree of collaboration, a mix of centralization and decentralization. CFOs can use the optimization table to benchmark where their finance function is today and the desired future state. Analyzing the experience of leading companies, we've observed that:

- Most organizations are moving towards more, not less, standardization.

- Optimizing, however, does not mean absolute ruthless standardization, but the leveraging of multiple change dimensions in a similar direction.

- Systems alone will not realize the benefits expected.

- The path to optimization is determined by a number of company-specific factors: its *culture*, its starting position, and the *rationale* for the change – be it regulatory or the pressure to perform.

Consider, in Figure 2.2, the finance optimization profile of a global media company – where it was three years ago, where it is now, and where it would like to go next.

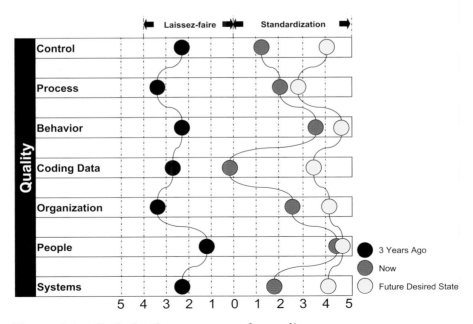

Figure 2.2   *Optimization case example: media company*

As CFOs embark on their latest round of finance developments, they should ask themselves the following:

Organizational realignment

- How should finance be organized and aligned to support the business?

- What are our spans of control and are they in line with what a well-controlled, cost-effective organization should be?

- How will organizational realignment affect our internal control environment?

- What levels of service are required and do we possess the appropriate mix of skills to deliver them?

Processes and reports

- What finance processes and reports should be redesigned, changed or eliminated?

- How are our processes performing? How do we measure up against high-performance finance organizations?

- What best practices can we leverage to improve performance?

Compliance

- How might implementation of cost improvements impact regulatory compliance and internal controls?

- What monitoring or compliance policies/processes are necessary to maintain internal control effectiveness and compliance rigor?

- How should compliance risks be managed? Is our approach aligned with organizational and business needs?

- How do we ensure that compliance is optimized without negatively affecting business performance, processes, people, culture, and technology?

- Are our financial reporting processes effectively designed in light of Sarbanes-Oxley?

SOX, along with other regulatory and internal pressures, is prompting many companies to reconsider their overall governance models and

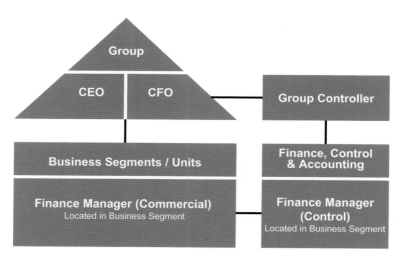

Figure 2.3 *Governance model: group control*

the effectiveness of their control functions. The model that is emerging defines finance as having two core components:

- Control – transaction processing and statutory reporting.

- Partnership – planning, analysis and finance operations.

Figure 2.3 shows how the role of the group controller – and his control organization across the business – is increasingly segregated from the business partner organization in the business units. In today's environment, this governance model facilitates:

- Clarity concerning accountabilities.

- Clear segregation of duties.

- Standardization and simplification of processes.

- Alignment of *growth* (commercial) and *control* agendas.

THE *NEW* FINANCIAL MANAGEMENT MODEL

Consider how Nestlé has gone about introducing its new financial management model – addressing the need for growth and innovation as well as its global standardization agenda. Wolfgang Reichenberger, until recently the group CFO, has now moved on to become CEO of an exciting new venture capital fund.

SHAPING THE FINANCE FUNCTION
Wolfgang Reichenberger, former CFO, Nestlé

Our strategy for Nestlé is based on four pillars for growth:

- *Innovation*
- *Product availability*
- *Communication*
- *Lower operating costs*

We knew that if we executed well on all four of these pillars, it would lead to the growth we wanted. We've been reshaping our organization to benefit from synergies at a global level – where appropriate, moving from a predominantly geographic country orientation to a global business and support service model.

There are certain aspects of our business, such as in food, where we need to be close to our markets and our organization remains country-based. But the back office – "behind the curtains" – can be standardized, organized into shared services, maybe even outsourced. We've called this project "Globe."

The finance change agenda
We thoroughly analyzed what was needed to align our finance function with our new business and strategy organization. We've set up shared services for finance and developed models based on SAP for global roll out. We have defined five key finance roles:

1. *The transactions processing roles: for example, on the purchase-to-pay cycle. These are being incorporated into our regional shared services organization and may be either insourced or outsourced.*
2. *Specialist technical roles: grouped mainly on a global basis, in centers of excellence – such as accounts consolidation, treasury and tax.*

3 **The co-pilot (role number 1):** *finance executives working in partnership with business units – driving performance, supporting innovation and growth, and, where necessary, assisting in lowering costs.*

4 **The co-pilot (role number 2):** *the same executives as in (3), but having a different, "double" personality – reporting to headquarters on target achievement, providing early warnings of problems, and being accountable for control governance and stewardship. It is through this role that we ensure compliance with our business principles and best accounting practice.*

5 **Decision-support specialists:** *these are aggregated together into centers of excellence, at a regional and market level. They support the co-pilots with analytics and data mining. This is a whole new way of managing our corporate information, particularly with the advent of Globe and the business warehouse "information pull" concept. We've covered twelve markets so far, but we've still got fifty to go!*

When you change an organization as profoundly as this, you have to fully involve the people affected and deal with their concerns. You also have to make people accountable, with clear ownership for the changes involved.

It's quite difficult for the co-pilots to balance their respective roles and double loyalties. They have local reporting lines and their salaries and bonuses are agreed locally, but I manage their careers (and promotions!) from headquarters.

In fact, the co-pilots for our three key geographical zones (Europe, Americas and Asia) are my closest allies. They have a dotted-line relationship to me and are encouraged to raise difficult issues with me. When you put the right people in charge, you have to trust them. The "proof of the pudding is in the eating" – we've achieved good healthy earnings without cutting corners.

Decision support

Our decision-support centers of excellence share knowledge about what works in terms of our investment in brands and campaigns. We also spend a considerable amount of money on promotions and look at the impact of promotions on revenue and value. We find quite often that it's not the finance people doing this, it's operational and marketing too – so we take a multidisciplinary approach.

Hermann Wirz, SVP Group Accounting and Reporting of Nestlé, comments on developments in financial management processes:

With the background of the accounting scandals in the US and Europe, we've got so much more legislation and regulation to handle. The danger with all this is that it can take the attention away from the real business issues. It's become too technical and too academic.

We need to avoid a complete disconnect between the financial world and what general management wants. General managers want simple key performance indicators – and some financial yardsticks that are sustainable, comparable, and devoid of accounting complexity.

My challenge is to balance accounting accuracy – a true and fair view with integrity – with the need to optimize profitability. We drive the business with EBITA measures, based on rock-solid reporting, and aligned with figures derived from International Accounting Standards. We have one set of accounts. Not easy!

Our Globe project should provide us with tremendous leverage in our ability to drill down for information – from headquarters into business unit data. We're also moving away from yearly budgeting to rolling forecasts. We want to break what I call the "wall of budgeting" at the year end – with 18-month dynamic forecasts using financial measures and a new set of key performance indicators (KPIs) that are tailor-made to the businesses.

In the future, we're likely to have fewer people in our central financial functions, but the skills mix will change. With our changing organizational model, we're going to have to adapt our reporting approach. We're moving from functionally-related and operating market profit and loss accounts to more of a process-driven income statement.

The downward pressure on the cost of finance will not abate, despite the temporary blip associated with the cost of SOX compliance. Finance functions are being forced to learn to do more with less. As at Nestlé, this means a review of all activities, systems, and processes across the entire finance organization. In addition to identifying quick wins, there are longer-term issues to address, including how finance operates and interacts with the rest of the business.

Business will increasingly have to provide forward-looking financial information, placing further strain on the finance function to produce appropriate information in real time. There is little doubt that most large organizations will have numerous initiatives at any one time that directly, or indirectly, involve the finance function. For the optimization process to move ahead, these initiatives have to be understood and managed within the overall business context.

However, many companies are not approaching these challenges holistically. Instead, they are conducting finance initiatives in silos. As a result, they are not seeing the "big picture" when it comes to various processes (how they integrate), the enabling structures (how far to go), and the constraints of the business itself.

Figure 2.4 provides a holistic model for shaping the finance function across business processes – ranging from the front office, to the mid and back offices. In this model, each process is optimized within the context of both *business specifics* and *enabling change dimensions*.

CFOs and their finance functions are migrating to integrated enterprise risk management and compliance processes, using SOX compliance as a core foundation. To sustain compliance, they're looking for efficiency improvements – and making the necessary changes in people and technology. They're also identifying and replacing "band-aid" remediation fixes with a holistic approach in order to minimize potential control breakdowns.

PROCESS OPTIMIZATION AND REPORTING

Increasingly, companies are coming to grips with their new financial management model – and entering the *beyond SOX 404* environment. They're going from SOX to "Ox" (operational excellence) – optimizing their operational processes. Where? In supply chain, in human resources, in go-to-market.

What's different? They're using the same discipline employed for 404 in assessing operational risks and controls. As a result, they're implementing wider process and related systems improvements. In so doing, they're really leveraging regulation.

There are a number of lessons to be drawn from the many process improvement cases we've analyzed for this book. Taken together, these lessons provide a sound basis for framing and implementing your company's process optimization efforts:

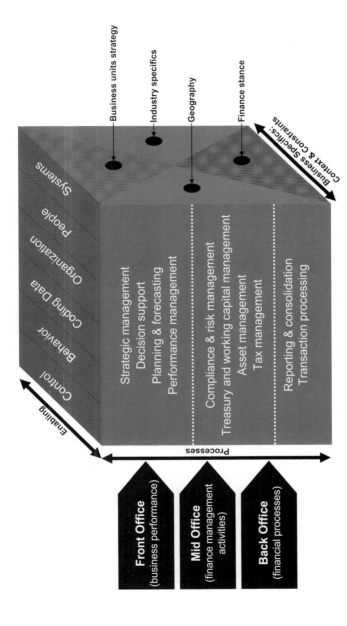

Figure 2.4 *Shaping the finance function: process perspective*

Lesson 1: Articulate a compelling case for change

For example, recently merged companies should make the case for timely reporting without having to revisit and revise input data.

Lesson 2: Build process-based expertise and knowledge

Success in process optimization often necessitates a community of experts and champions who are clearly accountable for completing the end-to-end process.

Lesson 3: Make transaction processing a pivot point

Standardization and simplification of transaction processes can lead to significant enhancements in decision support.

Lesson 4: Understand and address root causes

The foundation of any successful process optimization is getting to the root of the problem – through root cause analysis and a common set of process taxonomies for identifying problems and issues.

Lesson 5: Address issues through short-term focus

Focus on quick wins. Deliver incremental change at a pace the organization can absorb, establishing stability and process transparency.

Lesson 6: Work within the appetite for change

Strong communication and engagement of all stakeholders is critical; so is accepting the reality of an organization's culture.

Lesson 7: Embed program-management disciplines

Structure projects around the delivery of benefits, making the achievement of milestones unambiguous, maintaining visibility of inter-project dependencies, and effectively managing cost and quality.

Lesson 8: Measure and monitor results

Establish a scorecard for base-line and target performance levels – setting short-, medium- and long-term goals.

There is a tendency for newly implemented processes to degrade over time. This occurs as people shift roles and the business environment adjusts to new circumstances and new technology. However, continuous improvement is achieved only by introducing lasting changes in behavior.

We've highlighted the reporting process next in this chapter because, for finance, it's where so much comes together. It's also where the greatest concerns arise about transparency and control.

Typically, companies experience reporting "pain-points" in three areas: when closing accounts following a merger; when consolidating financial statements; and when providing broader reports, such as the Management, Discussion and Analysis (MD&A). Some of the most vulnerable aspects of the record-to-report process include:

- Multiple data sources and standards.

- Inconsistent data, its quality and integrity.

- Reliance on largely manual processes, reconciliations, and data re-entry.

- The time required to review and produce accurate reports.

- Differences between what's documented, *as the process,* and what actually takes place.

- Scalability of technologies and applications used in the reporting cycle.

Striking a balance between strategic and tactical initiatives is critical to successfully improving reporting. Examples of *tactical* initiatives include registering spreadsheets and automating data collection. *Strategic* initiatives might include the standardization of definitions, and the automation of production and validation of data using the latest technologies.

Nevertheless, investments in better reporting have returned mixed results. One CFO interviewed for this book said:

> *"I get only three hours to review the quarterly financials before I have to speak to the analysts. The pressure is unbelievable!"*

Companies still struggle to get the information they need to make well-informed decisions. People still spend too much time manipulating data instead of analyzing it. Manual, error-prone, and redundant processes are still common. Most organizations are not getting full value out of their ERP systems investment – or their data warehousing and reporting packages. There is still too much reliance on spreadsheets for tasks that create errors and risks. Effective controls can sometimes remain elusive.

As with Nestlé's Globe strategy, a well-controlled, flexible and integrated financial information environment should improve performance, achieve better insight, and action-oriented reporting. To improve finance effectiveness in reporting – quality, timeliness, efficiency, and relevance:

- Establish a vision and road map that links people, processes, and technology to meet measurable goals.

- Design a flexible, service-oriented architecture as the foundation for improvements.

- Improve and automate key processes.

- Embed controls and apply standards and streamlined processes to improve data quality.

- Measure goals and progress against critical attributes and industry best practices.

Figure 2.5 shows how best practices are being developed for the corporate reporting process – *from level 1* (ad hoc spreadsheets) *through to levels 4 and 5* (enterprise-wide business intelligence and integrated external reporting).

There are three building blocks for success in the reporting process:

Block 1: Foundation layer – the organization, policies and definitions, procedures and processes, reporting tools and architecture needed to source, consolidate, and deliver information.

Block 2: Analytical layer – the chart of accounts, performance measures, and analytical dimensions (*views* of financial information, for example by geography or by product).

Block 3: Financial and management reporting layer – the right reports for decision support.

Of course, optimizing processes such as reporting will help in simplification and standardization. However, streamlining the corporate structure itself can pre-empt the need for extensive process redesign.

Level 1 Ad hoc Spreadsheet Reporting	Level 2 Partial Spreadsheet Remediation & Control	Level 3 Complete Remediation & Control	Level 4 Enterprise-Wide Business Intelligence Reporting	Level 5 Internal / External Information Integration
• Heavy reliance on spreadsheets and manual tasks in key reporting steps (collection, preparation, storage, analysis & publishing)	• Heavy reliance on spreadsheets with limited automation along reporting steps	• Minimal dependence on end-user computing environment	• Enterprise-wide vendor solutions are leveraged to support automation along key reporting steps	• Enterprise-wide reporting extends outside the corporate boundaries and facilitates the preparation of regulatory and third party reports in interoperable formats such as XML and XBRL
• Data is locked within spreadsheets resulting in time consuming and error-prone data sharing	• Manual activities are reduced and control weaknesses identified, prioritized and partially addressed	• Data collection and preparation steps are automated & supported by IT	• Definition of process / data ownership is enforced via web-services, thereby reducing redundancy and the need to keep data synchronized	• Web-services are utilized to create real-time and bulk data-loading interfaces between data-sources and data-providers
• Processes are informally documented and suffer from key-person risk	• Data is stored in a database to facilitate sharing	• Data validation is automated and handled via exception based reporting	• Data aggregation and analysis supports automation as well as flexibility	• Data is fully tagged to support automated validation and analysis
• Data is secured via spreadsheet password or file folder restrictions	• Processes are documented to reduce key-person risk	• The reporting environment is 'departmental' in nature, which results in replicated data that may fall out of sync from the original source system	• A methodology exists to support ad hoc spreadsheet reporting within a controlled environment	• Business users define and control all aspects of key reporting steps
• IT does not support process and tools	• Data and process ownership is defined, but not enforced	• Trade-off between flexibility / automation can make processes rigid		
	• Data security is limited to the feature-set of the database system	• Ability to perform ad hoc analysis is limited		
	• IT provides limited support			

Figure 2.5 *Best practice corporate reporting*

STREAMLINING CORPORATE STRUCTURE

Consider the complexity inherent in a European headquartered company with operations all over Europe and the rest of the world. Signs are beginning to emerge that a unified corporate European entity may actually become a reality.

The European company, or Societas Europaea, has been a long time in the making. First proposed more than 30 years ago, the legislation providing the new legal structure only came into force in late 2005. So far, only a dozen or so companies have made the switch from a national corporate identity to a European one. These include Sweden's Nordea Bank and Austria's Strabag construction group. Take Allianz, the latest "convert," as an example.

CASE STUDY
Creating a one-European company

Allianz, Germany's biggest insurance group, is transforming its structure radically. This is leading to sweeping changes in its corporate governance and a buy-out of minorities in its Italian subsidiary. It plans to become the largest enterprise in Europe so far to convert into a truly European company. This new legal structure will enable it to avoid having to adopt different structural forms in each country-based jurisdiction in Europe. It will also empower it to behave as one company across the EU.

As part of this change, it intends to internationalize its two-tier board system to a degree unheard of in Germany. This involves consolidating into one new holding company all of its German insurance activities, from property and casualty to life and health.

A senior finance executive from Allianz commented recently in the financial press:

"We are the broadest European-based insurance operation. We think this sends a very strong signal that even though our headquarters are in Munich we are a European player and use that base to compete globally.

"There are several reasons for us changing to the new European company status – not least that it is the only legal way to do a cross-border merger. That's what we're planning to do with our Italian subsidiary, RAS, the country's second-largest insurer.

This allows us to reorganize our Italian operations and bring their other European activities in countries such as Spain and Austria directly into one holding company.

"Another important reason for the change in company status will be our ability to shrink the supervisory board and bring in more foreign directors. The management board will be expanded from ten to eleven members and will contain directors of six different nationalities. But the supervisory board, the subject of much criticism due to its unwieldy size and strong worker representation, will be shrunk to twelve members. Six will still be workers, but drawn from across the group's European operations.'

Allianz's decision coincides with its move to take full control of RAS. Groups in several EU states are now able to merge and operate throughout the Union on the basis of a single set of rules and a unified management and reporting system. This should save money by avoiding a complex web of subsidiaries subject to different laws. But questions still remain about tax and regulatory issues arising from the new statute.

Unifying a corporate structure in the way planned by Allianz should go a long way to relieving the administrative burden in reporting and processes. Consider next how far some companies can go with simplification and transparency when they are funded by the private equity market.

For small to medium-sized companies, private equity has always been a recognized mechanism for triggering a step-change in performance and focusing on longer-term capital growth. Today, however, the private equity market is moving up the scale continuum, with ever-growing funds available. For larger companies, there's much to learn from private equity players!

LESSONS FROM PRIVATE EQUITY

Although not subject to the rigors of the public market – public exposure and comparison – private equity based company investors are asking the non-execs to evaluate management, make their contributions to strategy, and to do this in private.

In private companies, you can get things done without public interference. You don't have to choose the safe options. You can focus on mission-critical decisions without the constraints of a sub-optimal, more public environment. You can go for the option that is truly the best.

There is a very real threat of a "brain drain" of executives from the boardrooms of public quoted companies to the private equity sector. Senior executives with experience in both unlisted and listed sectors predict that, in cases where individuals are mainly money-driven, the private equity sector has a winning edge.

As the private equity sector has acquired bigger companies, its attraction for top talent has grown. To quote one CEO of a privately held company:

> *"If you deliver, there is no question about how much money you are going to make – and no need for negotiation. It's very difficult for a public company to compete with that."*

Another CFO says:

> *"Some people like working for listed companies for the prestige. But why should I spend half my week dealing with shareholders, analysts, and PR advisors?"*

This debate prompts two important questions. First, is it really the case that talented candidates are being discouraged from working in public companies? Second, do investors have a role in ensuring that this does not happen? It would be unfortunate if the positive work done by companies, investors, and government to improve the governance of public companies has the unintended consequence of driving away talent.

Three major concerns have been raised about working in the public company sector:

- The greater regulatory burden.
- The complex nature of the job.
- The degree of press and investor scrutiny.

Investors in public companies should not put themselves at a disadvantage relative to other providers of capital, either through their own demands as owners or by supporting inappropriate government interference. Their role is to help create the conditions in which talented individuals are willing to take up directorships and do their job effectively. Let's look more closely at the debate among CFOs about the relative merits of private equity versus public listing.

Take the case of Phil Yea, who went from Group Finance Director at Diageo to a managing director at Investcorp to his current position as chief executive of 3i, a world leader in venture capital and private equity. 3i is a prominent FTSE 100 public company listed on the UK stock exchange. The company has invested in over 1,700 businesses. In the last five years alone, it has helped over 70 companies float on 16 different international exchanges and a further 540 companies achieve trade sales.

Phil, as the former CFO of a large public company and, more recently, as the managing director of a portfolio of private equity investments, is in a unique position to comment on *public versus private*, and also the transition from CFO to CEO.

A PURER FORM OF CAPITALISM
Philip Yea, CEO, 3i Group Plc

Private equity is a purer form of capitalism because the shareholders create the board for the period of their ownership. They sit on the board of the company and have a sense of responsibility for creating value. The shareholders are therefore more directly involved with management and with strategy. Communication between shareholders and managers is also much more straightforward.

In public companies, if there is bad news for shareholders, the board has to spend much of its time having to guess (and finesse!) how to communicate it. In private companies, because the relationship between the board and shareholders is so much closer, the public company game is irrelevant.

Public market regulation
As an investor across the world, I can appreciate the need for regulation. As a CEO of a FTSE 100 company in the financial services sector, I can also appreciate the frustration at "over-regulation" and why so many people are now deterred from joining the boards of public companies

Although obviously well intentioned, SOX is inevitably increasing the relative attractiveness of private equity boards. Its primary goal is to correct reporting imperfections. However, it is extremely costly and time consuming. In private equity, when we buy a company, we do extensive due diligence, we know what we're acquiring, and are in a position to change the management if we have to.

The key word in the regulation debate is "balance": taking positions at either end of the spectrum is unhelpful to business. There are many aspects of regulation that I support. For example, I am more in favor now of IFRS than I was when I was a Finance Director.

In an increasingly international business world, I see more and more value in having a common language. IFRS would certainly seem to be the solution to Europe's muddle. Having just two sets of standards, US GAAP and IFRS, is at least a step forward. Ultimately, IFRS is moving us to where we want to be, has a one-off cost of compliance – and, unlike SOX, should not add cost and complexity forever.

Shareholder dialogue

It's certainly hard to argue against the need for greater transparency in public markets. As a public company director, you want to have a realistic dialogue based on common data with shareholders. In 3i, the first thing I did was to make our targets more explicit. This means we are going to have to report progress against these targets. Some people said: "Well what happens if you miss them?" But how else can I have a meaningful dialogue with shareholders on how we are doing?

I think such disclosure is a good thing. If you have more realistic indicators against which to report, then you can have a richer and more meaningful dialogue with shareholders. We publish not just our returns but also our volatilities around them.

Volatility information can be helpful in explaining short-term variations in performance and in focusing the investor on longer-term trends and sustainability. If we are ahead of target, my message might be: Don't bank the good news without recognizing that there is the potential for bad news, which may be just around the corner! That's what I mean about the richness of dialogue.

Investor involvement

When I am talking to prospective shareholders who are interested in making a significant investment in 3i's shares, it concerns me that they seem to rely on just a few brokers' notes and a few hours with management!

At 3i, when we buy into companies, the extent of our due diligence is phenomenal! It includes customer interviews, detailed management evaluations, market assessments – we absolutely have to understand what we are buying. In the private equity sector, we have a more comprehensive review process – another reason why I believe it is a "purer form of capitalism."

Of course, the work of the board should be all about how to deliver for sharehold-ers. In a private company, you can focus on this. If there is bad news, it's shared immediately by the management. And then the discussion moves to what you are going to do about it. In my experience, this is the fundamental difference between most public and private companies.

The closer relationship between management and investor leads to greater immediacy – getting done what needs to get done quicker! What supports this sense of immediacy? Not just the presence of investors on the board but the senior man-agement incentive scheme. This just leads to a more efficient feedback loop – quick, proactive reaction.

Recreating option value

I also believe that public equity markets quite often destroy option value in compa-nies in some areas of the market. That's why private equity can be a really good asset class. What private equity firms can do is recreate option value – either by attracting a better management team or by taking the company to a strategy that the public markets won't allow it to follow. One example: a diversification strategy that takes the company away from a pure-play focus.

For a company whose traditional markets are in decline, this means that it can fall into a downward spiral of value destruction. The reason? Because it's not permitted by investors to get out of its straitjacket, get out of the box, and take advantage of its capabilities in developing fresh options for growth. In fact, the thesis of private equity is just that – recreating options for value creation.

It's not just the public equity markets that can limit the company's option for growth, but also the parent company of a subsidiary that doesn't fit. If you have the wrong parent then it is possible that it will under-invest in you and not have the management capacity to work with you to exploit the full option value.

So there is a valued skill in recreating options for companies. When those options have been recreated and represented as a much simpler value proposition back to the public equity markets, then the people who've done it are likely to go on and do it again!

Creating the tension and space for new business models

The area that really interests me is innovation behind the business models of the companies in which we invest. I was really stimulated during the dot-com phase by the emphasis on business models and their potential sustainability. What's really exciting? When someone has found a truly different business model – either because it is substantially lower cost or new technology or it's created a new market in which to grow.

Dell is one of the great icons of a business model that is different. What's interesting about Dell is that it continues to innovate around its business model. BP, too, is constantly challenging its business models within its markets.

When we are looking at investments, we're constantly asking questions about the business model – how sustainable is it? What threats are there from others changing their business models? To what degree is a model's success dependent on individuals? Is it scalable? How unique is it? Is it replicable by a competitor?

Capitalism creates the tension and the space for new business models to develop and flourish. Business models, driven by end-consumer needs – these are at the heart of capitalism!

Business models aren't static: the rate of change today is frightening! So you can't really take a snapshot, in financial terms, of the value of a business and view it as representative of performance, current or future. You have to look at the pace of change behind the scenes. This is what we're doing with private equity investment – we're managing change.

Big company-itus
The important thing for investors and managers alike is to avoid what I call "big company-itus'! At our company I'm focusing on regularly reviewing our business models, being very clear on our people management, their quality and potential.

For example, at 3i this isn't just about rehearsing our presentations to investors. It means exploring what we're doing with our business lines, re-evaluating their business models, creating international rather than single-country teams. We're working and reporting on our processes for investment selection, asset review, and exiting, as well as on compensation systems that support sustainability.

A big issue for many companies: How much change can they cope with and at what speed? Many translate this from a business model viewpoint: How much to insource, how much to outsource?

Take the pharmaceutical industry, for example – increasingly it is outsourcing R&D and production. The business models and investment processes of pharmaceutical companies today are very different from those of fifteen years ago.

Is the accounting world of today appropriate for our business models? There's no point in trying to value assets at a particular moment in time – particularly intangibles such as drugs under development or brands.

On the question of brand value – it is not the brand that's worth the money, per se. Brands are perceptions – what people think at a particular point in time. Most importantly, it's the ability of the company to sustain cash flow arising from investments in brands and business models. People and processes are the keys to brand value. What is important is to try to make transparent the underlying business processes so that the market can evaluate the sustainability of cash flows generated by such assets.

So, what we're interested in here at 3i is the sustainability of the business models of our investments. What's likely to change these business models? And therefore, how should we value them? A static valuation based on historic cash flows will not do the job. What we are looking at is the likely dynamics – a whole series of variables – behind future cash flows. We're evaluating information on the ability of the company and management to sustain performance.

CFO qualities

What do I look for in a CFO today? I rate highly CFOs who really do tell the truth, are hard working, and who "work smart." The role of a CFO, increasingly, is to act as the guardian of shareholder value – pulling out the relevant metrics and analysis and providing a complementary challenge to the CEO on strategy and its implementation.

However, with all the emphasis today on regulation and SOX, the CFO is almost being dragged back into being just a process manager for regulatory compliance. Despite the shared responsibility for this burden, the CEO is bound to look to the CFO to make sure everything is in order and increasingly the CFO has less time for the business. Not much fun!

What can the CFO learn from experience in handling private equity investments? Well, how to evaluate a management team, how to stimulate and discuss strategic change, and how to influence a senior management team – and how to hone man-agement judgment.

In the past, specialists who handled investment portfolios were largely passive asset managers; today they are more proactive. The skill base has increased, just as it has for the CFO. Key questions to consider: Where is this business going? What's the strategy? What are competitors doing? What's the value creation plan? The finan-cial numbers in the end are only reviewed in the context of the answers to these questions. Every asset we own has a value creation plan – this is so much more than just accounting.

Like Phil, most CEOs of public companies view their CFO as a full business partner. Yes, the CFO has to deliver on all the regulatory requirements, but the job is much more than that. Just like a strong CEO, a good CFO must have a vision. The CFO is more internally oriented, but nevertheless must act as a sounding board on issues in the outside world.

It's no coincidence that some of the best strategic business thinkers and practitioners – those that have focused on business models and how to make money – have ended up in, or around, private equity. As a share-holder you are placing much greater expectations onto the backs of the management and non-executives.

However, most readers of this book will be senior executives of public quoted companies. Business leaders today, whether they're in publicly quoted companies or private, have to get three things right:

- Create their own models for the business, shape these in their head, and get others to share their vision.

- Choose the right people for execution, focused on the right issues in the right way.

- Foster the right business culture and behaviors – a responsive and dynamic management environment for change.

If you get these things right, the company just hums! In upcoming chap-ters, we move away from the issues of complexity and control and onto the issues of value creation and growth. Our goal: to explore how com-panies are successfully managing their business models through these times of uncertainty and change.

STRAIGHT FROM THE CFO

- **Make conscious choices**

  Formulate a shared finance agenda. Take advantage of scale. Look for opportunities to standardize. Choose among your options: what should be centralized, what should be local? Is the mandate and "fit" of finance as a function well understood in your company? Is there clear accountability for financial control?

- **Make finance one function**

  Overhaul your control environment. Understand better the risks to the business – what *is* really key? Build a control culture. Do not compromise on reporting – solid black line to the center, dotted lines locally. Establish single-point accountability. Remember: avoid disconnecting finance from front-line business unit teams.

- **Go from SOX to "OX"**

  Challenge complexity – no one else will! Consider the impact on business processes – front office, mid office, back office – on the overall organizational, control, and cultural contexts. Focus on the reporting process – travel up the best-practice maturity curve. Spreadsheet mania? Go for common data, common systems.

- **Shape your new financial management model**

  Align your various finance initiatives. Do you need a project "Globe"? Separate transaction processing, from decision support. Encourage business-unit finance executives to be true co-pilots!

- **Streamline your corporate structure**

  Take the opportunity to rationalize the number of statutory entities, reducing structural complexity. Review your board structures to improve the speed and effectiveness of decision making – but don't compromise corporate governance. Consider the advantages of the one-company European model.

- **Learn from private equity**

  Build richness into your shareholder dialogue. Set and communicate clear, simple targets. Avoid big company-itus! Go for transparency in the underlying processes in your business model. Evaluate the sustainability of the cash flows of your major assets. Recreate option value. Have a value creation plan for every (significant) asset. Create the tension and space for new business models.

CHAPTER 3

Making Change Happen

The finance function has never before been in such a strong and powerful position to make change happen. But the reverse can also be true: finance can get in the way – unless it provides the necessary leadership, influence, and passion for execution. CFOs interviewed for this book understand the drivers behind change in their organizations, but their starting points vary tremendously.

As we've seen, CFOs are juggling many different change agendas – for example, *externally* with stakeholders (government, regulators, and investors), and *internally* with issues related to compliance, improving performance, and creating value. The various pressures on a CFO today are shown in Figure 3.1.

Managing all these different changes, balancing the often-conflicting demands for resources, and keeping everything moving in the right direction is the constant challenge. Maintaining the motivation of your finance staff in the face of the enormous additional workload is difficult to sustain.

Not surprisingly, many CFOs complain of initiative overload. The issue is not only how to prioritize, but how to identify project overlaps and avoid duplication. The real goal: going for the greater benefits of combining initiatives into an integrated change program that delivers not just incremental change, but also wholesale transformation.

Most CFOs and their finance functions, like in the case of Ahold, know all about the problems they've got today but are unsure as to how far to go on the continuum of change. Companies such as BP, with legacy issues, are working hard to get the balance right – reinforcing control, but also stimulating sufficient change to re-energize – and all this without sacrificing entrepreneurial flair!

The public sector – for example, central government – also has a finance change agenda: increasing accountability; introducing best practices and

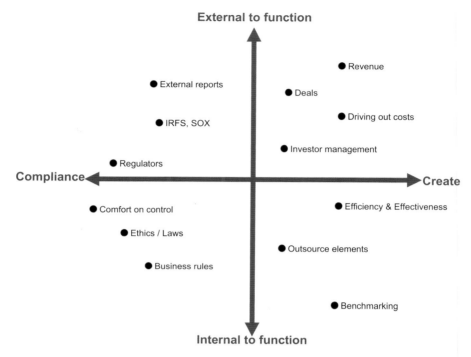

Figure 3.1 *Pressures on the CFO today*

private-sector financial management disciplines; going for cost efficiencies, for example with shared services; and wholesale systems renewal. What the public and private sectors have in common is the thorny issue of how to improve customer service at the front line.

What's particularly interesting about the public sector, is the massive degree of change required over relatively short timescales and the implications for culture and skills.

This chapter shows how various organizations in both the public and the private sectors are tackling the change process – but from different starting points. We consider the CFO as a leader and sponsor of change in the business, what it means to be best practice in the transformational change process, and how to benefit from change integration. The chapter concludes on how the role of the CFO is changing – from CFO to COO – and the search for new finance skills and talent.

We begin by looking at how Parmalat, an Italian company, recovered from scandal. The company achieved unwanted worldwide notoriety for its own "black hole" in accounting. It has since been restructured and is now fully back in business.

CHANGE, IN A HURRY

It's well known today that Parmalat Group had built up far too much debt and was not generating sufficient cash. The press coverage indicates that a very small group of senior managers, working in conjunction with banks, caused a major financial collapse. This could probably have been avoided by having the right controls, the right ethics and the right level of transparency.

Parmalat Group today, even after fundamental restructuring and a significant reduction in size, is still a company with revenues of €4 billion and 16,500 employees. Paolo Fietta, the new Group Financial Controller, talks about the challenges and changes required – some of which had to be implemented straight away.

FOCUSING ON THE ESSENTIALS
Paolo Fietta, Group Financial Controller, Parmalat

My past career has been wrapped up as a controller and as a director of finance and administration in a variety of industrial and commercial environments. I believe my past roles have prepared me well for Parmalat – international exposure, restructuring, financial discipline – I was never one for an easy life!

When I was appointed Group Financial Controller of Parmalat Group, I was confronted with a mess! There was no real group financial planning and analysis process in place. So there was no way to assess the ongoing business and financial situation. The financial team at the center was too small, and many people across the group were worried about their futures. And, of course, they were in a state of shock when faced with the reality of the scandal.

My challenges when I started were threefold:

1 *Transparency, internal and external – the market was looking for reassurance and for us to tell the truth. We quickly had to give them information about the company's real position.*

2 **Consistency** – *to ensure that the figures we produced were consistent and reliable. This was about changing behavior, the company culture and management style.*

3 **Financial planning and analysis** – *we had to put together the right people in a team and support them with the right processes and systems. We needed to achieve the right level of financial forecasting and control.*

Despite the pressure to turn things around quickly, this was always going to be a long journey. Today, we are well down the path to reassuring the market and providing the necessary transparency.

A new Parmalat has been born! We have merged the sixteen previous companies into a new single company traded on the Milan Stock Exchange. The former creditors of the bankrupt companies – largely bond holders, national and international banks, and suppliers – are looking to recover part of their losses through the new group. The alternative would have been to liquidate the assets.

We hoped to issue shares of the new company to creditors, but for this to be successful, we needed to have their approval and their confidence in our business plan.

All being well, "the Phoenix should arise from the ashes"! It should become clear as to who the new shareholders will be and, hopefully, we will have their support for continuing our restructuring. This will be seen as a success for the entire company.

The agenda for my part in the change process is as follows:

1 *Completion of plans for the development of a world-class team in financial planning and business analysis.*

2 *Continuing to introduce changes in systems and processes. For example, we hope to complete an enterprise-wide SAP implementation for the new Parmalat – before that, the sixteen companies had sixteen different system solutions!*

3 *Introducing common best practices for financial planning, analysis and control at headquarters and in the business units. We need a standard approach, for example in investment evaluation.*

My experience at Parmalat, coupled with previous turnaround experience, shows the importance of the following learning points:

- *Have a focal point for leadership that encourages teamwork at the top. We've achieved a lot in a very short space of time, thanks to the charismatic leadership of our Extraordinary Commissioner, while under legal cover of the "Extraordinary Administration.'*
- *Ensure that the business models that underpin your various management business units are substantive. Check that the basic assets – such as products, processes, and customers – are healthy and that the people involved really do add value.*
- *Make your organization simpler: reduce complexity in your organization structure and reduce the number of reporting levels for optimal efficiency. Focus on relatively few, but clearly fundamental, controls. Give high importance to standardization and consistent procedures.*
- *Ensure good, honest, and regular communication with all your stakeholders.*

Formalization and standardization is important. However, it's the implementation of key operational controls that ensures a successful transition. These controls include:

1 *Clear definition of roles, responsibilities, and accountabilities – both within individual companies, up and down the corporate hierarchy, and for management reporting.*
2 *The management of human resources – the selection of people, their career development, motivation, and the company culture.*
3 *Strong information systems, standardized and under change control. Clear, simple processes focused on fundamentals.*
4 *Defined measures of economic performance and constant, reliable tracking of the company's financial position.*

Ultimately, it's all about cash – cash is king! We have to check continuously: Does everything that happens in the profit and loss account and the balance sheet generate cash or not? Are we able to grow the company value, cover our debts, finance new investment, and still provide dividends to shareholders?

As the Parmalat situation shows, senior finance executives are responsible not only for keeping score – for governance, compliance, and effective preventive controls – but they also have to act as business advisors and integrators. Above all, the CFO and the finance function are seen as the *glue* in the organization – making change happen.

Increasingly, senior finance executives are seen as an organization's key communication channel: to the outside world of stakeholders in presenting how the business is actually doing, and to the inside world of management in sponsoring change.

CHAMPIONS OF CHANGE

Change programs are no longer unique events; they are part of the daily pattern of corporate life. On average, major companies are running four significant transformation projects – and anywhere between 300 and 1,000 smaller improvement initiatives!

Yet only approximately 30% of major change projects deliver any significant improvement in performance. Change efforts fail for two main reasons:

1 **Poor design** – the failure to address the underlying processes used to get the work done – for example, the resource allocation and performance management processes. Relying on IT to provide the "magic bullet" won't work, nor will avoiding the necessary behavioral changes.

2 **Poor communication** – change leaders should explain proposed initiatives thoroughly, letting employees hear the arguments for and against the options that were rejected.

CFOs often find themselves in the role of executive change sponsors. They must have the capability not only to initiate change, but also to continually manage it and to finish the job – driving specific change initiatives through to successful completion!

As in the Parmalat case, typical finance-led change programs involve both business process redesign and systems implementation.

Consider next the experience of Axon – specialists in mission-critical, complex business transformations. Mark Hunter, CEO and Executive Chairman, talks about his company's experience in supporting CFOs in making change happen.

BUSINESS TRANSFORMATION
Mark Hunter, CEO and Executive Chairman, Axon Group

We have an exceptionally strong management team. As CEO, this team looks to me to provide a strategic framework and to ensure that we have the capability to deliver it. I try to leave enough time to carry out a roving troubleshooting role, as and when required, to deal with the unexpected! Apart from this, I let managers manage.

Most organizations are going through some form of change. Be they private or public sector, there is a considerable amount of talk inside organizations about changes that are happening or about to happen. You get the impression that there's more change than ever before. There's certainly more activity, but I'm not sure that there's any more change being delivered today than there was yesterday.

In my view, the rate of change is the same, and the level of change productivity as unimpressive as it's ever been!

A transformation can only be considered successful when it pervades the organization – it's rather like injecting a virus, a cell with some foreign DNA. But most viruses aren't particularly malevolent – they're positive change agents. When we, as consultants, are working with a client, we try to build up the self-belief of the client's staff in its ability to change. It's also important to create a vision: to ask, "What will the organization be like in ten years' time?"

Doing the right things right

The pace of change in your industry is driven by the market. We measure the speed of change programs – how fast you get through your change program and how long it takes you to realize the benefits. Approximately 50% of our clients get through the first few phases of the change program very well, but only about half of these clients have the courage to see it all the way through to realize full benefits.

Do the right thing right! That's what I advise clients.

Too often, I find that companies want to do the wrong thing right. They want to implement the system well – but the system in itself won't resolve their problems. They may have broken processes or, quite simply, the wrong strategy for the market. So they won't get the real benefit from a systems implementation.

Other companies try to do the right thing but do it wrong! Implementing enterprise systems technology is the right way forward, but they either take the wrong implementation approach or select the wrong business partner.

We started our business in the UK, which is one of the more sophisticated countries in adopting enterprise technology to achieve change. Elsewhere, however, we're finding that although CIOs are motivated by the latest technical developments they have a lot more to do in applying current ERP technology to achieve its full benefits.

Accountability for benefits arising from a change program should vest in the person leading it. If the change program is about improving process cycle times and reducing inventory in the supply chain then benefits ownership, and the leadership of the change program, should rest with the supply chain manager.

The CFO is becoming what is effectively the COO of their company. CFOs today seem to be broadening their remit for change to cover other functional disciplines, quite often functions that the other top executives don't want! We're seeing functional integration between finance, IT, and HR – enabled by process integration and enterprise technology.

The CFO and change[1]

What is the role of the CFO in promoting change? When undertaking a transformational program, you're trying to alter behaviors, motivation, and personal objectives – as well as organizational structures and incentives. The CFO is often the principal sponsor of change in a broader, COO capacity. But time and again, the finance function itself seems to escape the transformational change agenda. It almost seems as if the finance department has a fence around it, with a notice stating "no change here!"

I believe the role of the CFO is to look forwards and see the business future as a series of "what if" scenarios. However, no one can really predict the future. But the CFO can help the CEO to prepare for the unexpected and to influence the outcome.

The CFO has to be able to visualize and forecast the business on a more holistic basis – not just financial. I expect a CFO to be an influencer, to have a natural charisma and to be perceived generally as authoritative.

CFOs must have the necessary skills for the job: to identify a problematic situation, gather the facts, assess the options, create an action plan and, most important, delegate! The trick is to move on once the delegation is successfully executed. That's not easy.

By contrast with the CFO, the role of the financial controller is to look backwards – ensuring that the past is accounted for accurately. However, triggered by SOX, the controller has a broadening remit – to embrace control across the depth and breadth of the organization. This is a big move for controllers to make, stepping outside the comfort zone of their training and discipline to play their part in shaping the future.

The public sector

We're also seeing a lot of change in the public sector at the moment. Building on private sector experience, central and local government organizations are implementing ERP systems and moving away from legacy in-house IT to externally supported services. As in the private sector, the case for change is based on cost reduction and process transformation. But, in some respects, it is a mistake for the public sector to emulate the private sector. The challenge is as much how to run a better public service for the same cost than it is about reducing cost per se.

What else is different about the public sector? Well, the impact of unionized labor for one thing, the sheer scale and complexity for another. Normally, what happens at the outset of a change program – for example, in a UK local authority – is that the unions instruct their members not to cooperate. So it's even more important for the leaders of the change program to get the hearts and minds of the employees engaged in the program – directly addressing their concerns as well as those of management.

It goes without saying – good communication is vital. But understanding the stakeholders, what motivates them and what doesn't – that's the key to the reality of transformational change. You need the collective will of the top management board led by the Chief Executive to sustain real change. This commitment is crucial, not only at the beginning, but also during the early stages of implementation – especially years two and three – as the reality of the change begins to bite.

Selecting the right "movers and shakers" is important too. In practice, you only need to really influence a relatively small number of stakeholders affected by change to get more general buy-in.

When asked why change projects fail, many CFOs say the answer is all about the lack of leadership. The primary issue is not the need to recognize that change must happen – that is inevitable in the current business environment – but *how*? To be effective, companies need a change process, a clearly articulated role for the change sponsors, and a mechanism for reviewing change effectiveness.

Studies of best practice in change management show that there are typically three phases in the design of successful change programs:

Phase I – Preparing for change: Understanding the vision, objectives, and key business drivers of the organization. Analysis of the gap between the current situation and future goals. Formulation of a customized approach to implementing change.

Change must be tangible and measurable so that the benefits case can be aligned with the initiatives and reviewed during the stabilization phase of the project.

Phase II – Implementing change: Planning and completing the necessary activities required to transition the business to the "future state."

Middle management support should be engaged by clarifying what needs to be done differently and conveying new roles and responsibilities. Managers and their teams should focus on benefits. Resistance to change should be managed proactively.

Phase III – Reinforcing change: Ensuring that the program has delivered the benefits targeted in the initial change agenda.

Effective support and monitoring should be provided during adoption of the changes and beyond – enabling a culture of continuous improvement.

A typical change management model, covering each of the three phases above, is shown in Figure 3.2.

Change should be like any other business process. There should be a procedure describing it, policies defining how it should be used, guidelines and roles explicitly stated. Most change programs have a clear beginning. Few, if any, have a defined end-point. Instead, initiatives tend to fizzle out, rather than being formally closed off and, if successful, celebrated.

CFOs should consider a post-implementation audit to compare the implemented solutions with an initiative's objectives and measures as

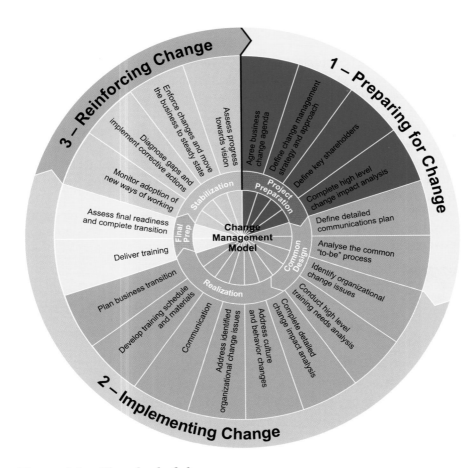

Figure 3.2 *The wheel of change*

defined at the outset. Just as important as identifying the effectiveness of a given change is analyzing the learning for the next initiative. This learning may be used to improve the core change process, or even to refine the sponsorship model itself.

When Mark Hunter talked about transformation, he referred specifically to what he saw happening in the public sector – the sheer scale of the changes involved, their complexity, and the impact on the finance function. We focus next on the public sector, what it can learn from the private sector, *and vice versa*.

TRANSFORMING THE PUBLIC SECTOR

As in many other countries, the UK Government is committed to maximizing efficiency within the public sector and reducing administrative costs while continuing an ambitious program of public service reform and delivery.

Building on past performance improvement and the evidence gathered by Sir Peter Gershon's review of public sector efficiency, the Government announced its ambition to cut administrative costs in real terms across the public sector by 2.5% annually over three years – equating to £20 billion worth of savings each year!

Sir Peter also chairs a private sector listed company in the electronic components sector, Premier Farnell, and contrasts his views on change between the public and private sectors.

EFFICIENCY IN THE PUBLIC SECTOR

Sir Peter Gershon, Chairman of Premier Farnell Plc and Head of the UK Public Sector Efficiency Review, 2004

Leading large-scale change in the public sector is similar to that in the private sector, with one notable exception – the need to work successfully with politicians!

The relationship between a senior government official and the relevant minister is not like that of a chief executive and his non-executive chairman. It has a more political dimension and no standard "governance" template. Each minister has a unique style: one may be "hands-on;" another may be "hands-off." Some ministers behave like executive chairmen, and are sometimes quite operational in their approach. Others are more non-executive and strategic. And, of course, the world of politics is subject to constant change.

Given the right leadership, government departments, such as HM Revenue & Customs (HMRC), should have the necessary capability to deliver the change required to meet savings targets.

The board of HMRC now has a Chairman from the private sector, David Varney, with the ability to lead the merger of two giant organizations of state – the Inland Revenue and Customs & Excise. A massive change by any criterion!

Efficiency programs

In the public sector review I led,[2] we had a number of recommendations. Those most relevant to the world of finance directors were:

1 **Departmental efficiency programs** – *agreed efficiency targets for individual major departments ranging from Health to Education, to the Home Office and Local Government. For example, in the Department for Work & Pensions a target was set to reduce the civil service workforce by a net 30,000 posts.*

2 **Cross-cutting efficiency measures** – *we recommended cross-departmental initiatives including:*
Strengthening financial management.
Improving procurement.
Instituting e-enabled transactional services.

Following my review, the Government announced a framework to ensure that planned efficiency gains would be realized. A strong central efficiency team, with specialist support, was set up to advise and to drive the agenda forward.

Back-office models

In looking at the back-office functions, such as finance, the review developed a functional model comprising three structural elements – the corporate strategic "core," core professional expertise, and transactional support. A generic reform map for government finance functions is reproduced in Figure 3.3.

Using the reform map, government departments developed strategies for change including:

- *Simplification and standardization of policies and processes.*
- *Adoption of best practice.*
- *Sharing transactional support to achieve economies of scale through cross-departmental "clusters."*

Benefit realization plans were drafted to ensure the reform plan was fully achieved and that costs were driven out as quickly as possible.

In addition to improving the efficiency of transaction processing, through the use of shared services and IT, the Government accepted my recommendation that the general standard of financial management in government needed to be strengthened. A significant increase is planned in the number of qualified finance directors

	Prepare	Consolidate	Transform	Improve
Corporate Core	• Rationalize staffing requirements • Simplify policies	• Professionalized CFO Group • Transactional performance standards in place • Standard accounting policies in place	• Finance information systems standardized on an up-to-date platform	
Core Expertise	• Rationalize staffing requirements	• Core and Transactional activities split • Expertise-based activities focused on risk management & decision support • Vendor management in place	• Expertise based activities consolidated e.g. management accounting	
Transactional	• Rationalize staffing requirements • Site Rationalize • Simplify processes	• High volume transactional activities e.g. accounts payable, consolidated into shared service centers • Co-sourcing or outsourcing employed	• Lower volume transactional activities consolidated • Scope of co-sourcing / outsourcing increased • Processes re-designed to exploit self-service e.g. purchase order authorization	• Transactional performance progressively raised

Figure 3.3   *Generic reform map for finance functions in UK Government*

and members of departmental management boards. We also intend to upgrade the quality of financial management information and to develop a stronger financial "community" for the sharing of expertise.

Government change agents

The review team proposed the use of "change agents" – specialists for supporting implementations. Change agents have relevant experience in delivering change and help by:

- *Providing expertise to enable departments to realize full savings potential.*
- *Identifying cross-departmental collaborative opportunities.*
- *Delivering savings earlier than would otherwise be possible.*

Figure 3.4 sets out the range of functions that a change agent could perform in, for example, the procurement area.

Local government

Procurement of goods and services by UK government departments from third parties will rise to over £120 billion annually this year. Nearly half of local government spending is on goods, works, and services that are commissioned or procured and the goal is to secure better value for money by more collective and professional purchasing.

Universal implementation of e-procurement should secure savings of £1.1 billion annually. There is scope for additional savings through aggregation of demand by local authorities via Regional Centers of Excellence (RCE) and back-office shared services.

There are examples of shared services already. One local authority in London has effectively outsourced its back office to Blackburn, a lower cost location in a joint venture with a private sector supplier, Capita. Clearly there is considerable scope left for further collaboration in services such as finance, IT and HR as well as procurement.

The Comprehensive Performance Assessment, which is the framework used by the Audit Commission to independently assess the performance of local authorities, has recently been enhanced to include a stronger focus on how efficiently resources are being utilized.

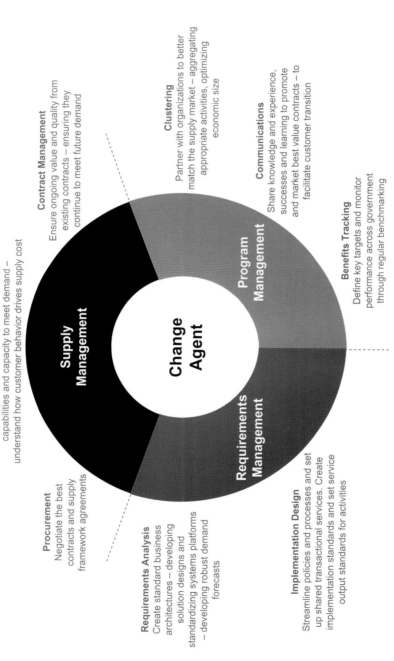

Figure 3.4   *Potential functions of a change agent*

Contrasting public and private sectors

In the private sector, the focus is on cash flow generation and creating shareholder value. Most CFOs in the private sector, from what I've seen, act as a strong source of challenge to the operating activities inside the company. They're not just a collator and reporter of the numbers. They help allocate resources where the opportunities are seen to be greatest.

Finance Directors (FDs) in central government are in a very different place. Because UK Parliament votes the departmental expenditure budgets, the pressure is on the departmental FDs not to overspend and to comply with the will of Parliament.

This pressure to spend budget, but no more, is phenomenal! Three-year rolling settlements, albeit only implemented at a relatively high level, do help to alleviate this problem. Nevertheless, the "spend-to-budget" discipline is ingrained throughout the public sector culture. The Government accepted my recommendation that such settlements should be cascaded down to lower levels such as local authorities.

Public sector FDs have to negotiate with the Treasury for resources – they have always started with needing more resources, not less! They are moving away from the traditional cash accounting to modern resource accounting. As a result of my review, I hope they will act as a much stronger source of challenge within their organizations to help embed the efficiency agenda. There's considerable scope now, in the public sector, to take the data coming out of the upgraded processes and systems and turn it into real management information.

It's these two areas – management information and challenge – where the public sector can learn most from private sector financial management.

But what can the private sector learn from the public sector?

Well, in the public sector you're exposed to a broader range of stakeholders with different interests. There is a growing awareness in the private sector that it's not just about making money; there are other responsibilities to consider too – for example, sustainability and social issues, and the growing impact of NGOs on private sector interests. There are also significantly greater transparency requirements in the public sector, and there are lessons here for the private sector as it faces ever-increasing demands for additional disclosure.

Clearly, change is all around us, and the traditional models of incremental improvement are not sufficiently dramatic to meet the challenge. Instead, the transformation of organizations has become a necessary pill to ensure survival in this ever-more competitive jungle. But how? Through the power of technology – at least if the investment dollars of the world's leading organizations are the test of where step-change is believed to come from.

For example, ever since SAP launched its pioneering Enterprise Resource Planning (ERP) package, the systems revolution has gone from strength to strength. The ERP phenomenon was closely followed by Customer Relationship Management (CRM), e-business, and a host of other supporting technologies such as mobile computing and workflow. This torrent of technology appears to have overwhelmed CFOs' appetite for investment, risk, and returns.

So step-changes are needed. Is technology the only answer? Does the pattern of investment fit the rhetoric of management? CFOs say that people, not technology, are their greatest asset. But what do the facts and figures of most major change programs show? That most transformation initiatives combine an element of technology and process redesign, as well as people change.

PULLING *ALL* CHANGE LEVERS

A survey of more than 70 corporations that have implemented ERP packages concluded the following: "two-thirds of companies surveyed have yet to realize the benefits they expected from implementing ERP. There are many reasons for this ... almost all of these reasons relate to people and their impact on business systems."

While technology may enable transformation to be achieved, the barriers to releasing that potential come back to the classic principles of change – leadership, commitment, politics, resources, and skills.

What most CFOs understand is that: if they are to reach for the prize, technology only enables. It is strategy, people, and process that deliver the benefits.

Strategy is one of the key levers for integrating change: it's a process and a mindset, not an event or a plan. Large-scale transformation programs cut through traditional organizational boundaries – whether they be functional or geographic. Designing business solutions that deliver real bottom-line improvement requires "joined-up" strategic thinking.

Most CFOs now use an integrated change management framework to help make all these connections. Figure 3.5 shows how these various dimensions of change link together to form a "pyramid" of change initiatives, all underpinned by a good strong program and project management discipline.

Using an integrated business transformation framework should ensure that all change initiatives are aligned to strategy and pull the organization in the same direction – *towards the prize*.

But how do you calculate the benefits? Too often, the answer to this question tends to be linear and one-dimensional. Cost cutting or just productivity gain? Yet the singular purpose of the modern enterprise is the creation of *total* value.

Consider next how two large government agencies are being integrated in the UK to generate both cost savings and productivity gains – but also to benefit the customer, *in this case the taxpayer!*

INTEGRATING TWO LARGE GOVERNMENT AGENCIES
Stephen Jones, Finance Director, HM Revenue & Customs

HMRC was formed from two very large public sector organizations – Inland Revenue and Customs & Excise. Together, they serve millions of people in the UK. We, along with other government departments, were challenged to come up with greater cost savings and efficiencies than we had in the past.

Savings opportunity
We started the change program with 98,500 staff in the two legacy departments. We had to reduce this by 16,000 staff over a period of four years, redeploying 3,500 and making a net headcount saving of some 12,500. Savings from this and other efficiencies are expected to amount to £507 million annually – a 12% improvement. There are three main cost-saving areas:

1. ***Transactional services*** *– streamlining and automating processes, such as the self-assessment process, pay-as-you-earn (PAYE), and VAT collection.*
2. ***Productive time improvement*** *(detecting non-compliance, countering fraud and tax evasion) – for example, by improving our yield-to-cost ratio for business tax investigations.*

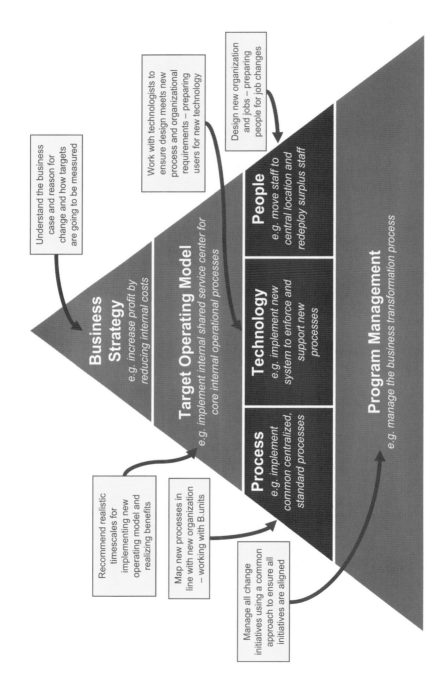

Figure 3.5 *Integrated business transformation*

3   *Procurement and back-office services* – as one of the UK Government's big-gest procurers, we have major opportunities to strike better procurement deals and reduce the number of our suppliers. Also, as far as the back office is concerned, there is considerable potential for developing shared service centers (SSCs). HR and finance are strong SSC candidates.

We have very specific performance targets for the next three years. In our public service agreement (with the UK Government) we expect to reduce dramatically the gap in direct taxes between what taxpayers should pay and what they do pay – by some £3.5 billion annually!

Systems changes

On the transactional support side, self-service is likely to accelerate. Already, for example, 17% of taxpayers carry out self-assessment online. The target is to achieve 35% self-assessment using the e-service in the next two years. So far, this initiative has yielded considerable benefits: We have found that half a million potential tax-payers do not need tax returns at all. This saves us both work!

Similarly, we are modernizing our PAYE system – employers will have to return their PAYE data at the end of the tax year electronically. We can then reconcile employers' payments made during the year electronically with returns. Again, the uptake of the electronic submission and payment service has been encouraging.

Most of these kinds of savings are visible to the public. We also hope to get "behind the scenes" savings based on what happens to e-tax data inside HMRC. Currently, this data has a complex path through our processes and systems, most of which are legacy and therefore disjointed. For example, PAYE is dealt with on one system and National Insurance contributions on another.

Currently, we have no single taxpayer database. If employees change jobs, their records can move to one of twelve different databases – depending on the tax office location of the new employer. We intend to move from a taxpayer database organized by "employer," to a database organized by "customer." This is a remarkably complex challenge, as both a business process and a technical IT integration, since the database involved holds around 30 million employment records.

With such an IT implementation change ahead of us, we need to have an absolutely safe method of migrating our data from our existing set of systems to a new integrated solution. Risk management is at the top of my and the CIO's agenda.

Integrating the "customer" experience

A single taxpaying business "customer" interacts with us for a number of taxes – corporation tax, PAYE, VAT, various excise duties, and more specialist taxes. We want to make things simpler for ourselves while also relieving the administrative burden on business.

We can also avoid unnecessary duplication. For example, VAT inspector site visits to taxpaying businesses are carried out separately from those for corporation tax or PAYE. If we had integrated processes and systems, we could combine some of these visits. Also, we could "join-up" our risk assessments of a business taxpayer – taking a more holistic view of a taxpayer's compliance picture.

Making change happen

We have almost 100,000 people working for us at the moment in some 800 different locations. Roughly half do basic transaction processing and first-line interactions with the customer. To make these processes more efficient, we are now asking:

1 *Do we need to have the interaction with the customers at all?*
2 *Can we make our customer interactions better and more efficient?*
3 *Can we improve our customer information processing?*

Above all, we need to make our technology work better. Our staff use two principal operational computer systems at present – the one for Inland Revenue, and the one for Customs & Excise. We also have two separate finance and HR systems. And when you consider that our staff cost base is nearly £3 billion annually and that we spend £1.5 billion a year externally – and that some of this is organized centrally and some locally – then the scale of change we face is really enormous.

We have an IT partnership, called "Aspire," with our IT outsourcer, Cap Gemini. Since our business is so dependent on information, we can't just outsource and leave it! We are a very large client and our outsourcers have to move with the changes we need to make.

We're looking at standardizing our processes on the best "out-of-the-box" systems – such as SAP and Oracle. In benchmarking our best practices, we make good use of our outsourcing partners. We observe what the rest of UK government is doing and look at advances in the private sector – for example, in the banking industry. Then we measure ourselves against other tax authorities in other countries – such as Australia, North America and the Netherlands. We also benefit from the fact that our management board has two members who have a private sector background – this helps bring an "outside-in" view on our change program.

Joined-up tax accounting

We have a complicated "product" range. For each tax we administer, there is a different payment, late payment, and non-compliance penalty regime. Not surprisingly, this has led to separate accounting systems for each regime. Standing back from this, we can see that improvements can be made and we're planning to make changes.

Cultural change

You've got to take the workforce with you. We have to work with our people to persuade them that this change is necessary. They need to understand where we are going as a business and get their buy-in on the benefits. Our stakeholders vary considerably – more than you would expect in the private sector. Not only do we have to consider staff and the general public but also the politicians!

From my experience, there are a number of lessons to be learned:

- **Clarity and determination** *– you have to be absolutely clear about the change that you want and determined to see it through.*
- **Accountability** *– you need to break down the overall change program into manageable chunks to which individual accountabilities can be assigned.*
- **Leadership** *– your change leaders need the capabilities and resources for implementation. Anticipation and preparation is everything! So is being honest in all your staff communications.*

We have to sustain the motivation of our staff through this period of change. In the public sector, we are limited in what we can do in using money to solve our problems. We have to find other ways to motivate staff through carefully constructed and negotiated packages for benefits and opportunities. This is a personal journey for them. They need support and encouragement. The trade union representatives, as well as the staff themselves, have to be fully involved.

We, at the top, need to be very clear on the detailed impact of changes on individuals. We need to spell out the impact – for example, what will the job of a small business tax investigator look like in three years' time? So, you're looking at the big picture, and at the same time you're considering the micro level.

Not only do I have to view this change as a three-year window, but also, as the Finance Director, I have to work within my annual cash limit for the department on a year-to-year basis. This is a constraint you don't find in the private sector. This cash limit has to cover the cost of the staff I expect to have, inflationary pressures, the funding for the change investment (including any exceptional costs) and the one-off costs. A complex financial jigsaw!

Iron discipline

What keeps me awake at night? Risk. The size and scale of the challenge – just taking on too much. If I screw up, it affects a vast number of people, potentially the nation. Because we have to operate in a highly disciplined financial environment, it's vitally important I don't spend more than the government-voted limit. Iron financial discipline is a fundamental. Parliament holds me accountable – if I overspend then, theoretically, my Chairman is personally liable as the legally responsible accounting officer. This sharpens your focus. Iron discipline is equally important on delivery. We are obliged to deliver our headcount savings in two years' time – not a month or two later!

In conclusion, I see my role in this change as having two key sensitivities. First, treating the staff affected as individual human beings, not just numbers on the payroll. Second, awareness of the impact of the change levers at my disposal – the calibration of the impact. Pull one of those levers too weakly and you underperform. Pull it too hard and you could put the entire HMRC at risk.

As with the HMRC, a tightly integrated design for all aspects of a change program – stakeholders, processes, systems, training, accountabilities, and communications – should, from experience, deliver the best results. An example of a best practice integrated change program design is illustrated in Figure 3.6.

By focusing on implementation, best practice change programs minimize adverse effects on business performance and accelerate benefits delivery. Summarized below is the advice that a number of CFOs offered for managing change successfully:

> "Whatever your *strategy*, whether it's low prices or innovative products, it will work if it is sharply defined, clearly communi-

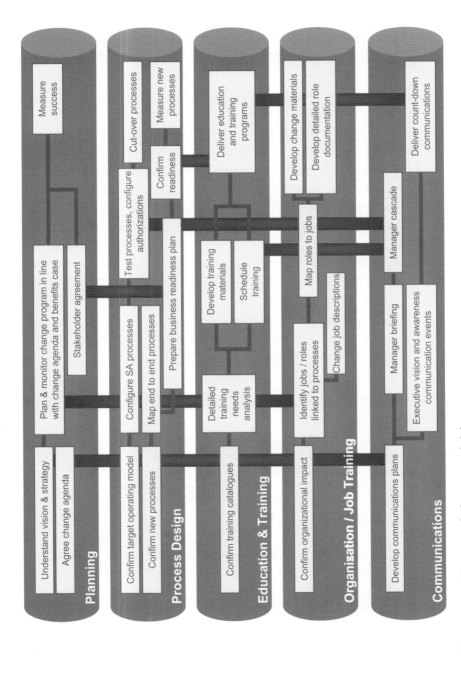

Figure 3.6 *Integrated change activities*

cated, and well understood by employees, customers, partners, and investors."

"Develop and maintain flawless operational execution. You might not always delight your customers, but make sure never to disappoint them."

"Corporate culture advocates sometimes argue that if you make the work fun, all else will follow. Our results show that having very high expectations and inspiring people to do their best matters a lot more."

"Managers spend hours agonizing over how to structure their organizations. Winners show that what really counts is whether structure reduces bureaucracy and simplifies work."

Here are some guidelines for designing change programs:

- **Articulate a finance end-state:** Define which strategies the company should adopt to achieve its vision and then decide how to execute aggressively.

- **Consider all the change dimensions:** Real efficiency gains are realized through a comprehensive review of the entire organization – from corporate to business unit levels.

- **Learn from others:** Identify and understand the relevance and potential application of efficiency and cost-reduction models used elsewhere.

- **Practice change control:** As you adopt new practices and processes, build in appropriate mechanisms to monitor performance and drive continuous improvement.

- **Link to other strategic initiatives:** Coordinate your finance change program with other initiatives, such as those in market and product development.

Consider next how one CFO became so involved in change across his organization that he is now its COO!

FROM CFO TO COO

Zurich Financial Services is a global insurance company headquartered in Switzerland. It aspires to become the leading global insurer in the general and life insurance markets. With its long-established network, it serves global customers in more than 120 countries, has 57,000 employees, and manages more than US$190 billion of group investments.

Zurich's business philosophy: customers are at the center. Earlier in this decade, the company had suffered along with most other insurers; the stock market decline weakened its capital structure and balance sheet. The company had grown through a series of mergers in the late 1990s, making integration a big management issue. Subsequently, the business has been through a successful turnaround.

Thomas Buess, who had been the group CFO and is now the COO of the Group Life business, has been actively involved in changing his company's business model. The challenges he and his director colleagues faced were low profitability, weak organic growth, and low productivity. The opportunities: strong distribution in major markets, a large customer base, and a great value proposition. Thomas picks up the story below.

FROM CFO TO COO
Thomas Buess, COO Zurich Life, Zurich Financial Services

Zurich Financial Services is one of the few truly global insurance companies – we can service customers all over the world. But we've got to be more focused and more flexible in our cost base.

We've learnt from the past – you can't be all things to all people! You have to specialize. Our strategy today is to focus our business on core markets – geographies and customer segments – with core products and our preferred distribution channels. In the life business, for example, we're generally not number 1 in any of our geographies, but we do hold the top position in specific segments.

Recently, I moved from my role as group CFO to COO of the life business. There was much to do! Returns in our life business were relatively low: we've made great strides in streamlining what was a fragmented and underperforming organization. We are now focused on investment and creating value.

The Zurich Way
We've changed our business models. We needed to make cost savings, improve administration, de-risk and release capital. We aim to capture higher margins through redefining market segments – selecting those segments with scale, profit-

ability, and growth potential. Our aim: to be a leader in each segment, differentiating our products based on quality, value, and service.

'The Zurich Way" is our one best approach to achieving operational excellence in all core processes. Figure 3.7 shows the Zurich Way framework for building value through the sharing of resources, platforms, and global skills.

The Zurich Way is divided into seven work streams:

1 General insurance claims
2 Large corporate and commercial underwriting
3 Personal lines underwriting
4 Life – with four sub work streams: product development, distribution, service management and administration, capital and risk management
5 Tied agent distribution
6 Talent management
7 Financial discipline

As COO of the Life business, I'm driving change along the value chain in work stream number 4.

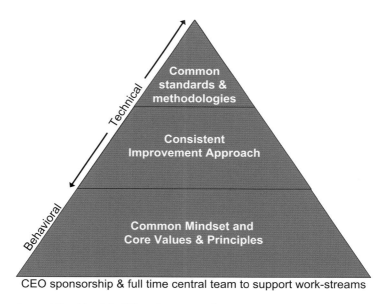

Figure 3.7 *The Zurich Way framework*

Analyzing the value chain

In the life business the value chain has five key components – the product, distribution, manufacturing (customer service and administration), capital management and actuarial, and finally investment. Investment has been outsourced completely to Deutsche Bank, so our turnaround is focused on the rest of the value chain, as shown in Figure 3.8.

The operational improvement program for manufacturing (service management and administration) consists of changes where we've completely remodelled the business – big transformational change! We benchmarked unit costs internally and externally and found substantial potential for improvement. Our US operations were the most efficient; Germany performed well too. The least efficient countries for us were Switzerland and the UK.

Our service management and operational improvement program had four main thrusts:

- *Business process outsourcing: Exploring outsourcing of new business processes, servicing, and claims for our existing and new product portfolio.*
- *UK protection products: Introducing new IT platform and manufacturing processes for new products.*
- *New operations model in Switzerland: Establishing a cross-border manufacturing model, based on German products and platform.*
- *Lean operations: Improving operations in the UK and Germany using Zurich Way metrics and methodology.*

We approached our outsource provider – CSC – to whom we had already outsourced our entire applications service provision (ASP). CSC is also in business process outsourcing (BPO), and specializes in life insurance and pensions. In the UK we found that we could save up to 50%; in Switzerland we found that if we moved our administration to the German platform we could also save another 50%!

So we're now implementing business process outsourcing in the UK and we're streamlining further our German operations – we call it the "lean" approach, similar to Six Sigma for continuous improvement. In the US, our operational platforms are already very efficient but outmoded. We will need to think about replacement and perhaps partnering up with a BPO provider.

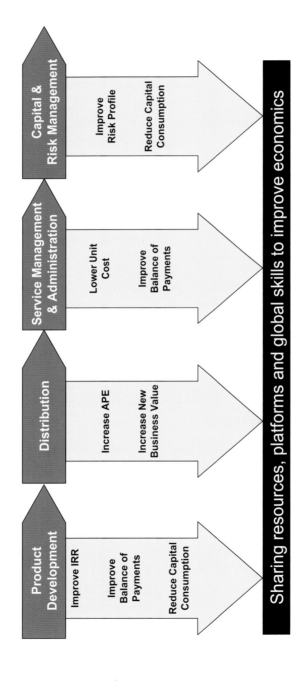

Figure 3.8 *Driving change along the value chain*

Over the last two years the Zurich Way initiatives have generated approximately US$460 million, largely attributable to savings in expenses.

New metrics

In the past, we only looked at net profit after tax on an IFRS basis. Today, we have two additional targets: cash and embedded value. Life is a long-term business, so we don't want to concentrate just on short-term earnings; we want to encourage long-term value creation. The embedded value metric enables us to measure the long-term value to us of life insurance contracts and the value we add from one year to the next from new business.

One of my first jobs as COO has been to introduce new metrics for performance management. We now call our three key metrics the Zurich Life Triangle, as shown in Figure 3.9.

Cash is still king! We have a clear dividend target for all the business units. So at the top of the triangle is cash; embedded value is in one corner, traditional returns in the other.

Continuous improvement

We've implemented metrics for the ongoing change initiatives of each value chain component:

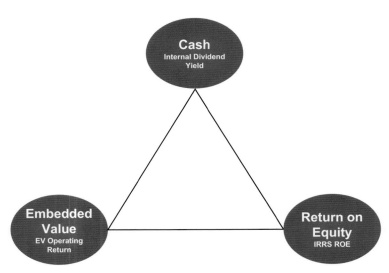

Figure 3.9 *The Zurich Life metrics triangle*

- *For the products*: Product screens – metrics for profitability and market attractiveness.
- *For distribution*: Metrics for better leveraging our tied-agent sales force and customer base and sales productivity metrics.
- *For manufacturing or administration*: Metrics for unit costs – cost per policy for both new and existing book business; process times for sales cycles; metrics for distributor/customer satisfaction.
- *For capital management*: Market "consistent" embedded value – the European approach – market discount rates, option and guarantee values, net present values.

This will give us a better understanding of the profitability of our different products, market segments, and distribution channels. It will also allow us to better match our asset and liability positions in our major life balance sheets in each regional market.

In the two years I've been COO we're already showing strong progress. Business operating profits have improved by 35% to US$1 billion. New business margins, a great indicator of value creation, have improved from 4% to 11%. However, we've still some way to go.

Our future agenda
Our agenda for the next three years in the life business:

1. *Growth* – once our "house" is in order, the right economic model in place, the next step is to grow the top line. We're competing with banks, with mutual funds in the savings market – so we need to innovate new value propositions.
2. *Efficiency* – the market will demand more transparency in the way we present our costs and expenses. This will force us to become even more efficient.
3. *Re-risking* – the insurance industry over the last three years has shifted risks back to the customer, moving away from guaranteed returns along with commensurately high capital charges. The pendulum is now swinging back to customers wanting product guarantees, at least for their capital principal invested. We would then price that risk back into the product – re-risking!

What are the key drivers of future value? The number of customers is extremely important. Persistency, or retention: how long a customer stays with you. Also, how many products you're able to sell to an existing customer – cross-selling. And, of course product margins.

Changing from CFO to COO

Traditional number crunchers have to "let go" of the numbers and put more emphasis on sales, growth, and operational efficiency. You have to really under-stand what drives value and how the business value chain changes over time.

As CFO, you strive hard to understand all this. But when you change roles, as I did, to COO it's only then that you really "see it and feel it." I feel I can "move" more now; I'm really empowered.

My advice to CFOs? Don't get completely buried by the accounting standards and the IFRS debates. The finance function should resist the urge to retrench back into accounting theory – but continue to develop along the path of true business part-ners.

As we've seen at Zurich Insurance, the world's leading CFOs are increasingly taking on a broader agenda, in some cases doubling-up with the COO role, and in others moving across into general management and away from finance as a specialty altogether.

We've witnessed a steady evolution and expansion in the role of the finance function. As one CFO put it:

> "The job used to be transaction intensive, now it's knowledge intensive."

Finance experts are now expected to contribute to strategy. Because the finance function is in the centre of corporate infrastructure, senior finance executives are now thrust to the corporate front line.

TALENT FOR THE FUTURE

The CFO position today demands, as it always has done, a high degree of technical competence in financial control and reporting. But the current environment, with its intense focus on corporate governance and transparency, also calls for CFOs to be exceptional communicators.

Why is developing talent in finance such a critical issue? The demands on finance professionals have never been greater than at present:

- Regulators demand ever-higher standards.

- Shareholders and audit committees expect more assurance and independence.

- Management still wants the help of finance with value-creating decisions.

- New initiatives, such as IFRS and SOX 404, are placing an exceptionally heavy project management burden.

- Company leaders generally want better value for money from their corporate infrastructure and headquarters.

Given these pressures and the shortage of talented finance people, CFOs realize that a renewed focus on attracting, developing, and retaining a strong finance team is not a luxury – it's a necessity!

When one CFO was asked the following questions he responded thus:

- In these times of great uncertainty, how do I keep my finance agenda moving and my team flexible?

  "By delivering change. I start by working with the team in building the case for change, focusing on what's wrong with our current behaviors and culture, and what can be done about it. We put enormous effort in developing our finance people in their capability to manage change, teaching them the importance of engaging and communicating with stakeholders. We're coaching them to be the business leaders of the future."

- How do I keep the skills up to date?

  "By defining in a structured way, with full involvement of the finance team, the competencies and behaviors required – identifying and plugging the gaps with training and tailored personal development programs. These include web-based learning and personal performance support tools."

- With all the additional pressures and workload today, how do I maintain motivation?

  "We're constantly reviewing and updating our organizational model, redefining roles, responsibilities and accountabilities for governance. Careers in finance seem to be going in three separate directions:

1 *Down deeper technical tracks, for example in accounting, risk, and regulation.*
2 *Across a much broader spectrum of responsibilities, for example finance now encompasses other functional disciplines such as IT, HR, and logistics.*
3 *Into the newly specialized shared services channel, developing more general management skills, quite often in a near-shore or off-shore location."*

GE has a terrific reputation for developing future management talent – recruiting top graduates directly into operational audit, giving them broad exposure, and then developing the candidates on either a specialist finance or general management track. In a further extract from the interview with Bjorn Bergabo of GE, he talks about its structured approach to finance executive skills development.

FINANCE SKILL BUILDING

Bjorn Bergabo, CFO GE Commercial Finance, Corporate Financial Services Europe, General Electric Company

GE has a long tradition of moving finance professionals into various roles. When recruiting, we tell people, "You are not really joining one company but many different ones"! Typically, we have fast-track career paths. So the people who work for GE share a common background. This is reinforced across our corporate culture by the disciplines we foster through training, processes, and day-to-day execution. I've been at GE for twelve years. This service length is common for my level; we are all here for the longer term.

Our internal finance network is very strong. If you meet a GE finance person in another part of the business there is a cultural similarity – an intellectual rigor with a bias for action. For example, finance staff are trained to take a complex issue and explain it clearly, concisely, and quickly to management.

This explains how GE can run a company that is so diverse, while still avoiding diving into too much unnecessary detail. There is a strong emphasis on people priorities:

"We typically do things the same way and share a common vocabulary. Above all we're passionate about our people – sharing our values and developing techni-

cal competence. We evaluate our people on their ability to communicate. It's so important to have the right people in the right places."

Undoubtedly, much of GE and Corporate Financial Service's success in its finance function is based on its very sophisticated and enduring training program. This program, outlined in Figure 3.10, is not new. The program's entry level has been going since 1919!

Currently more than 700 candidates go through the Financial Management Program (FMP) from all over the world every year:

> *Entry level (FMP)* – GE attracts top university talent, and provides a two-year program combining business and functional experience. It puts candidates through six-month rotational assignments and supports them with formal training, examinations, presentations, and case studies.
>
> *Mid-career/advanced training* – This takes candidates through Six Sigma and then onto controls and strategy. They are also mentored by senior leaders. The advanced financial management courses (AFMC) – professional training – deals with those at the mid-career stage. This program includes analytics, "growing the business," advanced technical finance skills (including M&A), controllership, decision support, and risk. At the **senior level** there are regular executive updates with current topical flavour, and then onto a senior leadership track, with symposiums for the very top company officers. Training never stops!

The FMP prepares candidates for their promotions to finance positions at various levels in the organization – from analyst to controller to business unit CFO, VP, and beyond. The academy approach not only applies to the finance function, but to other disciplines such as HR and commercial.

Companies like GE are responding to the challenge of developing finance talent by investing in focused training. Such companies share knowledge and best practices, and establish finance academies to coordinate learning activities. The goal: to ensure that the skills of their people are aligned with their strategies.

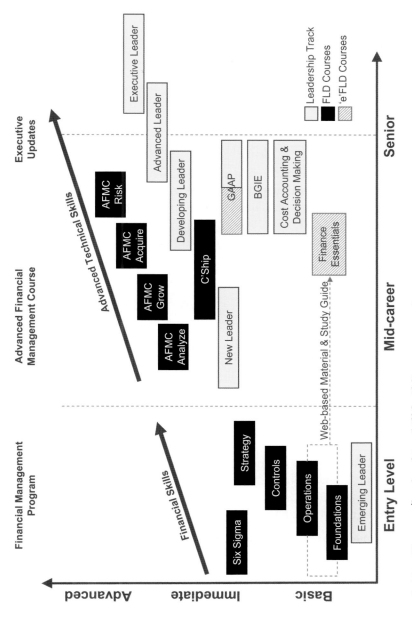

Figure 3.10 *Finance/leadership skill building progression*

Finance, like any other function, needs a clear strategy and processes for managing its talent. A talent management program typically involves:

- International assignments and rotations; diversity: proactively identifying and filling specialist skills gaps.
- Identifying and nurturing "high potentials;" building a global leadership team and providing for succession.
- Rewarding the right behaviors through career-enhancing redeployments and globally networked finance communities.

Subsequent chapters explore in greater detail how leading CFOs and their talented teams are managing the drivers of value creation in a regulated world. *We start, in the next chapter, by showing how they release the value of intangibles.*

STRAIGHT FROM THE CFO

- **Focus on the essentials**

  When looking at the bigger picture, consider what's likely to happen at the micro level, to the affected individual. Decide where you want to go in principle, then work out how to get there in detail. Aim for relatively few targets, single out the most fundamental.

- **Sponsor the change**

  How fast is your change program in achieving real benefits? Create a focal point for leadership. Encourage team working at the top. Don't just initiate, see it all the way through; inject change, just like a virus!

- **Do the right things right!**

  There's no point mending broken processes or implementing new systems if you've got the wrong strategy. Change course if you have to.

- **Pull all change levers**

  Consider people, process, and structure – as well as technology. Visualize the business change holistically, as a series of integrated scenarios. Don't forget to weigh the impact on each stakeholder group, especially customers.

- **Go from CFO to COO**

  Let go of the numbers. Don't get completely buried by the accounting! Really understand what creates value. Drive change along *all* components of the value chain. Remember: what gets measured gets done.

- **Refresh your talent pool**

  Determine the skills gap. Focus on what's missing. What needs fine-tuning behaviorally and culturally? Consider three finance career tracks: technical, cross-operational, and shared services. Like GE, commit to a really long-term Financial Management Program.

REFERENCES

1 Mark Hunter (2003) *The Executive Role in Sponsoring Change – Making it happen, www.axonglobal.com.*

2 Sir Peter Gershon CBE (2004) *Releasing Resources to the Front Line, Independent Review of Public Sector Efficiency,* HMSO.

CHAPTER 4

Releasing Intangible Value

Over the last few decades, we've seen a revolution in the corporate world: a transition from industrial capitalism, where business was based on tangible physical assets, to today's economy, where value creation generally relies upon *invisible*, intangible assets.

In the world's leading companies, more than half of all investment goes into so-called intangible assets that are not reported on a company's balance sheet. The proportion of a company's reported net assets, compared with its market value, has in many cases become so small that the balance sheet is rapidly becoming irrelevant.

In fact, intangible assets represent more than 80% of the total market value of the Fortune 500. As a result, on average, only 20% of a company's market value is reflected through traditional accounting methods.[1] For knowledge-based companies, such as Microsoft, or companies with strong brands, such as Coca-Cola, that figure is even lower – often under 10%.

The findings of a recent study[2] of corporate value derived from intangible assets, analyzed by industry sector, are summarized in Figure 4.1. This shows the market values as multiples of the net book values of companies in a range of industries.

Not unsurprisingly, industries with strong R&D pipelines like pharmaceuticals and industries like media/entertainment, with extensive intellectual content, have very high market-value multiples. Industries with traditionally heavy investment in physical infrastructure, like construction, utilities, and transport, have low market value multiples.

This raises a critical issue: managers who rely on standard accounting data to make investment decisions and optimize business efficiency are often acting in the dark. The traditional financial tools they are using are relevant to only 10% or 20% of the resources for which they are responsible. So there is a big disconnect between what traditional accounting

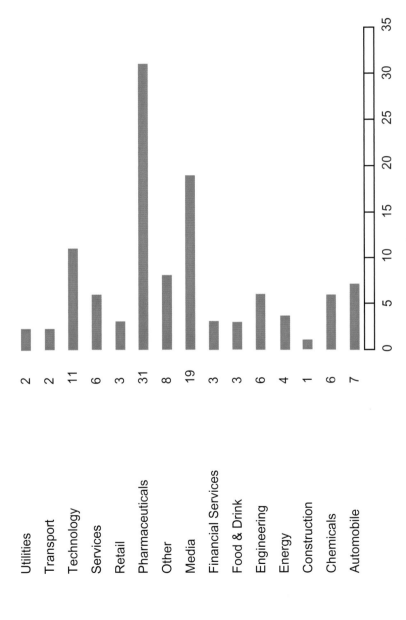

Figure 4.1 *Market values as multiples of net book values by industry*

systems capture and how financial markets value companies. The message? CFOs must take a closer look at how their companies are creating economic value.

This chapter explores how leading companies value intangibles, for example, to account for an *external* transaction – and how they make transparent *internally* the underlying business processes that create value. We make the case for maximizing the value of intangibles and look at what leading CFOs say about this critical issue.

EXECUTION *NOT* VALUATION

The most important value drivers to many companies are product and process innovation, coupled with customer relationships. For example, a recent study of the chemical industry revealed that the R&D investments of 83 chemical companies over a span of 25 years yielded a 17% after tax return, while typical capital spending earned just 7%.

Here, we look at what the CFO of BASF, the world's leading chemical company – with a portfolio ranging from chemicals and plastics to crude oil and natural gas – has to say about intangibles.

Innovation and growth at BASF flow from biotechnology, nanomaterials, material sciences, and energy technologies.

INTANGIBLES: EXECUTION, NOT VALUATION
Dr Kurt Bock, CFO BASF

At BASF, we strive for global scale in all we do. We're in one of the world's most innovative industries and have a huge R&D program. Our industry is also highly cyclical, environmentally demanding, and extremely cost competitive. And yet we've enjoyed very strong financial performance. We attribute our success to our ability to change with the times and to highly effective execution.

We use four strategic guidelines to chart our path to the future:

- *Earn a premium on our cost of capital.*
- *Help our customers be more successful.*
- *Form the best team in our industry.*
- *Ensure sustainable development.*

We have been expanding on our value-based management strategy for a number of years now. We measure every business decision and our performance based on how it influences earnings after cost of capital, both in the short and the long term.

Achieving gross margin targets is very high on our agenda. Overall, GDP growth is not a long-term feature of this industry, although we still achieve 5% annually. But it's very easy for spending to get out of control in chemicals. So as CFO, I'm very keen on financial discipline.

Driving R&D and innovation

We achieve profitable growth through innovation: this includes developing successful new products as well as more competitive production processes. Our operating units are in close contact with our R&D center – we call it the "Verbund." At our German headquarters alone, we have 5,000 employees in R&D; a further 2,000 researchers are deployed elsewhere in the world.

We pride ourselves on the efficiency of our innovation processes. This is particularly important in an industry where less than 1% of ideas, on average, give rise to successful innovations. We use a phase-gate process in our innovations pipeline:

- *Stage 1: Ideas for new products, processes or systems.*
- *Stage 2: Business potential evaluation.*
- *Stage 3: Prioritization of project portfolio.*
- *Stage 4: Laboratory phase.*
- *Stage 5: Pilot project management and market launch.*

As CFO, I'm most concerned that we evaluate, in Stage 2, the net present value of future cash flows of projects – that we turn R&D investment into successful returns. Yes, we back the projects that seem to be succeeding, but we also have to have the courage to abandon projects quickly which seem to be failing.

The introduction of value-based management to our R&D function was an uphill struggle, but we're there now. It's very important to measure ongoing performance of a project after investment. We have a rigorous approach to post-project appraisal.

We share quite detailed R&D information – such as potential sales and stage in the product development life cycle – with our investment analysts. We also have to

*comply with SEC reporting requirements for developments in our exploration busi-
ness.*

Valuing intangibles

*Intangible assets? In accordance with accounting standards, we expense our normal
R&D as it is incurred. However, as a result of acquisitions, we have more than €3 billion in goodwill and intellectual property – concessions, trademarks, and licences.
All this is on our balance sheet. We amortize it, and write it off quickly according to
market, or fair view, principles.*

*Since we're not in the consumer sector, we don't really have to deal with brand
value. So I found it surprising when the BASF brand was voted number 10 in a recent
national survey of top German companies!*

*Our image and perception in the chemical industry is especially important to
us, given the impact of the environment and the green lobby. We are as open and
as transparent as possible in our reporting on social and environment issues. For
example, we now publish targets for reduction of emissions and for reducing industrial accidents – and report annually on how we're doing in meeting these targets.
Recently, we won an award for being the most "sustainability minded" company in
Germany.*

Rationalizing goodwill

*What do I think of the value gap on the balance sheet? Well, this gap is between the
market capitalization of some €30 billion and the net book value of some €15 billion.
When we make acquisitions, we have to identify and attribute value to intangibles.
But this is still more of an art than a science.*

*I believe the value gap doesn't really represent the intangible assets per se. It
reflects the strength of the organization, the efficiency of our processes and management's ability to deliver results. Our ability to manage gross margin and cost, our
market access worldwide, our technical capabilities – all these attributes are what
makes up our share price. The market is confident in our ability to execute and to
exploit the intangibles at our disposal.*

The range of resources for the twenty-first-century business – some of which are measurable, but many of which are intangible and not capable of measurement – is set out in Figure 4.2.

Tangible goods – such as property, plant and machinery – have traditionally been relatively easy to measure; their ownership is also clear and enforceable. Intangible *goods* – such as intellectual property in the form of brands and patents – have rights that can be bought, sold, readily traded, and more or less protected. They, too, can be valued.

However, intangible *competences* and latent *capabilities* – variously referred to as R&D, core competences, human or structural capital – are almost impossible to measure by traditional means, difficult to identify separately, and their ownership is difficult to enforce.

Reflecting on what Phil Yea, CEO of 3i, said in Chapter 2, there's no point in trying to value intangible assets for valuation's sake. Such valuations can be largely spurious exercises. What's more important is a company's ability to sustain cash flow. It's the people and processes that are key to value creation.

However, when a company acquires another company, it frequently pays a price considerably in excess of the value of the net tangible assets acquired. Why? What is being paid for? Historically, the excess has been described as "goodwill."

THE GOODWILL DILEMMA

The goodwill dilemma: intangible assets are a vital source of value and accounting standards are encouraging increased transparency in acquired intangible asset values. Yet, intangibles, by their very nature, are difficult to value.

Most CFOs argue that while intangible assets are a vital source of value and must be proactively managed, their valuations are inevitably imprecise – and should not be required for accounting and reporting purposes.

Nevertheless, CFOs do seek to persuade the market of the advantages that their most recent acquisition offers – usually represented as the value of synergies, cost savings or other commercial benefits.

Not all agree with this strategy. Goodwill has attracted a fair degree of skepticism – many see it as representing an overpayment that should be written off. Others consider it simply an accounting entry to balance the books. However, in practice, the price paid for an acquisition often does reflect a value for the various intangible assets acquired.

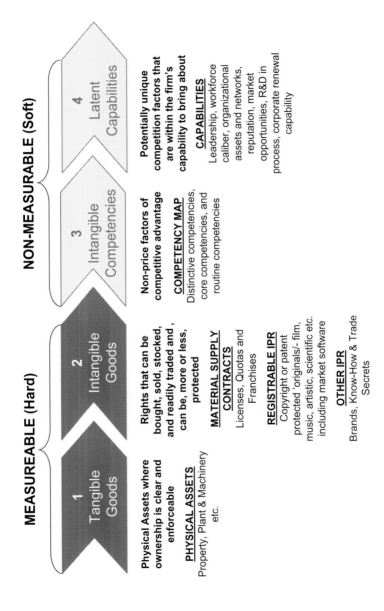

MEASUREABLE (Hard)

NON-MEASURABLE (Soft)

1 Tangible Goods

2 Intangible Goods

3 Intangible Competencies

4 Latent Capabilities

Physical Assets where ownership is clear and enforceable

<u>PHYSICAL ASSETS</u>
Property, Plant & Machinery etc.

Rights that can be bought, sold, stocked, and readily traded and, can be, more or less, protected

<u>MATERIAL SUPPLY CONTRACTS</u>
Licenses, Quotas and Franchises

<u>REGISTRABLE IPR</u>
Copyright or patent protected 'originals/- film, music, artistic, scientific etc. including market software

<u>OTHER IPR</u>
Brands, Know-How & Trade Secrets

Non-price factors of competitive advantage

<u>COMPETENCY MAP</u>
Distinctive competencies, core competencies, and routine competencies

Potentially unique competition factors that are within the firm's capability to bring about

<u>CAPABILITIES</u>
Leadership, workforce caliber, organizational assets and networks, reputation, market opportunities, R&D in process, corporate renewal capability

Figure 4.2   *The resources of 21st century business*

The concept of "fair valuing" of all acquired assets and liabilities is generally accepted. However, the degree to which the goodwill element of the purchase price must be analyzed varies from one part of the world to another. But there is a move to greater transparency as investors seek to understand with greater precision what a transaction means to an acquiring company. Why was the transaction ever undertaken? What actually has been acquired?

The new accounting standards require goodwill on acquisition to be identified and allocated to individual intangible asset classes. Figure 4.3 shows how intangible assets are interlinked. It also highlights the importance of identifying the primary intangible assets – in this case, customer relationships – that drive value.

Techniques for identifying the relative contributions of intangible resources to the goodwill acquired, or indeed to the total market value of the company, are in a formative stage. Most of these techniques rely on management's subjective judgment to:

- Identify which intangible assets contribute most.

- Determine values for intangibles with the help of proven valuation methodologies or market values, if they exist.

- Allocate goodwill accordingly.

Most intangible assets, other than goodwill, are regarded as having a finite life and therefore continue to be amortized over their expected useful lives. However, under new accounting rules, goodwill is no longer deemed to have a finite life and is not amortized. Instead, it is treated as having an indefinite life and reviewed for impairment at least once a year. But there are still differences in international (IAS) and US GAAP treatments:

- IAS will only recognize intangible assets to which the business has a *legal* right; US standards also recognize those to which it has an *economic* right.

- Under US GAAP, in-process R&D acquired must be immediately expensed; under IAS, this asset is capitalized and amortized.

- Goodwill is still amortized under IAS, usually over a maximum of 20 years, unless a trigger event has occurred to suggest that the goodwill is impaired.

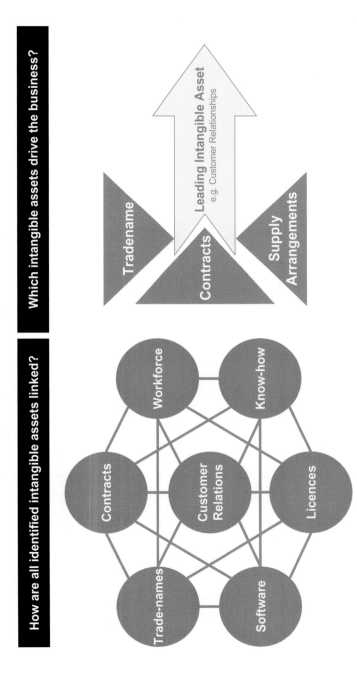

How are all identified intangible assets linked?

Which intangible assets drive the business?

Figure 4.3   *Hierarchal relationships linking intangible assets*

While it's unfortunate such differences exist, we are likely to see a greater convergence in the accounting treatment of intangible assets worldwide and greater clarity in financial statements. *Some CFOs and analysts even believe that true transparency will not be achieved until accounting standards permit internally generated intangible assets to be recognized too!*

VALUE CENTERS

Some companies are going one stage further in managing intangible values by disaggregating their shareholder value into its component parts, which we call "value centers."

Nestlé, for example, groups its brands into global strategic business units and looks at return on invested capital (ROIC) on a comparable basis – comparing investment in internally generated intangible brands with those acquired externally.

COMPARING INTERNAL AND EXTERNAL INVESTMENTS
Wolfgang Reichenberger, former Group CFO of Nestlé

I estimate that two-thirds of Nestlé's enterprise value is tied up in intangible assets. When presenting to external investors, we provide non-financial information, such as market share, pricing, margins, and the impact of currency fluctuations – as well as general indications on the business environment.

Non-financial information is, by its very nature, imprecise and cannot be subjected to a formal audit. Nevertheless, over time, we have developed a "sign" language to signal externally how things are going.

It's really difficult to get an accurate fix on your intangible values – such as for brands – but maybe that's not too important anyway. What's important is that we understand how to grow the value of our intangibles through the discretionary investments we make – how we place our bets – by growing brand awareness and creating ever better sales promotions.

Goodwill on acquisition is only a fraction of our total intangibles value. Intellectual property, brands, and patents are becoming ever more important to us. Like all companies, we're looking for return on investment (ROI). If the investment is not on the balance sheet, how can you hold people accountable? This goes to the heart of value creation in our business.

Value center models
Jean-Daniel Luthi, SVP Group Controller of Nestlé, continues:
My job is to ensure that we follow the strategy of our executive board. We're very keen on accelerating innovation – bringing new ideas, products, and product extensions to market.

We treat our product strategic business units (SBUs) as if they were virtual companies. The SBU heads are like CEOs – they're responsible for taking the long-term view on strategy and investment across our worldwide organization. But unlike CEOs, they're not responsible for the P&L account. We, and they, are especially interested in the shareholder value implications of each SBU – for example, how it will increase value in three years.

We've done theoretical exercises to look at the net present value (NPV) of the corporation and its various constituent product groups. If we only took the balance sheet investment in calculating returns, we would have a distorted picture. On coffee, for example, we've made few acquisitions, but we've spent an enormous amount to build the Nescafé brand. In contrast, in the petcare business, where we've made a big acquisition, there's significant goodwill on the balance sheet.

So we have to have like-for-like ROI comparisons between internal and external investments. What we're really looking for is the trend in year-on-year improvements. Our investors encourage us to deploy invested capital internally – on new products and brand extensions – rather than on acquisitions. If there was a system out there for highlighting better the value-add of internal launches, I'd have it! But I suspect we're flying in the face of accounting convention.

The bottom line? Innovation activities, not tangible capital investment, drive the value and growth of companies like Nestlé today. These innovation activities provide customers with a unique set of value-creating products and services. Measuring economic value added therefore gives you only "half a loaf." Companies must also measure the effectiveness of their value-creating processes for intellectual property (IP).

MANAGING INTELLECTUAL PROPERTY

Not surprisingly, CFOs and investment bankers have increasingly focused on understanding the importance of IP when undertaking mergers and acquisitions (M&As), or when seeking to raise capital. Among the IP issues faced by CFOs:

- In M&As involving a pharmaceutical company, the CFO has to understand the patent position of key products being acquired and the patent protection options available.
- When raising venture capital to exploit potentially valuable IP, CFOs and their banking advisors must consider joint ventures that are attractive to investors.
- In taking a company public, the CFO must explain to investors the attractions of IP, licensing options, and associated risks.
- When raising finance, CFOs may wish to exploit IP that is expected to generate future royalties, utilizing resulting cash flows to raise low-cost securitized debt.

Raising equity capital from public capital markets for an IP-based company is a very different challenge from that posed by traditional fixed-asset-intensive companies. Consider the situation it faced when ARM Holdings went public.

ARM HOLDINGS: IPO OF AN IP-BASED BUSINESS MODEL

ARM is a UK-based company that licenses high-performance, low-cost, power-efficient microprocessors and system chips to international electronics companies. The company's product-licensing business unit licenses the ARM architecture, as well as microprocessors, system chips, peripherals, and software tools.

According to Business Week, "ARM almost single-handedly created a new business model: hawking intellectual property instead of selling actual chips. That has earned it the trust of customers such as Texas Instruments, Philips Semiconductor and even Intel, which uses ARM technology in a line of speedy, power-stingy chips.'

During the preparation for ARM's IPO, it was observed that the development of a business relationship with a potential licensee was a very lengthy process. However, once the relationship was established, tremendous earnings leverage resulted because there were no capacity constraints.

The company's prospectus explained in great detail the revenue model for IP licensing, which consisted of certain milestone payments as the licensee developed the product, supplemented by ongoing per-unit royalties every time the licensee sold a product utilizing ARM's IP. The barriers to entry created by this IP-based business model were potentially very attractive to investors.

It was also important to ensure that investors were aware of the risks associated with this business model. Disclosure in the Risk Factors section of the IPO prospectus included the following four paragraphs:

- *"There can be no assurance that pending or future patent applications will be approved, or will not be challenged by third parties.'*
- *'In addition to patents, the company also relies on copyright, trademarks and trade secret laws to protect its IP, and such protection may be limited or unavailable in some jurisdictions."*
- *"Litigation is common in the semiconductor industry, and questions of infringement involve highly technical and subjective analyses; such litigation, whether settled in favor of the company or not, would be costly and would divert the attention of the company's management from normal business operations."*
- *"Loss of litigation could have a material adverse change on the company's business and financial condition."*

In the end, the IPO was very successful, with the offering ten times oversubscribed, and the price set well above the initial filing range. Moreover, since the IPO, ARM's market capitalization has continued to increase; it has been less affected than many other semiconductor companies by market volatility. The analysis of IP conducted for ARM's IPO is applicable to companies in other industries that derive their value largely from IP.

There are a number of reasons for moving intellectual property and intellectual asset management up on the CFO agenda:

- Intellectual assets can generate additional revenue streams and value.
- Effective intellectual asset portfolios create competitive advantage.

- Accounting and reporting for intangibles is changing to give more transparency.

- Capital markets are increasingly taking information on intangibles into account.

- Poorly managed intellectual assets are costly and create risk.

One of the reasons that many CFOs are skeptical about placing a value on intellectual property is that there is usually greater risk associated with potential revenues. Can intellectual property be reliably measured? The answer is yes, provided that the appropriate methodology is selected and properly applied.

Figure 4.4 provides an overview of the three main approaches to valuing intangible assets – **market** value, **income** or **present value of earnings**, and **cost** or replacement value.

SELECTING VALUATION TECHNIQUES

How much is the Coca-Cola brand or trademark worth? $50 billion? $100 billion? An Interbrand table of "The 100 Top Brands" once listed it at a value of $70 billion. How would you check whether you agreed with this assessment?

Most intangible assets generate premium returns for the businesses that own them, either through increased revenues or a reduction in costs. All valuation methods focus on capturing the value of these premium returns. The principal methods of valuing intellectual property for financial statement purposes are as follows.

- **Excess operating profits method**

  This method determines IP value by capitalizing the additional profits generated by the business owning the property over and above those generated by similar businesses that do not have the benefit of the property.

  A drawback of this method is that the business with which you seek to compare the subject's margins or return on assets is likely to have some intangible assets of its own which are increasing its margins and returns on assets. For example, it may have a more efficient production facility. Such factors will mask, to a degree, the apparent excess profits

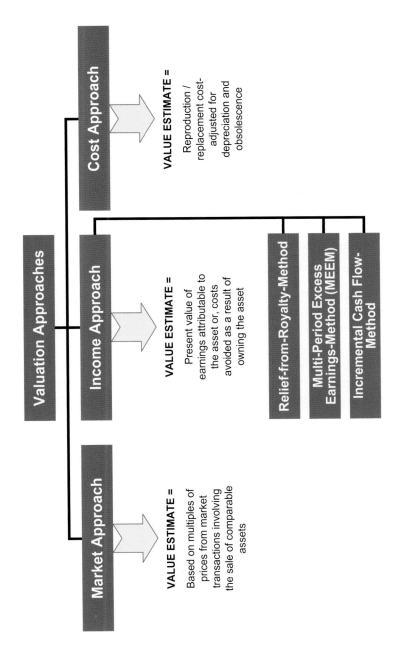

Figure 4.4 *Intangible valuation approaches*

that the subject is earning and should be taken into account in the valuation.

- **Premium pricing method**

  This is a variation on the excess profits method and is often used to
  value brands in the consumer products sector, where it is common for a
  branded product to be more expensive than an unbranded equivalent.
  The value of this additional revenue is projected over the life of the
  brand – net of the marketing and other brand support costs incurred
  to achieve this result – and discounted to the present day to calculate
  brand value.

  *A drawback of this method is that it is very difficult these days to find a
  truly unbranded product. In the food sector, where stores often sell their
  "own label" products as well as branded products, the store's "brand"
  itself has a value.*

- **Royalty savings method**

  This approach is based on the principle that, if a business did not own
  a particular asset, it would have to in-license it to earn the returns the
  asset provides. Alternatively, the business could out-license the asset
  if it did not wish to use it. The value of the asset is calculated based on
  the present value of the royalty stream that the business is saving by
  owning it.

  *While this method is popular, its major drawback is that, although there
  is extensive licensing across most industry sectors, details of royalty rates
  are rarely made public, and if they are, they are difficult to compare.*

- **Cost savings method**

  This method values an asset by calculating the present value of the
  cost savings that the business expects to make as a result of owning it.
  Such cost savings are often the result of an especially efficient process
  or secret technology.

  *While a business can usually calculate the costs it has saved since it
  introduced a new process, it can be more difficult to estimate whether a
  third party would save more or less if it introduced the same technology.*

- **Market approach**

  This approach values an asset based on price multiples of key financial metrics, such as sales or profits. The market price multiple used is based on the prices paid in other similar transactions involving the sale of comparable assets. Different multiples for different metrics help validate the price paid.

This approach is the one preferred by accounting standard setters. And in an ideal world, this is the best method for companies, since it offers the best approximation to "market value" available.

In practice, however, the world is not ideal. It can be difficult to find sufficient publicly available information on the multiples and prices paid for similar assets. Nonetheless, this method can usually be applied as a cross-check to other valuation methods using industry rules of thumb.

- Cost approach

  This technique values an intangible asset by accumulating the costs that would currently be required to replace it. The premise of this approach is that an investor would pay no more to purchase the asset than to reproduce it.

  While this approach is suitable for some assets, particularly those that are not directly generating income, care should be exercised since this approach is not always a reliable guide to value. Think of the vast amounts of money spent on pharmaceutical research projects that come to nothing!

Figure 4.5 tabulates the common methodologies for valuing frequently encountered intangible assets.

Perhaps the most important guide to your choice of valuation method is to consider how the asset creates values for its owner. Does it generate additional revenues? If so, then a method based on revenues is probably most appropriate. Does it save costs? If so, then a method based on costs saved is probably best. Does it provide a competitive advantage without directly generating additional revenues or saving costs? In this case, a method based on replacement costs is likely to be most useful.

As noted earlier, one of the reasons that many CFOs are skeptical about placing a value on intellectual property is that there is usually greater risk associated with the potential revenues from an intangible asset than from a tangible asset.

How can these risks be dealt with in the valuation process, so that it is reasonable, robust, and reliable enough for financial statement purposes?

Common methodologies for valuing frequently encountered intangible assets

Asset	Valuation Method				
	Excess Operating Profits	Cost Savings	Royalty Savings	Market Approach	Cost Approach
Brands	X		X	X	
Customer Lists				X	X
Patents	X	X	X		X
Know How	X	X	X	X	X
Franchises				X	X

Figure 4.5 *Common methodologies for valuing intangibles*

By using differential discount rates, one can recognize the level of risk inherent in different asset classes when projecting the net present value of future cash flows.

In conclusion, intellectual property *can* be reliably measured by applying the appropriate methodology. To answer the question at the beginning of this section, we believe the best way to value the Coca-Cola brands is to use the **excess profits** method *and* the **royalty savings** method, *and* to cross-check the results using the **market** approach!

BRANDS: THE MISSING HALF OF THE BALANCE SHEET!

A leading CFO with experience in several large consumer goods companies refers to organically grown brands as the "missing half" of the balance sheet. In his analysis of one of his company's balance sheets, he broke down the enterprise value as follows:

Fixed Assets	12%
Working Capital	3%
Acquired Brands & Goodwill	66%
Inherited Brands	19%
Actual Enterprise Value	**100%**

The inherited brands, and any acquisition synergies not given away, represent the unpublished part of the balance sheet. They are the balancing figure in the enterprise value – since fixed assets, working capital, acquired brands and goodwill are all treated as net asset costs and reported in the balance sheet.

But the CFO believes that the value placed on the enterprise by the market undervalues the company substantially – and, therefore, the inherited brands are substantially undervalued too. The CFO went on to estimate what the company's board might accept as a price per share in a takeover bid situation – a surrogate for what he would regard as the true market value.

In his view, the takeover premium increased the enterprise value by a further 30% after an estimate of the synergies the acquirer would be prepared to take. He therefore places a value on the unpublished part of the balance sheet which, in a takeover situation, he estimates to be as high as 49%. The missing half!

This CFO concludes by offering advice for internal brand value management:

- Value all brands on future sales basis.

- Drive brand values by brand marketing.

- Capitalize marketing and amortize over three years.

Companies like Beiersdorf, a leading global consumer goods company headquartered in Germany, state their accounting policies for intangibles as:

> **Purchased intangible assets** such as patents, trademarks, and software are measured at cost and amortized on a straight-line basis over their useful lives. Intangible assets are generally amortized over a period of five years. Additional write-downs are made for permanent impairment. If the reasons for impairment no longer apply, write-downs are reversed.

> **Goodwill** arising upon consolidation and acquired goodwill is capitalized and amortized on a straight-line basis over a useful life of five to a maximum of twenty years. Goodwill is also regularly tested for impairment and is written-down as required.

Unfortunately, because of the volatility created by impairment adjustments to goodwill, some companies are letting accounting treatment affect their business decisions about whether they invest internally, externally via acquisitions, or not at all.

Other companies are not letting accounting get in the way of doing business. Consider brand valuation at Beiersdorf.

INVESTING IN INTANGIBLES
Rolf-Dieter Schwalb, CFO Beiersdorf AG

We focus on fast-moving consumer goods, now 85% of group sales. Our biggest brand is NIVEA – voted the most trusted brand in Europe in the skin product category. Other strong international brands in our stable include Eucerin, La Prairie, Atrix, and Labello.

Our strategy: We want superior brands that "delight" consumers. Our products are mass market, but at the upper end of the quality scale with a brand premium. So we need excellent advertising, innovation, and point-of-sale presence. Central to our strategy is a superior integrated supply chain.

Business model

With our focused brand portfolio, we have taken leading positions in skin care, face and sun care, men's care, and deodorants. Our systematically implemented business model emphasizes:

- *Research and development: Innovation is our growth driver. We invest heavily in R&D to constantly satisfy consumers with new products. A large proportion of our sales is generated by products launched within the past few years.*
- *High-quality brand growth in three dimensions: Increasing market share, establishing new market segments, and expanding the range of products available in new countries.*
- *Synergies from brand families: Grouping products under one umbrella brand allows us to leverage potential synergies – for example, using NIVEA's uniform brand communication for the benefit of all related products.*
- *Global strategies, local execution: Developing international strategies that are implemented and, if necessary, adapted locally.*

Some of our branded competitors are bigger than we are, but we don't see them as having advantage in scale per se. We believe more in the scale of the brand, such as NIVEA, which is number 1 worldwide. We're always looking for the top positions for brands by category in country markets.

Last year, we had 180 brand categories in the number 1 position; this year it's 200 and growing! This positioning is our most important brand value driver.

Measuring innovation

R&D is the lifeblood of our business. Innovation is what makes us stand out, particularly when compared with private label brands. Our innovations are based on more than 100 years of experience in skin research, emulsion technology, and adhesive development.

Some companies measure innovation by the "sales in the current year by stock-keeping unit (SKU) that did not exist the previous year." However, this is only a reflec-

tion of, say, repackaging, relabelling or a minor ingredient change. We do not regard this as true innovation.

We measure our R&D performance in terms of the number of patents registered and our innovation rate: the amount of this year's sales generated from new products that did not exist five years ago. Currently, our innovation rate exceeds 30%.

For example, our NIVEA deodorant Pure is a new product. We're also launching a new sunscreen that works immediately on application. Consumers have to see the innovation – they have to feel it and understand it for it to be real, since it is an intangible! So we spend considerable sums on advertising and promotion.

Marketing investment

We see marketing expenses as an investment. Last year, we spent 34% of consumer sales on advertising and trade marketing. This is more than what we spend on our product cost of goods sold, and is high by industry norms. But the accountants treat it as an expense.

We don't report on marketing investment in detail in our annual report because we view this information as competitively sensitive.

Knowing how much to spend on marketing is always difficult in our industry; it's also difficult to evaluate the results. There is a saying: "Half the advertising expenditure is really effective, but we don't know which half!"

Valuing intangibles

Brands – along with patents and our people – are our biggest asset. However, their true value is not reflected in our balance sheet. But, of course, intangible value is built into our share price.

Only when we acquire someone else's brand do we put it on the balance sheet. We use quite a different accounting treatment from internal brand investments. The accounting treatment can sometimes dictate your investment policy choices – whether you either invest internally in marketing or acquire a brand externally. I think this is quite wrong!

I'm not in favor of the goodwill accounting recommended in the International Accounting Standards – the impairment tests can lead to volatility and inconsistency. I prefer the straight-line approach, writing it off regularly – and getting it off the balance sheet as soon as you can.

With the right valuation methodology, I would be in favor of putting both sets of brands – acquired and organically grown – in the balance sheet. But it is notoriously difficult to establish brand values. I've seen three different methodologies but they all came up with quite different results. In NIVEA's case, for example, they ranged from €1.5 billion to €6 billion!

When we've tried to value patents with valuation advisors, we've also come up with a huge range of outcomes. But we do use an in-house patent valuation tool when taking advantage of licensing R&D opportunities.

Some CFOs harbor reservations about brand valuation on the grounds that there is no one standard method for making the calculation. Our experience shows that these concerns are outweighed by the advantages of carrying out such an exercise.

Absolute accuracy is less important than the learning generated by undertaking the process in order to better understand the drivers of brand value.

As an alternative to cost-based, market-based or income-based approaches to brand valuation, the economic-based approach is generally preferred for ongoing brand management. Economic-based methodologies have been developed by organizations such as Interbrand. Their attraction lies in a comprehensive assessment of factors that affect a brand's ability to generate value.

Although economic-based techniques differ in practice, the steps in the valuation process are broadly similar, as shown in the economic value added (EVA) case below.

Step 1: Calculate overall economic value added

Use the forecast cash flows from future brand sales and calculate a fair charge for the use of assets at the risk-free cost of capital to determine overall EVA.

Step 2: Identify the brand value added

Identify the proportion of EVA attributable to the brand in question. A quantitative and qualitative research-based approach enables managers to understand and model the drivers of demand and estimate a brand's contribution.

Step 3: Calculate the discount rate

This takes into account relative economic, market, and brand risks. The cost of capital is adjusted for the specific brand relative to the geography of its market and its risk profile.

Step 4: Calculate brand value

Work out the brand value by applying the risk-adjusted discount rate to the brand value-added cash flows. On the assumption that the brand advantage continues beyond the forecast period – effectively in perpetuity – calculate an annuity based on the final year's earnings.

Step 5: Manage brand value

Establish clear ownership and accountability for brand value. Assess your brand portfolio and overall brand strategy. Establish a performance management system for tracking the development and execution of brand value generation strategies.

TREATING CUSTOMERS AS ASSETS

A company's customer base is often its biggest asset. As its guardian, the CFO is charged with finding customer-centric solutions. Since achieving customer profitability usually requires substantial investment, it is crucial to know where customers are in the life cycle – which ones deliver positive value, for example, and how close others are to breakeven. Yet even today, customer value is not measured regularly. And, typically, customer value measures are based on past history or outmoded business models.

Understanding your customer capital, and analyzing customer relationships from a value perspective, is critical for business success. This depends on achieving a complex set of goals:

- Building your asset base by acquiring profitable new customers.
- Strengthening relationships with your largest, most reliable customers.
- Transforming minor customers into more profitable ones.
- Increasing your share of sales revenue (and hence your share of wallet).

- Exploiting cross-selling or up-selling opportunities.

Consider the energy industry – specifically, electricity. Customers have a value: the difference between the retail price and the wholesale cost of electricity transmitted and distributed. Take E.On, the world's largest investor-owned utility. Headquartered in Germany, it operates in 18 European countries and the USA. The E.On UK market unit has a number of businesses – electricity distribution, power generation, and energy wholesale and retail.

Simon Richards, Finance Director of E.ON UK Retail, describes how finance is increasingly focused on customer value.

ALL CUSTOMERS ARE NOT EQUAL
Simon Richards, FD E.ON UK Retail

I'm the Finance Director of the retail business, which sells electricity and gas to both domestic and industrial consumers. Our portfolio is the result of both acquisition and organic growth.

Integrating resources
Our systems strategy has been to replace legacy systems with in-house modules. Having integrated the businesses, products, and customers onto one modern service platform, we can further improve customer service. This puts us in a better position to target our electricity, gas, and emerging products to different segments of the customer base.

Our value drivers include the number of customers, the volumes we supply, customer retention and churn. It's a lot more cost effective to keep a current customer than to lose it and have to go out and find another one!

We started with a fairly traditional accounting function, but we soon realized that our growing product complexity and demands for more customer information meant that we had to upgrade.

We found that we needed skill-sets that took our eyes off the rear-view mirror and looked forward to growing value. So we set about recruiting, restructuring, and putting in new systems. Today, we support our customer marketing and service colleagues so that they can act on our insight to attract new customers and retain existing higher-value ones.

Understanding customer value

We've been through an initial exercise of apportioning costs based on services to customers in order to determine customer segment profitability. Of course, all customers are not equal! As shown in Figure 4.6, some customers generate more profit than others.

The figure shows a fairly typical curve of cumulative annual profit per customer – 19% of customers lose us money. This exercise confirmed that there is an opportunity for the business to grow value.

We've completed a phase of analyzing customer segment characteristics. For example, an individual customer in a small, well-insulated bungalow consumes far less gas and electricity than a customer with a large family in an old Victorian house with a swimming pool! There are some very practical things we can do to sell different products to suit different customers.

When we looked at the cost side of serving customers, we found that costs also varied by segment. We've also found that some costs have nothing to do with the customer – they're the result of internal process inefficiencies.

So discerning the real customer attributes that drive revenue and cost, and deciding how to act on this information – that's the challenge for us in finance. We've looked at other industries, such as banking, to identify proven tools to manage differential customer lifetime value. From a process efficiency viewpoint, we've also learned from manufacturing's "lean" approach and applied it in a customer service environment.

This development program has led to changes in almost every aspect of finance – in governance (cost center and process accountabilities), in process redesign (end-to-end, customer driven), in management information (customer and performance granularity), and in restructuring our finance team. We're now much more externally customer facing – we're on the front line!

Achieving results

The size of the prize? If we could make our non-profitable customer segments profitable, it could generate an additional £30/40 million annually. In reality, our customer value/process improvement program is already generating £10 million in margin annually from some quick wins.

Figure 4.7 shows how the longer-term value of each customer is affected by our loyalty improvement initiatives.

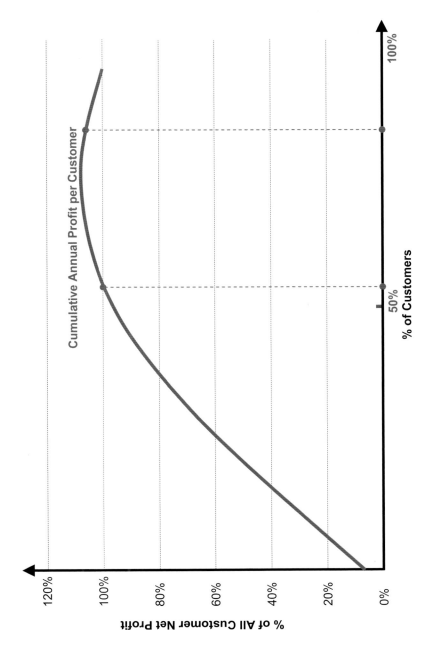

Figure 4.6   *All customers are not equal!*

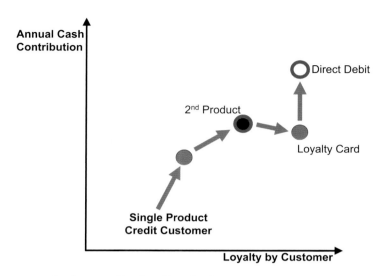

Figure 4.7 *Cash contribution/loyalty by customer*

We measure customer value as NPV of future cash flow generated over their lifetime with us. For example, in Figure 4.7, a customer taking a single product, say electricity, on quarterly credit can be motivated to take a second product, say gas, and in conjunction with our loyalty card scheme pay by direct debit. The outcome – the customer stays with us longer and is worth more.

Integrating finance, operations and marketing

We're working to build long-term relationships with customers. Our marketing and sales efforts are now better directed and achieve results that we are better able to measure.

In Figure 4.8, we demonstrate how we're integrating processes and systems for customers.

Our base IT systems are rich in terms of the data they offer on customer interactions. We map cost and revenue information from the ledgers to operational activities and then onto customer accounts – determining customer profitability from both an operational and a marketing viewpoint.

Moving from mass marketing to customer segmentation takes time. The theory of customer value is relatively easy to understand; the practical challenge of getting

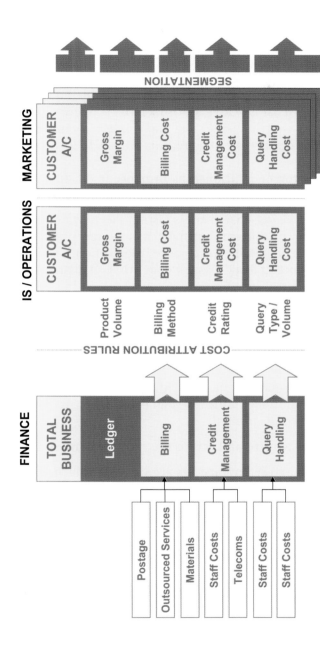

Figure 4.8   *Integrating customer value processes and systems*

a large organization to pull in the same direction is tougher! Don't underestimate the extent of the cultural change required.

A well-defined customer value framework can and should be used to measure the health of your customer base and improve performance. This said, in almost all cases, CFOs lack the framework or tools to attain this customer-centric vision. The major issues facing the CFO today in implementing customer value programs are as follows:

- **Do our customer relationships promote loyal, long-term profitable growth?**

  The cost of losing customers is rising. Fleeting customer loyalty has always been a problem, but today's consumers are more fickle than ever. They have more choice, more information, and are more willing to chase a "better deal." Little wonder that churn rates are surging!

- **Do we really understand who our customers are and how much they contribute?**

  For example, phone companies often find it hard to consolidate all their contracts with large commercial customers. Many banks also have difficulty consolidating a customer's file if that customer has several accounts and uses multiple financial products. One large Japanese bank was astounded to learn that 1% of its customers accounted for almost 99% of its profits!

- **How do we acquire and retain the right customers?**

  Acquisition and retention costs are skyrocketing. In response, companies are searching for new strategies to build customer and shareholder value. The key is tailored marketing: defining all value-driven activities at an individual customer level so that products can be personalized.

- **How can we monitor customer value on a long-term basis?**

  It is important to track changes in customer value over time to determine which customers are increasing or decreasing in value. Analyzing historical customer value data can help pinpoint the reasons for customer changes, making it easier to make decisions about future interaction and investment.

- **Why do we need customer value tools – isn't a customer profitability system enough?**

  Customer value is more than just financial measurement. That's why calculating it requires ongoing tracking of many non-financial measures. Some organizations use activity-based management to measure the cost and profitability of customers, products, and services.

So how are CFOs and finance functions exploiting their learning on customer value, partnering with marketing, packaging their capabilities, and developing their skills?

VALUE TIERING

Consider the success of Vodafone in Italy, as described by Margherita Della Valle. Unusually for a CFO, she has a background in marketing, which she uses to create value through focused customer investment.

THE CFO: PROACTIVE MARKETING
Margherita Della Valle, CFO Vodafone Italy

As employee number 35 when we started Vodafone in Italy, I was the marketing department's first staff member – the Head of Marketing Analysis. Later, when we reached 10 million customers, I became Head of Customer Base Marketing and helped define our first customer loyalty program and churn prediction models. Tools like these are now the backbone of our customer management activities, which have become extremely sophisticated as Vodafone Italy has grown to over 23 million customers.

I moved to finance to become Head of Planning and Control – an example of cross-functional job rotation that's typical of our company. My background in marketing analysis was considered to be very valuable in my new role. I moved on to the post of CFO one year ago when my predecessor became CEO!

Impact of customer behavior
As a very large mobile telecom company, we have the benefit of an enormous amount of data on customer behavior. We have two key customer segmentation approaches – one based on socio-demographic and usage characteristics, and one

based on value. The first is based on seven segment categories – such as teenagers – which are common across the Vodafone group.

Our value segmentation uses a scoring model to identify our most valuable customers: Vodafone's top 30% of customers generate over 75% of its revenues! Scoring is based on the margin per customer.

We use segmentation to differentiate our relationships with customers at every touch point – be they marketing campaigns or new tariff offers – in order to maximize customer satisfaction, loyalty, and service usage.

Customer acquisition and retention

Historically in Italy, customer acquisition costs have been relatively low compared to other countries. These are around €20–30, allowing us to break even on acquisition very quickly. In most other countries, service providers offer handset subsidies – and as a result, acquisition costs range from €100–200.

Figure 4.9 shows how Vodafone calculates the breakeven point for a customer contract and highlights the importance of retention.

The lifetime value curve provides us with valuable information to make tactical decisions – for example, reducing cost to serve or extend a contract expiration date.

A new competitor entered the Italian market two years ago with a "free handset" strategy. This has increased competition significantly and we have had to face the risk of increased churn. When customers have the opportunity to buy their mobile phone and connections for free, it is difficult to resist!

However, we've successfully counteracted this by leveraging our customer knowledge and taking advantage of existing marketing initiatives – such as our 10-million-member loyalty program.

We've put statistical models in place to compare actual versus "normal" patterns on a customer-by-customer basis and provide us with advance warnings – what we call "churn-prevention signals." For example, a drop in call numbers may indicate churn intentions. In such circumstances, we contact the customer with specific offers to retain them.

Thanks, in part, to these targeted actions, we've maintained our position as the highest growth company in our market.

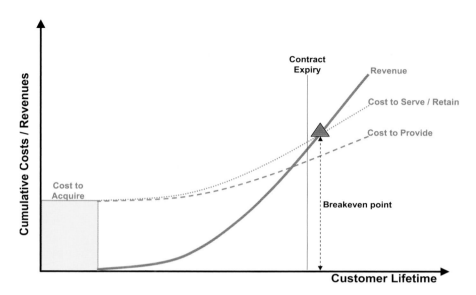

Figure 4.9 *Customer lifetime value at Vodafone*

Capability development
We've invested enormously in IT and systems. Customer relationship management with our scale and complexity is an expensive activity!

Our customer processes are supported by different systems – our customer data warehouse is held on Oracle, we use SAS for modelling and analysis, and in the call center, we use Clarify for customer contact management.

We are currently rolling out best practices on relationship management across the whole Vodafone Group. For example, we now have a call center system of "alerts." Depending on customer behavior, we identify the best actions to increase loyalty or up-sell new products in order to maximize the benefits of the interaction.

Partnering with marketing
The financial analysts working with marketing "live" together on the same office floor. Their role is to support marketing on all economics-related decisions, analyzing trends, and suggesting potential corrective actions. Financial and marketing analysts share the same tools and speak the same language.

We also encourage job rotation between the two disciplines. In finance, on the revenue control side, we want people who have a background in marketing as well as finance. Equally, we want people in finance to go on and develop a career in marketing.

I'm responsible for the decision-support program in our global finance academy. This includes two training courses: "Generating Revenues" and "Cost Optimization." The revenues course uses case studies – for example, how to assess a new price plan and how to appraise customer-based marketing initiatives.

As the CFO of a mobile telecoms business, I'm very focused on revenue growth. We have to make sure that the new products we launch in the market, as well as our customer management interventions, are the best in terms of return on investment!

Vodafone shapes its marketing activities according to whether customers are high or low value. Figure 4.10 shows how the company differentiates such activities for customer service, development, loyalty and retention.

Customer value drivers are reshaping pricing, services, and processes. Today, a well-planned customer value strategy encompasses:

- Unified customer intelligence.

- Customer profiling and valuation mechanisms.

- Customer tracking by household and buying patterns.

- Breakeven analysis for investment and retention programs.

- Enhanced sales and marketing capabilities.

- Pricing based on customer lifetime value.

MOVING FROM BACK OFFICE TO THE FRONT

Consider next how CFOs and their finance function can effectively restructure the business by reviewing existing models from the "outside-in" – from the external customer viewpoint *and by moving from the back office to the front.*

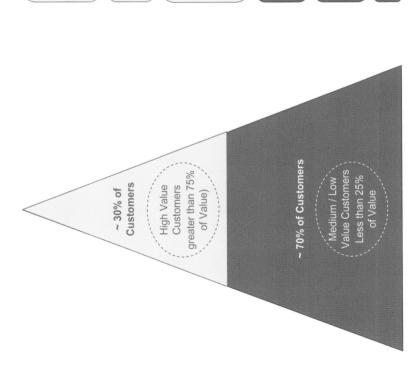

Figure 4.10 *Vodafone: value tiering marketing activities*

CFO AS SALESMAN
Juan Carlos Stotz, CFO Fixed Networks, Communications Division, Siemens

Fixed Networks is a worldwide business in the telecommunications equipment sector, structured in four product groups – Access, Solutions, Transport, and Control. This part of the Siemens group has annual revenues of €3 billion, and employs around 10,000 people worldwide. Our headquarters are based in Germany and we operate in 120 countries.

Under our customers you will find the big telecommunication operators – the major incumbents in each country. Today our customers also include the new challengers to these incumbents, such as the cable operators and smaller service providers.

We're in a very dynamic and highly competitive market. This market has been shrinking over the last five years, but we're now experiencing some growth in volumes – although not in price. So the good news is that revenues are rising, currently 8% pa, in a shrinking market. So we're gaining market share. We constantly increase our product portfolio through acquisitions and new product development – with a drive towards systems and applications business, rather than just hardware product. To increase our focus we separated our product business from our service operation.

However, because of price pressure we constantly need to re-adjust our business model to reduce cost. In the last three years we reached productivity gains of €2.5 billion.

We're being forced to look for new ways of making our R&D more productive, for new ways of streamlining our go-to-market organization, redefining our sales channels, and concentrating our manufacturing on fewer sites. We've also moved manufacturing and R&D resources from high-cost to low-cost locations.

From the back office to the front
I find my role has changed – from the back office to the front. As CFO, I believe you have to be very close to your customers to understand changing market demands. I spend 25% of my time with external customers. My role with customers includes not only financing, but also closing the deals and sustaining relationships at the highest level.

If you're spending this much time on external customers, then of course you do need back-up internally. I'm lucky in having a reliable controlling department, good systems, strong project management and accounting disciplines inside the company.

As a CFO, I'm neither a salesman by background nor a technology expert. I'm in a position to negotiate with chief executives and ministers in our customer organizations because typically they too have a non-technical background. But both sides are empowered to take business decisions; we understand the business behind the technology. The technology is supporting your business idea.

Facing reality

Talking to customers is absolutely essential for me to do my CFO job. We invest nearly €500 million each year in R&D, so I need to know first hand where the market is going and that the investment is addressing customer demands.

For example, different countries have different telecommunications regulations and restrictions that can affect the commercial feasibility and viability of new technologies coming down our development pipeline. By working with customers I can also learn quite a lot about our competitors.

In this way I can save the company a lot of money. You can avoid much of the internal misunderstanding and miscommunication of market realities. Working with the customer you can solve the problems from the very beginning before they work their way into your organization. You can influence the customer and the process of value creation from the customer's point of view as well as your own – the customer can see the CFO as a "sparring partner," not as a salesman, but as someone with whom they can mutually share problems and thrash out a solution which works for both parties.

Conversely, I've found, from mistakes in the past, that if the CFO doesn't have this direct customer contact then you have to mend the broken parts of the internal business model after the event.

Juan Carlos's advice to CFOs? Get out there, meet the customers – all major decisions start with them. After you've put the finance function in order, the best way to play a valuable part in restructuring business processes is by going to customers and understanding their needs. From the outside in!

STRUCTURAL AND HUMAN CAPITAL

So intangible assets – be they brands, customers, or human capital – have become more critical in value creation for the CFO. Many companies, like Siemens, have been through dramatic restructurings to reflect this shift. They have invested in what we call "structural capital" – business structures and processes for managing the value of intangible assets.

Structural capital has been referred to as *packed* human capital: it permits individual human capital, individual knowledge, to be used again and again to create value. It belongs to the organization as a whole and can be reproduced and shared, creating the conditions for rapid collective knowledge growth.

Structural capital comprises all resources that support people in their work: all those intangibles left behind when they go home at night. These include internal processes and structures, databases, and customer relationships. Structural capital helps people work smarter, not just harder.

In an increasingly knowledge-based economy, everything starts with people: they are the source of innovation and renewal. It is people who conceive new organizational processes, and managers who come up with strategies that outsmart the competition.

Many CFOs interviewed for this book talk about their people first, the variety and quality of the skills in their teams – and the growing importance of people in their organizations as a whole. They see the process of resource allocation – one of their key responsibilities – as having more to do with human capital than financial capital. Financial capital is often seen as a commodity – it's relatively plentiful, and relatively cheap. But human capital is relatively scarce, difficult to sustain, and very expensive!

For example, when a CFO is making an acquisition, key questions arise: Who will stay and who will leave? How motivated are those who remain? How much value are they going to create? When a company considers an acquisition target, and how much to pay – along with brands, intellectual property, and customers – it takes into account the value and costs of the people involved, the *human capital*. Such factors include:

- Workforce adaptability

    1 The flexibility of the personnel structure has a material financial impact on purchase price and future earnings.
    2 Remember: most restructuring programs do not realize expected savings.
    3 Future efficiency programs often involve higher costs than projected.

- Employee liabilities

    1 Remuneration and fringe benefits are often not transparent and costs are usually higher than expected.
    2 Contracts are often difficult to terminate and future costs are a risk.
    3 Management contracts: change-of-control clauses, transaction bonuses, and other costly arrangements may be ongoing factors.

- People performance

    1 Identifying key employees and ensuring retention.
    2 Personnel costs relative to productivity benchmarks.

- Human sustainability

    1 Analysis of HR provides a reality check of the business plan: often future development has little or no anchorage in personnel development.
    2 Commitment of employees to the new ownership.

Human capital can only be preserved if the managers and employees who matter strategically constantly upgrade their skills and add new ones. Investments in this form of human capital are not only of vital interest to the company, but also to the people themselves – they really *own* the capital; the company just *rents* it!

As CFO, how do you identify strategic human capabilities? As your business model and strategy changes over time, what are the changing requirements of your human capital? How do you avoid the risks of increasingly obsolete skills? How do you secure valuable new competencies and refresh innovation capability in order to improve competitive edge and generate shareholder value?

Techniques are emerging for valuing human capital. They range from the simplistic to the complex. For example:

- **Value-add per employee:** the revenue-earning capacity of people employed. In professional services, this can simply be a matter of evaluating the revenue that individuals can be expected to generate – for example, in professional sports, the "crowd-pulling power" and marketing potential of the individual sportsman. In industry, as in sport, premiums may be placed on teams. In entertainment, musicians have a value based on their future royalties discounted to present values. In pharmaceutical companies, scientists and top innovators are rewarded with exceptional bonus packages. *However, in most other industries, the value-add of individuals or teams is difficult to ascertain.*

- **Human asset valuation:** the market salaries of managers and employees are used as a surrogate for capitalizing, over a number of years, their human asset value. There are formulas for adjusting the market salary calculation to factor in the competitive "knowledge duration" period, the annual cost of investment in knowledge refreshment, and a motivational index. Such formulas are beginning to gain credibility, but can be difficult to apply in practice.

Many companies in knowledge-intensive businesses – professional services, software or hi-tech – have begun to identify and track the skills they require, not just currently, but in the future.

However, assessing individual skills is not enough. If people don't interact, if knowledge does not flow between them, then there is no collective brilliance. Real leading-edge knowledge and innovation come from exchanges between knowledge workers, from the sharing of ideas and experiences. To make this happen, a company needs the right organizational infrastructure, and a stimulating culture that emphasizes innovation. In the next chapter, on innovation and growth, we look at how the CFO can help increase the effectiveness of knowledge-based value creation.

STRAIGHT FROM THE CFO

- **What's missing from your balance sheet?**

  Make your intangibles tangible! Identify intangible assets, such as brands, which provide competitive advantage. Select the right mix of intangible valuation techniques.

- **Focus on execution, not valuation**

  Identify the changes your business model needs to maximize intangible value. Consider new processes, new structures, new measures – structural capital for packaging and sharing your company's potential!

- **Invest in value centers**

  Break your value chain into components for value center reporting. Rebalance your capital investments. Optimize internally generated returns. Manage the investment of internally grown intangibles on a like-for-like basis with those acquired externally.

- **Exploit intellectual property**

  Carry out an inventory of your IP. Determine which assets generate revenue – be sure they're protected. Avoid any unnecessary cost and risk. Make IP transparent – internally, for investment management, and externally, for investor communications.

- **All customers are not equal!**

  Focus marketing investments on customer lifetime value. Understand customer behavior. Distinguish between customers who create value and those who destroy value. Integrate customer value management processes, systems, and knowledge.

- **Move finance from back office to the front**

  Review your business model and restructure it from the "outside-in." Spend more time understanding the impact of your business on the economics of your customers' business. As CFO, do you see yourself as a "salesman" for the company?

- **Grow your human capital**

  Discriminate between those people who are likely to make a difference and those who can't. Identify the skills and competencies required tomorrow to innovate and grow your business. Put a premium on scarce human capital and the processes for attracting talent. Develop mechanisms for measuring the investment required, and the returns achieved.

REFERENCES

1 Juergen H. Daum (2001) *Intangible Assets and Value Creation*, Wiley.

2 Morgan Stanley, PwC, Moody's *Building and Enforcing Intellectual Property Value, An International Guide for the Boardroom*, Globe White Page (2003).

CHAPTER 5

Driving Growth and Innovation

Competing today comes down to leadership. Going forward, your only weapon is systematic, radical innovation – making innovation an "all-the-time," everywhere capability. Yesterday's success has never mattered less; today's success has never been more fragile; and tomorrow's success never more uncertain – and the courage to lead never in such short supply!

To quote Gary Hamel,[1] of London Business School:

> "I hear this from executives all the time: 'I know we need to innovate, but why now? This is the time to get back to basics.' I don't object to getting back to basics. Every company has to grow revenue, raise prices (if it can), and cut costs. But you can't grow revenue by flogging the same old stuff to the same old customers through the same old channels in the same way!"

We're living in deflationary times. Most companies can't increase prices, but they can bring new products and services to customers. Customers will always make room for something new, useful, value-packed, unexpected, and exciting. That's not easy if your corporate energy is focused on retrenchment.

Most companies reach a point of diminishing returns with traditional cost reduction strategies. Few are cutting costs faster than their rivals. What's needed is radical thinking – imaginative ways to improve efficiency. Hamel suggests three tests for radical ideas:

- Do they change customer expectations?
- Do they change the basis for competition?
- Do they change industry economics?

The dilemma for the CFO: how to encourage the business to grow and stimulate radical ideas at a time when most companies are not built for radical innovation at all but for perpetuating their existing business models. Innovative behavior in the business is often heavily influenced, for better *or for worse*, by the finance function.

Finance either enables or inhibits such behavior in the way it allocates resources, measures performance, exerts control, and interacts with other functions. Worse, finance can actually get in the way – by reinforcing the status quo and hierarchy at a time when the business needs to be flexible and to make change happen.

Most people who succeed at radical innovation inside large companies tell you that they did it despite the system! There's nothing wrong with control and hierarchy but it has to be balanced with demands for growth. Investors place innovation and growth high on their agenda, but they're also looking for consistent results from one quarter to the next. What a balancing act!

The CEO and the CFO have to lead from the front. Real business innovation should not be seen as an exception, or corralled within an R&D function or a new product development. Rather, innovation comes from the *whole organization* looking at the world through different lenses – challenging the status quo, spotting trends that have gone unnoticed, learning to live *inside* the customer's skin, and thinking of the company as a portfolio of assets and competencies.

So how do you generate breakthrough ideas? And how do you manage the innovation process? Not in one gigantic leap! Through a series of steps – building new skills, metrics, processes, and values that turn rhetoric into reality.

We begin with how one company, which wishes to remain anonymous, manages to innovate and revise its business model to meet today's challenges.

SUSTAINABLE ADVANTAGE

CHANGING THE BUSINESS MODEL
CFO, Global Manufacturing Company

Despite our success, we still face a lot of challenges and have further opportunities to exploit. From a cost perspective, IT expenditures continue to grow for us, mainly because we have multiple IT platforms and lack harmonization in our business proc-esses. Our administrative systems are somewhat outdated: we're challenged to pro-duce timely information and our dependence on manual processes is higher than we would like.

Furthermore, our customers expect us to operate and present the company as a "collective," as one company rather than as individual business units. Many of our competitors have consolidated and standardized their internal operating plat-forms. We now have to go down that path, too.

As part of the investment in our future, we're creating an efficient platform for growth: supply chain, finance, and HR processes, which will provide us with vital, timely information and with productivity gains for re-investment back in the busi-ness. We need business process transformation:

- To standardize our fragmented processes and systems
- To address our customers' needs
- To secure greater productivity to fund investment.

So what's our approach? We're starting this transformation by considering the con-sumer – by mapping real-time marketing and sales processes right back through to supply chain and execution. Our objectives: to ensure we bring innovative prod-ucts to full production and to market as quickly as humanly possible; to manage "demand to execution"with accurate, consistent data; to develop a flexible planning and execution capability; and to provide an adaptable technology infrastructure for the future.

Our traditional vertical product-based divisions are the core strength of the company. The divisional general managers enjoy a great deal of freedom to achieve results in their markets. But we're now supplementing this model with horizontal functions that will work across the vertical divisions, taking advantage of opportu-nities for efficiency without compromising our market-facing focus.

For example, we hope to achieve significant productivity improvements in our supply chain, where we can spread the cost of our transportation network, assets, and information across product divisions. We're combining top customer teams from our various divisions. We also see the opportunity for implementing best prac-tices in horizontal processes such as purchasing, IT, and information management.

The change process for this transformation has to start with the culture and people. The organization has to buy in to the notion of one way of doing things. We're staffing this transformation project with full-time dedicated resources, providing strong central coordination, and plenty of discipline! We're trying to overcome the usual resistance to change by establishing clear criteria for determining what processes should be included in the project and therefore standardized, and what should be excluded as being unique to a product and its market requirements. Of course, there will be circumstances where variation is valid, and we're not trying to stifle the creativity we need in the front line of our businesses.

We're securing support from the vertical divisions as well as the horizontal support functions. If someone wants to make a case for a process which differs from our standard, we ask: does the difference create a core competitive advantage for the individual business unit inside the company? And does this difference produce an "overwhelming" big dollar improvement in productivity? Are there specific regulatory and compliance issues? But if the reasons for the difference are insubstantial, then we're going down the route to standardization.

Once we've aligned the people and culture, we're harmonizing the processes and then we're going on to implement new systems. Oracle has been selected as our ERP system of choice. This is supplemented by best-of-breed software in certain situations. Generally, however, we're biased towards standardization on the Oracle platform.

Our finance function has the opportunity to work outside the boundaries of traditional accounting. We work in a "data-rich" industry and we're a "data-driven" company. Our finance professionals already support decision-making across the company, but the broader transformation initiative should provide the timely, standardized information to enable finance to make an even greater contribution to our future success.

Innovating on how to do things better – this is an area where finance people could always do more. Sometimes CFOs get locked in their patterns and have trouble seeing that there are fundamentally different and better ways of doing business.

Radical innovation implies jettisoning the past. Certainly, the central challenge for radical innovation is to learn how to escape the dogmas that blind a company to new opportunities. At the same time, companies have to continue leveraging the

brands, assets, and competencies that have been built up over time. You never want
to "throw the baby out with the bathwater"!

   You build on the infrastructure you've got already – improving what you've got.

DECISION SUPPORT TAKES CENTER STAGE

As CFO, one of your prime goals must be to improve strategic performance and ensure that the right disciplines are in place. Best-in-class companies want finance to be proactive – advising managers of the financial impact of decisions, helping them to simulate alternatives, and pushing operations to support strategic goals.

The CFO is not just the scorekeeper, or just a business partner – the finance team now has to play the role of the *independent business partner.* They continue to be involved in creating value, but put fresh emphasis on being the external voice of the business. To quote one CFO:

> "The CFO is essentially the business conscience of the company. In times like these, however, pressures for radical change increase dramatically. The CFO must produce new strategies to sustain and grow corporate value."

Finance has to challenge and validate business decisions. Business plans and financial projections must be tested, accepted, or rejected. Ongoing performance has to be measured and monitored, and the need for action has to be flagged. The board can make informed decisions only based on rational information provided by finance.

As such there has to be a healthy tension between management and the finance function. Increasingly, the CFO will have to say "no" to management decisions and behaviors that are contrary to the interests of stakeholders.

Our CFO research has shown that decision support is the one area in which the finance function is expected to expand within the corporation. Every company has oceans of data and acres of knowledge. However, only those businesses able to transform their disparate data streams into timely, relevant, and coherent information will ultimately achieve real competitive edge.

Today's integrating technologies – such as portals and data access tools – supposedly provide users with insight. But they do not address a fundamental flaw – today's decision support systems present users with problems, not solutions.

For the CFO, this means decision making has to be intuitive rather than explicit. It is based on individual mental models – an individual's experience and understanding – instead of collective corporate experience and understanding. The decision support discipline of the future has to address the following questions:

- How can you communicate and implement strategy throughout the organization?

- How can you help managers make informed, value-based judgments on predictive information?

- How can you share knowledge based on what works best across the organization?

Next in this chapter, we look in some detail at what Diageo is doing to develop its decision support discipline to help grow the business.

NEW WAYS OF WORKING

Diageo is the world's leading premium drinks business, with an outstanding collection of beverage alcohol brands across spirits, wine, and beer categories. Its brands include Smirnoff vodka, Gordon's gin and Johnnie Walker whisky.

Like so many companies, when it first considered setting up a decision-support discipline, Diageo had a number of issues to resolve and obstacles to overcome:

- Talent and people
  - Limited leadership capabilities.
  - Uncertain career development opportunities.
  - Little experience in business partner collaboration.

- Structure
  - Multiple faces to the same business partner.
  - Unclear lines of responsibility and accountability.
  - Limited involvement in strategy and decision making.

- Processes and systems
  - Complex, non-transparent operation.
  - Minimal end-to-end ownership.
  - Inconsistent financial information.
  - Significant manual intervention.

Today, all this has changed and much has been achieved. At the core of Diageo's finance strategy was the desire to become *"Great business partners at world-class cost."* Its success so far is based on four pillars:

1 **Developing people** – allowing everyone to realize their full potential.

2 **Expanding decision support capabilities** – tools and techniques to significantly enhance value creation.

3 **Embedding business performance management** – unlocking the potential of the business.

4 **Developing world–class processes and systems** – operating at maximum efficiency.

For Diageo, this means driving for *exceptional* rather than just acceptable performance. It also means finance must develop "high-performance relationships" with business managers that emphasize *stretch* goals and improved decision making. It also means a ruthless focus on end results and creating value. The vision and strategy for Diageo's decision-support capability in North America is represented in Figure 5.1.

What's interesting about Diageo's decision-support vision is its emphasis on the individual – the impact on the way people work, the decision-support academy for skill building, and the mechanisms for sharing. "Search and spin," for example, is a process for *searching* for ideas and *spinning* them across the group.

Jim Grover, head of Diageo's Global Business Support (GBS) comments:

> "A distinguishing feature of the people who work in decision support at Diageo seems to be their passion and energy. They challenge themselves, and are really committed to beating the competition and achieving the company's brand-growth objectives. We try to 'bottle' this enthusiasm!"

We also interviewed Thorsten Knopp, currently CFO of one of Diageo's biggest markets, Africa. At the time, he was SVP finance and strategy for North America and led the decision-support function there.

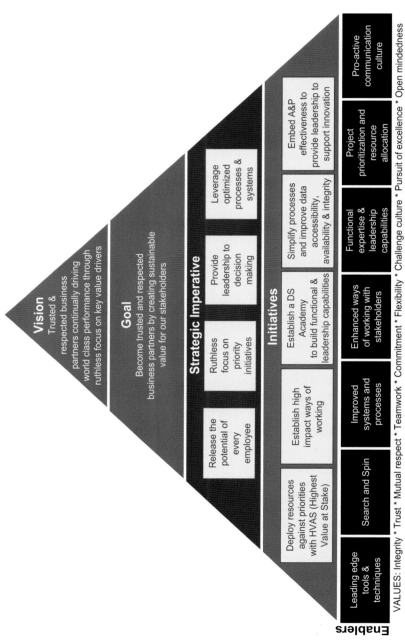

Figure 5.1   *Diageo: vision and strategy for decision support*

BUILDING DECISION-SUPPORT CAPABILITY
Thorsten Knopp, CFO Diageo, Africa

What's different about Diageo's decision support? It's in the organizational set-up – its agenda is broad and multidisciplined. From a finance viewpoint, our decision support is holistic. It's a fundamental part of GBS – covering strategy, M&A, tax and treasury at the center and also includes change management and specific finance skills to support individual markets and brands as well as support for the supply chain. GBS operates as one team but is geographically dispersed. In North America, everything other than financial accounting, shared services, and reporting is included in decision support. Figure 5.2 shows how we regrouped responsibilities.

Our decision-support people provide their business partners in the line with timely, accurate, and action-oriented data to steer the business. Their key responsibilities include:

1 Lead strategy planning and development.
2 Support all commercial analysis requirements.
3 Lead competitive understanding and financial goal setting.

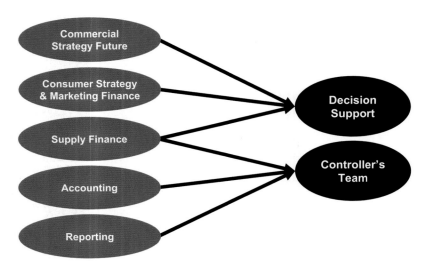

Figure 5.2 *How Diageo changed finance responsibilities*

4 *Develop and deploy tools for value creation – for example, advertising and promotion efficiency and effectiveness tools.*

5 *Reduce complexity and optimize business processes.*

6 *Provide resources for projects with major impact on in-market performance.*

Value architects

In order for the decision-support community to allocate scarce resources against a challenge, "a certain level of value has to be at stake." We have to "pay our way" with a performance promise to generate, for example, additional economic profit of £100 million over three years.

We're quite purposely moving away from value protection activities and process re-engineering, which tend to be reactive, relationship neutral, and concerned with fixed infrastructure. As a result, they have limited impact on growth and innovation.

We, in decision support, focus on unlocking opportunities for creating value – we call this "value architecting." Value architecting is concerned with discretionary investment in processes that are value-adding and that depend on a deep knowledge of relevant "customer" groups. Our support has to be "relationship rich."

To be successful as value architects, we have to be proactive – not hiding away in the back office looking merely for cost reduction, but working with marketing and sales on the front line – looking for growth opportunities and new ways of doing business with our external partners.

We believe that we are good at improving the bottom line – driving out unnecessary capital, increasing cash flow, and achieving cost synergies. As a company, however, we see more opportunities in substantially improving our top-line performance. We believe we have the best portfolio of brands in our industry and this ought to give us a fantastic platform on which to compete and improve our performance. So we're committed to continually doing things better.

New ways of working

We operate very much as an integrated, multifunctional internal resource. Our internal business partners, such as those in marketing, ask for help – we respond by planning and managing the project, and then move on to the next one!

We assign projects a relationship "partner" from within GBS. This partner pro-vides one clear point of contact for the internal business partner and ensures that projects are scoped sufficiently to allow for optimal resource allocation.

We have more than 200 people working on decision support – about 25% of these in North America – and 40% of resources required for this work are seconded into the function and onto our projects. Even so, demand for our decision-support services exceeds supply! Decision-support projects are prioritized based on contri-butions to shareholder value and according to the following criteria:

- *Fit of projects with business strategy.*
- *Expected value creation.*
- *Project urgency.*
- *"Search and Spin" potential.*
- *Resource requirements – time and capability.*

There are plenty of opportunities for cross-functional working and we put a lot of emphasis on team skills, personal flexibility, and on promoting a "challenge and feedback" culture.

The decision-support team, is deeply involved in the entire innovation process. This ranges from what I call "ideation," idea generation combined with innovation, to the commercialization:

1. *Turning idea generation into a project pipeline.*
2. *Identifying the most promising, value-creating ideas and turning them into reality.*
3. *Commercializing and implementing ideas.*

This approach is not just brand specific, it spans our entire portfolio. The key ques-tions we are addressing in this process include:

- *How do we find the pearls within the many ideas?*
- *How do we identify all the relevant options?*
- *How do we ensure we don't close off options too soon?*
- *How do we build a manageable innovation pipeline in times of uncertainty?*

Diversity and challenge

Unusually, our "value architects" have a variety of backgrounds. In my North American team, we had people who were physicists, historians, or chemists by training. Of course, we had financial, commercial, and marketing skills as well. But what we were trying to achieve in the team dynamics was diversity and intellectual curiosity.

More than 50% of all decision-support resources in our North American team were either new to the company or new to the country. In addition to many different nationalities:

- *55% were female.*
- *40% had lived or worked outside North America.*

This diversity of talent led to better ideas for improvement and a wider range of options for action.

We were also looking for behavioural change: we want our decision-support staff to truly own the business challenge. This means a proactive stance over and above that of the internal adviser or quantifier of problems. We want people to understand the issues, to take part in focus groups with external customers, and to challenge our thinking internally.

We also engaged a behavioral psychologist to help the team understand our business partners' views and perceptions. Often the assumption is that your business partner does not understand a challenge. Quite often, they actually do, but through different filters, individual paradigms. Also, a business partner may come up with a proposed solution, but it might not be the most value-creating one for either party. We needed to align our organization with that of our business partner through challenge, debate, and jointly developed solutions. Understanding this challenge to our existing paradigms was a major breakthrough in our capabilities.

Diageo has put a lot of thought behind developing its decision-support capabilities and understanding what it means to be a business partner in practice – the commercial acumen, and the tools and techniques required. Diageo evaluates these capabilities and how well their people are doing against various skill levels: baseline, developing, experienced, and mastery. Much of this evaluation is based on observed behavior. We show how this capability matrix works in Figure 5.3.

Theme	Baseline	Developing	Experienced	Mastery
Business Partner	Displays tenacity and a sense of urgency – collecting all relevant data. Can naturally express opinions and capture attention of business partners (e.g. sales teams) EXAMPLE: *"Here's my report showing the profitability of a, b, and c customers"*	Actively contributes to commercial discussion supported from the conclusions gained from Tools & Techniques. Credibly challenges the input to the decisions EXAMPLE: *"Based on my analysis of customer profitability, I believe we should do x, y, and z with our top customers."*	Will recommend options and influence others' recommendations. Will gain appropriate business alignment to the right decisions. Drives teams towards conclusions EXAMPLE: *"Here's my report and recommendation – and all the sales teams have agreed to it."*	Will / can take 100% accountability for the business decisions. Will personally engage the executive team on the decisions and the outcome EXAMPLE: *Hard to see who is the primary decision maker. Key decisions are not made without input of the individual sought.*
Tools & Techniques	Can use specific analytical tools in certain areas – seeks expert help when required. EXAMPLE: *able to own a distinct piece of analysis relating to a specific area of the business*	Working knowledge of a range of analytical tools. Able to acquire mastery of specific techniques when their use is required. Can contribute to business debates / decision making process EXAMPLE: *able to use a range of analytical approaches, identify the most appropriate & contribute to business debate*	Acknowledged expert in the use and application of a range of tools. Uses / adapts / flexes Tools and Techniques for specific requirements. Can lead the debate to make decisions EXAMPLE: *tailors and develops tools to help make pricing decisions, coaches others in the use of tools and techniques*	Leads global development and deployment of DS tools & techniques. Proactively addresses new areas of focus EXAMPLE: *identifies gaps in the DS tools & techniques across markets – forming teams to address them*
Commercial Acumen	Understands how decisions impact their immediate commercial area and sees where to add value EXAMPLE: *"if we changed the way our distributor was compensated (volume vs. margin) we could add value to the business in this market"*	Delivers value in immediate area of influence by developing and action commercial insights EXAMPLE: *Able to identify a latent opportunity in the local brand portfolio and work with sales and marketing to capture that opportunity*	Continuously develops business insight, in & beyond immediate area of influence. Demonstrates the ability to influence business resources to drive value EXAMPLE: *"we have a problem sourcing a product for our market. If we worked with neighbouring markets, we could all save money – let's team to go after that value."*	Displays restless bias for action to continuously create significant value by deploying analytical expertise and insight to commercial issues EXAMPLE: *Constantly identifying opportunities and generating ideas to drive value for the business. Able to tap into internal and external resources to capture that value*
Capability Building	Develops a network of contacts from which to source information tools and skills. May be an expert in own area EXAMPLE: *Uses a range of information sources (e.g. colleagues, intranet) to access best practice. Actively interacts with key contacts to build own expertise*	Contributes to search and spin process across a range of areas. Can roll out and embed existing tools. Builds capabilities across local environment EXAMPLE: *actively shares and spins local solutions with broader community e.g. by facilitating cross-functional workshops to embed local tools and techniques.*	Builds, refines, enhances, and embeds existing and new tools across a number of markets / functions. Develops capabilities in own team and externally – standardizes tools for global application EXAMPLE: *maintains global network, uses that to drive global initiatives to next phase and delivers in local markets*	Champions & leads initiatives effectively sponsoring and allocating resource to key priorities. Owns identification of gaps, development and roll-out of new capabilities through to delivery. EXAMPLE: *champions roll-out of tools and associated capabilities across a region*

Figure 5.3 *Decision support capabilities*

Diageo now believes it has the people and talent to create effective business partnerships. Their people have broad commercial understanding and acumen – just the right amount of analytical expertise to provide insight and ensure a bias for action.

Consider next some examples of how Diageo's decision-support function in North America is proactively helping develop innovative ideas across the company's value chain.

IN-MARKET INNOVATION

Spirits suppliers in the United States are spending more heavily on advertising, focusing investment on priority brands and learning to operate efficiently in a fragmented, often unstructured media landscape.

Evolving demographics, particularly in ethnic populations, are opening new opportunities for spirit and wine growth – especially in premium brands. Changing consumer attitudes are driving wider acceptance of beverage alcohol and ongoing innovation is renewing interests in specific spirits categories. For example:

- **Vodka** – an explosion of flavors is spurring a robust cocktail culture! Rum is also shifting from light to flavored products.

- **Tequila** – high-end, more mixable brands are helping to extend occasionally beyond the Margherita shots!

- **Brandy** – international brands are capitalizing on consumer trends among ethnic groups.

Diageo has a broad set of premium brands and leads its industry in innovation. It views itself as a clear leader in spirits advertising and believes that, with a renewed focus on the consumer, it can capitalize on the latest trends. The goal: giving customers the experience they want in products, services, and shopping and drinking.

The consumer shifts driving key stakeholders – such as suppliers, retailers, and distributors – are illustrated in Figure 5.4.

Diageo believes that its industry data, tools, insights and capabilities – such as relationship marketing, on-premise activation, media-buying clout – should enable it to capture growth opportunities. Thorsten Knopp provides four brief case studies on how decision support has fuelled innovation:

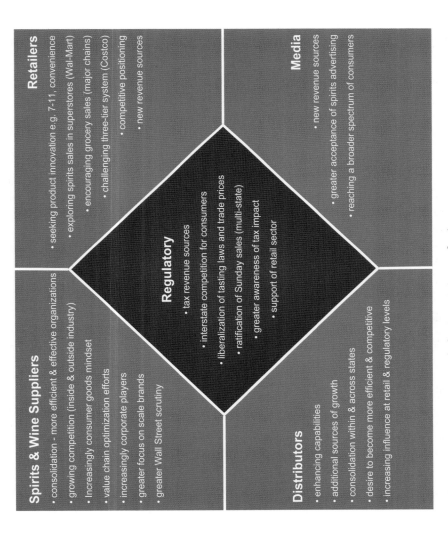

Spirits & Wine Suppliers
- consolidation - more efficient & effective organizations
- growing competition (inside & outside industry)
- increasingly consumer goods mindset
- value chain optimization efforts
- increasingly corporate players
- greater focus on scale brands
- greater Wall Street scrutiny

Retailers
- seeking product innovation e.g. 7-11, convenience
- exploring spirits sales in superstores (Wal-Mart)
- encouraging grocery sales (major chains)
- challenging three-tier system (Costco)
- competitive positioning
- new revenue sources

Regulatory
- tax revenue sources
- interstate competition for consumers
- liberalization of tasting laws and trade prices
- ratification of Sunday sales (multi-state)
- greater awareness of tax impact
- support of retail sector

Distributors
- enhancing capabilities
- additional sources of growth
- consolidation within & across states
- desire to become more efficient & competitive
- increasing influence at retail & regulatory levels

Media
- new revenue sources
- greater acceptance of spirits advertising
- reaching a broader spectrum of consumers

Figure 5.4   *North America: Consumer shifts in spirits and wines*

DIAGEO CASE STUDY 1: ADVERTISING AND PROMOTION (A&P)

In North America, Diageo spends about $650 million a year on A&P. The purpose of its decision-support project was not to save money but to reallocate it where it was needed most – to brands that promised to have the biggest impact on the top- and bottom-line performance of the company.

Smirnoff vodka and Crown Royal whiskey are good examples of how the decision-support team made a difference. Together, these two brands made up a significant slice of North American profit. Despite an increase in A&P, the two brands were not responding as expected.

The purpose of the decision-support project was to build volumes, brand equity, and loyalty. First, it focused on the lower-hanging fruit – the volume-building activity. Once it had understood what brands in what regions were responding in what way to advertising, the project team shared this information across the business through the "Search and Spin" initiative.

The decision-support team came up with a different way of allocating A&P resources. The new approach meant there had to be clarity on why the money was being spent and the value it created.

DIAGEO CASE STUDY 2: PRICING EFFECTIVENESS

This project focused on better understanding traditional pricing sensitivities and how they were changing, given a changing competitive environment. Although Diageo is selling through third-party distributors in North America, and then onto the retailers, its focus was very much on end-consumer pricing. The aim was to harmonize pricing structures across the country, which differed from state to state.

The decision-support team looked at the impact of pricing on the competition and on the different customer segments they served.

In a high-margin spirits environment, with the North American three-tier system of supply, it's very important not to lose the focus on the end consumer. So the team also looked at the linkages between market price and associated A&P investment. It developed a best-in-class pricing diagnostic tool to understand the impact of various pricing decisions.

Subsequently, it linked the impact of promotional investment on consumer behavior and associated pricing implications. For example, to maximize value from seasonal variations in consumer behavior, Diageo provided additional offerings, such as Christmas packaging combined with free gifts. This initiative saved significant money in non-value-adding packaging, and maximized the benefit of free gift offers.

 ## DIAGEO CASE STUDY 3: SALES FORCE EFFECTIVENESS

The "New Generation Growth" project focused on improving the effectiveness of resources and their allocation to the sales force in its dealings with distributors. The decision-support team reviewed the relative roles of both Diageo's sales force and its distributors. They found significant overlap.

The result improved Diageo's "way of working" with distributors, and also helped the distributors upgrade their own sales forces through Diageo-led training, improved communications, and a stronger focus on partnering. Diageo didn't see the distributor as an external customer anymore – but as part of its seamless value chain organization linked to its overall value proposition to the end-consumer.

The distributors were pleased with the help. They now had dedicated sales teams trained in Diageo brands, and were better able to articulate to retail customers the benefits of different Diageo pricing structures. Diageo also benefited because distributors were less inclined to promote competing brands.

For Thorsten Knopp and his North American decision-support team, one of the challenges was to prioritize some 250 projects. They included their internal business partners in the prioritizing process – agreeing on the "size of the prize," and trade-offs between brands and margins.

They extended this approach to include external business partners, either on the supply side or the customer, such as distributors. The marketing projects were particularly aimed at optimizing the balance of discretionary investment between long-term brand equity building and short-term volume increase.

The supply initiatives were all part of a much larger program of identifying the total profit pool in North America, looking at how the company placed its bets in the value chain.

DIAGEO CASE STUDY 4: SUPPLY INITIATIVES

The decision-support team is working with its internal business partners in the supply organization in four main areas:

1 *The R&D process*
2 *Procurement*
3 *Manufacturing*
4 *Supply logistics*

Each of these four work streams had very specific requirements. For example, in procurement, the focus was on moving from the more traditional zero sum price negotiations to the generation of options that would improve the value creation within the entire end-to-end supply chain. The goal: value creation for the entire end-to-end process. By working with the supplier – its business partner – it created a win–win situation.

Diageo developed tools around strategic thinking. Value chain analysis started with the total industry profit pool, the allocation and segmentation of the profit pool to participants, understanding the basic processes involved and identifying how participants and profit can be shifted from one part of the value chain to the other.

The decision-support team was looking closely at the perceived end-value of the product: would customers pay for up to four warehouses, for example? Would consumers pay for higher-quality vanilla from Madagascar versus vanilla substitute? The answer to such questions was only if they perceived value and if they would be willing to pay for it!

Thorsten concludes:

"The decision-support team in North America created value for the company, and we were clearly able to measure the top- and bottom-line improvement to Diageo North America. Diageo is still a young organization and we are constantly adapting to the external market challenges. In the future, I see a more holistically integrated environment as a key challenge for management – integrating customers, consumers, and suppliers to create value."

FROM THE OUTSIDE, IN

Few technologies or product ideas are inherently sustaining or disruptive when they emerge from the innovator's mind. Instead, they go through a process of being fleshed out and shaped into a strategic plan in order to win funding.

In his book *The Innovators Solution*,[2] Clayton Christensen sets out three different approaches to creating new growth businesses: sustaining innovations, low-end disruptions, and new-market disruptions. These approaches are defined and contrasted in Figure 5.5.

> **Sustaining innovations** focuses on performance improvement in *existing* product attributes, targeting the most profitable *existing* customers and/or improving profit margins by exploiting *existing* processes and cost structures.

> **Low-end disruptions** target *existing* over-served customers in the low-end of the mainstream market by utilizing *new* operating or financial models.

> **New-market disruptions** seek to improve performance in *new* product attributes and by targeting *new* customers who've historically lacked the money or skill to buy and use the product.

Christensen makes the case: disruptive business models are potentially valuable corporate assets.

Take the case of Procter & Gamble (P&G). It has implemented change at all levels to complement its shift to the low-income consumer market. As one of the world's greatest consumer companies, it has an outstanding reputation for marketing. The CEO, A.G. Lafley, has led the company through a difficult few years – shifting P&G's focus to health and beauty brands. The company's track record since he took over has been impres-

Dimension	Sustaining Innovations	Low-End Disruptions	New-Market Disruptions
Targeted performance of the product or service	Performance improvement in attributes most valued by the industry's most demanding customers. These improvements may be incremental or breakthrough in character	Performance that is good enough along the traditional metrics of performance at the low end of the mainstream market	Lower performance in "traditional" attributes, but improved performance in new attributes – typically simplicity and convenience
Targeted customers or market application	The most attractive (i.e. profitable) customers in the mainstream markets who are willing to pay for improved performance	Over-served customers in the low end of the mainstream market	Targets non-consumption: customers who historically lacked the money or skill to buy and use the product
Impact on the required business model (processes and cost structure)	Improves or maintains profit margins by exploiting the existing processes and cost structure and making better use of current competitive advantages	Utilizes a new operating or financial approach or both – a different combination of lower gross profit margins and higher asset utilization that can earn attractive returns at the discount prices required to win business at the low end of the market	Business model must make money at lower price per unit sold, and at unit production volumes that initially will be small. Gross margin dollars per unit sold will be significantly lower.

Figure 5.5   *Three approaches to creating new growth businesses*
Source: *The Innovator's Solution*, Harvard Business School Press

sive: sales have grown by more than 40%, profits have doubled and P&G now boasts 17 "billion-dollar brands" – and that's without including the Gillette acquisition. With Gillette, P&G becomes the world's largest household goods empire, with brands ranging from Duracell batteries to Pampers nappies and Pringles snacks.

Clayton Daley, the Group CFO of P&G, says:

> "There are roughly 6 billion people in the world. For most of this company's history, its strategy was pointed at the billion at the top of the economic pyramid. Where did that leave P&G? It meant we were only appealing to the top percentage of people in developed markets. When A. G. Lafley, our chief executive, arrived he said, 'We're going to serve the world's consumers.'

> "That led us to realize that we don't have the product strategy, the cost structure, to be effective in serving low-income consumers. What's happened has been one of the most dramatic transformations I've seen in my career. We now have all our functions, including finance, focused on that goal."

P&G devotes about 30% of its $1.9 billion annual R&D budget to low-income markets – a 50% increase from five years ago. Developing markets are expected to grow twice as fast as developed markets over the next five years. P&G's transformation includes three areas:

1 How it identifies what consumers want.

2 How this affects R&D.

3 How it has retooled all its global manufacturing systems to make products more cheaply and sell them more profitably.

P&G has changed its approach to consumer research: Rather than focus groups and quantitative research, it spends more time in consumers' homes to gain insights into daily habits.

Four years ago, P&G decided to get half its ideas from outside sources. The company has also improved manufacturing efficiency and cut costs by developing a network of suppliers in China, Brazil, Vietnam, and India.

In P&G's top finance role for more than eight years, Clayton Daley has supported the business through difficult times and helped orchestrate its current success. He reflects on how P&G's structure has changed to a global organization that has fuelled innovation and growth. He goes on to comment about how finance is playing a lead role in strategy and doing its part in innovating with customers.

COLLABORATING WITH CUSTOMERS
Clayton Daley, Group CFO, Procter & Gamble

The background and context for our success today is well chronicled. Growth slowed for us in the mid-1990s. The foundations of the structure and strategy that we later followed were laid down then, including the move to a global business unit (GBU) structure and increased emphasis on R&D. The objectives were sound, but execution at that time did not stimulate growth fast enough. We took our eye off the core business and no amount of new product activity can substitute for a weakening core.

When A. G. Lafley came in as CEO, he took us back to the core, leading with a focus on customers and stressing the necessity for flawless execution of our core product strategies. You could say – "back to basics."

Since then we've established revenue growth rates of 3–5% annually; when you include acquisitions, this is nearer 6%. We've also achieved double-digit EPS growth. This makes us a high performer.

Threat of commoditization
From a growth standpoint, the biggest threat we face is commoditization. Unless you create innovations that justify brand premiums, consumers, and retailers – our customers – will inexorably lead us down the commoditization path. If you look at what's happened to many packaged food businesses – for example, cereals and flour – they've been overtaken by private label manufacturers supported by retailers. As a result, they've lost their brand-value advantage. So the key for us is developing products that actually perform better – that really do offer something to consumers that's different from the private label market.

So we've got to develop product innovation and marketing programs to stimulate sufficient value-add in our products to win market share from not only competing branded products, but also private label competitors. We have to do all this while maintaining a reasonable brand premium. Quite often it's difficult to patent, or protect, the intellectual property in the product design advantage, so you have to keep innovating to stay ahead.

Acquiring Gillette

We've got to sustain our margin of superiority just to stay in the game. We've got to back this up with the right marketing and branding, and excellence in our in-market execution. We tailor execution locally where absolutely necessary, but we try to secure the benefits of global standardization and scale.

That's why we've acquired Gillette – it's a scale business, offers consumers good-value products, and earns an acceptable price premium with a decent return for shareholders. We see the potential for growth and savings from the additional scale that Gillette will give us in the market. For example, Gillette is exceptionally quick at go-to-market – often launching across Europe in less than three months.

I've temporarily stepped out of finance to lead the integration with Gillette, working jointly with its CEO. During the transition, we need to make sure that the existing businesses stay healthy. Gillette's branded business units will retain their identity and structure, but we will see synergies in our respective back offices and eventually, in our go-to-market organizations (everything that happens to a product from the factory gate to the customer).

Our business model has 18 global business units (GBUs) – shortly to be 21 with the inclusion of Gillette. These GBUs are based on brand groupings and focus on innovation for their respective consumer groups. The GBUs "own" globally their R&D, product and marketing initiatives, but have to collaborate closely with in-country sales teams or market development organizations (MDOs). They draw on global services for back-office support and go-to-market capability.

Looking for leaders

Our finance managers provide dedicated support to both the GBUs and the MDOs. In addition to their finance skills, they have to understand the improvement programs running through the businesses. They also need the ability to think strategically and to be the alter ego of their general manager. In a nutshell, I'm looking for leaders – leaders in strategy and projects who are proactive.

P&G doesn't have a separate strategy or business development group. Its general managers own the strategy. But the finance leaders in the businesses are responsible for leading strategy planning. That's my job at the group level, and that's what we expect from our finance people cascaded down through the business units. It's much more a business role today than a technical financial role. Nevertheless, we stress the importance of financial competencies – we wear two hats – and we cele-brate the success of those who demonstrate deep, technical financial mastery too.

The "CFO Circle"

Some years ago, we recognized that we had a number of experts across the organization who were undervalued. The high-flyers on the fast-track career path had more general management background. There wasn't the same opportunity for advancement for technical specialists.

We have about 4,000 people in finance across our company and we needed a better balance in our finance community. So we have a CFO Circle – made up of approximately 20 or so specialists, nominated each year by their peer group. Mem-bership is based largely on individual accomplishment – and is drawn from a number of seniority levels. Because the CFO Circle is selective, almost an elite, it's seen as something special and valuable in developing and sharing new ideas and best prac-tice.

Role of finance in sales

In one of our finance specialties – sales – our Circle expert in "direct-to-consumer retailing" understood what was important in the business model for home delivery and channel success. That's why we now have finance people in all of our customer teams. We've stimulated internal demand. It wasn't the finance function's idea to put people on sales teams; our sales organization demanded it!

The only way we're going to really penetrate the customer – retailers such as Wal-Mart and Tesco – is if we understand how they do their accounting and how they reward their people, for example, their buyers. We're looking at how our actions at P&G impact their systems and reward structures. In some cases, we've even had dis-cussions with customers about changing how they evaluate themselves internally. We think there's a better way for them to do their business and, in doing so, help us too!

For example, retail customers traditionally had buyers who were rewarded on gross margin. They weren't rewarded for sales volume or shelf-space utilization. Today, there's a lot of financial sophistication in retail: it's not just about maximizing gross margin, it's as much about the economics of volume and capital productivity. So the sales guys have to have the finance guys at the table when they're negotiat-ing, not after the event, when it's often too late for them to have impact.

Working with Wal-Mart

I believe our finance folks have made a difference in our dealings with Wal-Mart. Wal-Mart pursued a strategy three years ago of going for what they call "opening price-points." It wanted to shift its strategy towards lower-priced goods. Of course, such a strategy was not in our interests. Our Wal-Mart team, including our finance manager, helped persuade Wal-Mart that this low-price strategy had taken it away from more attractive consumers and from higher-price baskets moving out of the store!

While Wal-Mart competes very effectively for lower-income consumers, it was losing "shopping baskets" to other retailers. So it's shifting strategy back to more branded merchandise – bringing more traffic back into the stores with attractive pricing on high-quality branded products. Once the shoppers are in the store, then Wal-Mart can attract them into other categories – what we call "soft lines," such as automotive, where margins are higher.

Getting outside exposure

We have to avoid our finance community becoming too insular, which can easily happen when you consider the strength of P&G's internal corporate culture.

One of the best assignments we can give a promising member of our finance team is working with a customer. They get the "outside-in" exposure they need by getting involved in:

- *competitive analysis and benchmarking*
- *consumer research*
- *working with suppliers (on materials and packaging)*
- *negotiating with customers on pricing.*

We hope to avoid the death struggle evolving in our industry between the manufacturers and the retailers. Retailers get bigger, stronger. Manufacturers will lose, certainly their branded premiums if they're also manufacturing for private label. I believe that the leading retailers understand that they can have a true partnership with a short-list of leading branded manufacturers, such as P&G – jointly developing a mutual understanding of the end-consumer.

We share a lot of our market, shopper, and consumer research. We're bringing out new trade-up products that retailers want in order to reach for additional sales and margins.

In summary, as the CFO of P&G, I try to set an example through what I do in my role – leading with strategy, with the integration of Gillette, and playing my part in supporting innovation and growth. This sets a cultural expectation and a role model for the finance function across the company, about constantly seeking new ways to add the most value.

P&G aspires to be the leading consumer products company in sales, profitability, market capitalization, shareholder return, and – particularly important – in each of their core strengths: scale, branding, go-to-market, and innovation.

INNOVATION CENTERS: A "WIN–WIN"

As a branded products company, P&G's challenge is always to add value for consumers. The key to that challenge lies in technology – developing and marketing products that are demonstrably better to the consumer than competitive offerings.

P&G is a pioneer in marketing and consumer sales. Recently, it has built *innovation centers* in the US and Europe to forge even closer links with its first-line customers, the supermarket retailers, in order to jointly create value. Wade Miquelon, Vice President Finance for Western Europe, takes up the story of how he and his finance team get involved in the Geneva innovation center.

THE GENEVA INNOVATION CENTER
Wade Miquelon, VP Finance, Western Europe, Procter & Gamble

We're building stronger partnerships with customers and suppliers. This results in stronger retail partnerships. In a recent industry survey of US retailers, P&G was ranked number one in six of eight categories: clearest strategy, most innovative, most helpful consumer and shopper information, best supply chain management, best category management, and best consumer marketing.

On the supply side, you have to share risk with suppliers on new product develop-ment. Supply partnerships are also important in execution – in bringing products to market more quickly than we have in the past.

Achieving value

At P&G, there is a relentless focus on achieving value for the consumer. Better prod-ucts at cheaper cost! How can we, in finance, help? Through business leadership around value creation – providing the financial metrics, strategic guidance, and resource allocation. Brands have their own inherent business models. How can you stretch those brands over time, while evolving your business model and getting more out of it?

During our careers in finance, we will be rotated through country-based, GBU, corporate, or shared-service finance management positions. This broadens our perspective and is a major strength. Although we play a significant role in spotting opportunities, perhaps our greatest contribution is to spot the " icebergs" – unex-pected, submerged obstacles to sustainability and growth. Also, we are ruthless in maintaining discipline over cost and overall margin structures.

Focus on shoppers

David Lang, a senior P&G finance manager for sales in Western Europe, joins the discussion and comments on his unusual job title, CFO Circle: "I'm an expert in work-ing externally – supporting the sales organization by collaborating with external customers. We bring our total shareholder return (TSR) objectives to life in our rela-tionships with retailers.

"When we do business plans they are very focused on shoppers – and consumers – to offer retailers a range of solutions that drive value across the complete retail value chain. We focus on driving value well beyond just negotiating with our retail customers on margin. We want to grow the total pie available to both parties and deliver a 'win/win'."

Figure 5.6 illustrates the P&G approach to growing the value pie with its retail customers.

Wade goes on to say: "Creating new categories and segments is a lot easier than taking business away from determined competitors. P&G can help retailers grow their businesses even faster by taking fuller advantage of their intangible assets – leadership brands, product innovation, shopper understanding, consumer mar-

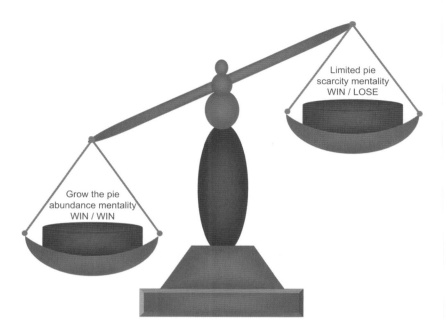

Figure 5.6   *A bigger pie for manufacturer and retailer*

keting. Having finance work with external customers in this way creates a leading edge.

For example, by jointly targeting mothers who buy or should buy Pampers, bringing them into the store for the product, you can grow total consumption – not only building valuable brand loyalty for P&G, but also increasing the overall shopping basket for the retailer. One brand in the 'right shopping moment' can provide a shopping basket net present value (NPV) to the retailer that's far greater than a one-off product purchase ... a win–win–win (consumer–retailer–P&G)."

P&G's finance directors in the GBUs have two metrics on their scorecard: sales delivery and innovation delivery. The company creates indispensable partnerships with customers. David picks up the story again: "Leading manufacturers, such as P&G, can collaborate with leading retailers – such as Tesco – to generate more growth and more consistent business results by innovating more closely together."

Innovation centers

Our innovation centers represent a major investment. Each of 13 major product categories has its own brainstorming studio. These studios innovate jointly with retail customers by reinventing the consumer experience of new products in the home.

We operate with a mindset that believes we can create more value – for shoppers, customers and P&G. By understanding better both the consumer and the retailer needs, shoppers reward us through the sales line. We secure improved sales penetration, increase customer loyalty and higher spend. There is a clear link between TSR and measures of shopper and consumer satisfaction.

In our Geneva innovation center, we take the opportunity to explore together with retailers new shopping experiences. We've built mock-ups of various retailing concepts, ranging from up-market boutiques to cut-price discount stores.

Baby care is a product category where global scale is important to fund investment and research. We need to really understand babies and their mothers' needs. For example, P&G's innovative use of advanced technology in the paper diapers product has decreased leakage from 30% to 5%! We've also been able to extend the nappy brand from the 1–3 year age range to ages 3–7 with the Kandoo toilet tissue – a great example of an innovative brand extension.

Pringles is a snack brand which also works well globally. Ariel, on the other hand, is a laundry product, and has to be varied to suit different market requirements, for example, in France and Spain.

Working closely with Tesco, the UK's largest supermarket retailer, we plan our future business in these categories together. Business planning and performance measurement are major opportunities for the finance function to get involved – at the sharp-end of the business.

With the retail customer, it's not just about margin negotiation, it's about understanding how you can both create shareholder value. The finance function, more than any other, has many touch points inside and outside the organization.

When business planning in the innovation center with retailers, P&G takes a structured shareholder value analysis approach – breaking the top-line measures into detail, as illustrated in Figure 5.7.

Ultimately, it's the end-consumers, or the shoppers, who have the power. They want choices in brands and products that are easy to shop for and a delight to use.

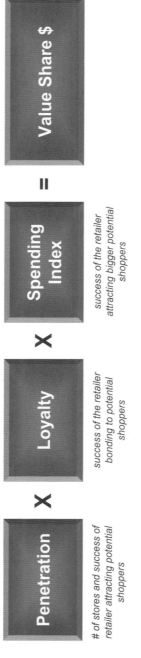

Figure 5.7 *Creating value for shoppers, customers and P&G*

Wade summarizes: "Many of our finance people spend up to 20% of their time working externally, particularly with customers. We must continue to drive sustainable sales and value growth. We cannot be complacent. We, in finance, must play our part in helping to transform shopper insights into innovation – not only in the product offer but also in the store."

Fast-moving consumer goods companies like P&G are looking for perpetual growth and sustainability. This means finance involvement in perpetual reinvention, in staying ahead and in working against perhaps the biggest threat to brand value – the speed with which private label competitors can imitate products.

P&G makes a clear case for the role of finance in all this and undoubtedly their finance capability is at the leading edge.

STRAIGHT FROM THE CFO

- **Define your model for sustainable advantage**

  Treat innovation as the most important corporate asset. Consider, holistically, how your company generates breakthrough ideas. Are all functions involved? Disaggregate your shareholder value algorithm – defining who contributes what to innovation and financial performance.

- **Introduce an innovation scorecard**

  Establish metrics for measuring sustainability. Ensure that finance encourages, rather than hinders, the innovation process. What's in the pipeline? Is it enough? Screen the "forest" of ideas, look at the "trees," the "roots" – every "leaf."

- **Build a transformation platform**

  Leverage the brands, assets, and competencies built up over time. Transform the infrastructure and standardize business processes to free up investment for growth.

- **Create a new decision support discipline**

  Develop new capability "bundles." Like Diageo, become great business partners at world-class cost. Drive for stretch – exceptional performance. Focus ruthlessly on end results. "Search" for ideas for improvement and "spin" them around the company.

- **Become the value architect**

  Work with marketing and sales at the front line, looking for growth opportunities, for new ways of working, and new ways of doing business. Move away from just value protection and re-engineering – it's limiting. Focus on discretionary investment, deep customer knowledge. Become relationship rich!

- **Innovate in-market**

  Encourage diversity in your decision-support team – a really broad skill spectrum, a range of nationalities. Get the team to own the business challenge. To confront their preconceptions, to filter ideas. Change the rules, go for breakthrough! Develop capabilities – commercial acumen, insight, and a bias for action.

- **Form a CFO circle**

  Encourage peer groups to nominate their "best and brightest" to join the circle – the network of your finance high-flyers. Put them on a career fast-track. Give their achievements the highest profile.

- **Invest in an innovation center**

  Assign top finance executives to work with customer sales teams. Like P&G, establish joint business planning with your top external customers and innovate together to entice end-consumers. Go for a win–win–win!

REFERENCES

1 Gary Hamel (2000) *Leading the Revolution*, Harvard Business School Press.

2 Clayton M. Christensen (2003) *The Innovator's Solution*, Harvard Business School Press.

CHAPTER 6

Looking *Forward*, Not Backward

CFOs of companies driving rapid growth and maximizing intangible values are concerned about whether their finance disciplines and processes can keep up!

Their priorities: attracting and allocating the *right* resources to the *right* investments, staying on top of what's *really* happening in the front line, and taking corrective action quickly. They also have to prepare their organizations to deal with the unexpected. But one thing's certainly true – CFOs can't predict the future!

EXPECT THE UNEXPECTED

The CFO of a leading Fortune 500 company comments on the pressures he faces to constantly reinvent the business:

> "As Group CFO, I am looking forwards as much as looking backwards. I am always looking ahead to the end of this quarter, the end of this year, and the year that follows. Then, I'm worrying about the future beyond that! We're in a business that has to keep reinventing itself every ten years or so. When the patents for our current products expire, we need to replace them with new ones. I'm very focused on the innovation pipeline – where we are, where we need to be.

> "We used to have a rigid and excessively time-consuming strategic planning process – a five-year plan, with fixed financial outcomes. But we found that the debates around possible outcomes were a lot more useful. So we don't really have strategic plans

anymore. We now have a long-range forecast based on multiple scenarios with different outcomes – more of a considered and realistic look into the future than a financial projection."

The emphasis of best practice in financial management has therefore changed from reviewing accounting results in the past to preparing for the future. Consequently, the processes for allocating resources and for monitoring performance, which historically have served CFOs so well – and for that matter, kept the business under such tight control – no longer seem as appropriate.

Consider this as well: in too many companies, there is a grand, and overly vague, long-term goal on the one hand, but only short-term budgets and annual plans on the other – with nothing in between to link the two. To quote Gary Hamel of London Business School:

> "We often come across companies that have set an ambitious long-term goal, perhaps to double revenue and profits over five years, or to dramatically increase the proportion of revenues coming from new businesses. But they have devoted almost no intellectual effort to thinking through the medium-term capability-building program that is needed to support that goal."

So this gap poses a series of dilemmas for the CFO: which aspects of planning should you preserve and which should you throw away? How should you build capability for the growth envisaged? How far should you plan into the future, and to what extent should you prepare for the unexpected? How can you be sure that top-down strategies are executed properly and that bottom-up reporting tells you what's actually happening? And are your supporting processes and systems up to the job?

Organizations cannot rely on chance or luck. CFOs the world over realize that attaining a long-term goal requires a series of logical, achievable, sequential steps. Having a strategy and a plan is not the issue. It's the failure to implement that can prove disastrous.

Michael Coveney of Extensity, the lead author of *The Strategy Gap*,[1] singles out two major reasons why companies fail in executing their strategic plans:

- Management's inability to convert vision into operational reality.

- The limitations of their traditional financial management processes – such as budgeting, forecasting and reporting – which underpin strategy implementation.

Management can actually create the gap between strategy and execution, either through its actions, or through *inaction*. Quite often this gap is caused by a failure to secure support for a new strategy, failure to communicate it, failure to adhere to the implementation plan, and failure to adapt to unexpected changes in the external environment.

Strategic plans typically have to be action based. They should measure strategic implementation activity. Measures for strategic initiatives do not always fit easily into rigid accounting and cost-center-based structures, so the CFO must find new ways of measuring strategy implementation – traditional accounting won't work.

Furthermore, traditional budgets tend to be too short term, too financially focused, and too internally oriented. *Blow up the budget*! Many CFOs secretly wish they could abandon the straight-jacket of budgets and focus more on rolling forecasts and lead key performance indicators (KPIs). However, business forecasts, if based solely on past performance, can lead to unrealistic and misleading predictions.

But *organizational behavior* is perhaps the factor that contributes more than any other to the strategy gap, because of:

- A lack of accountability and commitment.

- Wrongly focused incentive plans.

During research for this book, we've observed that senior finance executives in companies that are generally regarded as demonstrating best practice in finance tend to focus on five new financial management disciplines:

1 **Closing the strategy gap** – building medium-term capability to deliver strategy, reorganizing the business model around strategic initiatives, giving priority to execution, and revamping their incentive schemes.

2 **Optimizing value** – modeling the future, linking strategy and operations, valuing the value chain, and pulling the right value levers.

3 **Rolling forecasts** – basing forecasts on the same goals and drivers as strategy, having one consistent view of the future across the enterprise, using forecasting as a collaborative tool to gather the richest possible insight into future performance.

4 **Monitoring reality** – delivering timely information on the progress of strategic initiatives – a single version of the truth, shaping per-

formance management processes to focus on decision-making ... and action.

5 **Connecting the dots** – integrating processes and systems, building a global enterprise platform for strategic and medium-term planning, shorter-term forecasting, and performance reporting.

Next in the chapter, we feature an interview and case study with Glaxo-SmithKline, the pharmaceutical company. We explore how its finance function is helping to fill the company's strategy gap, building medium-term capability – the research and development (R&D) pipeline of the future!

CLOSING THE STRATEGY GAP IN PHARMACEUTICALS

GlaxoSmithKline (GSK) has done much to fill its strategy gap. The finance function has played a proactive part in restructuring the organization for accountability in execution, changing the internal management processes to stimulate growth behavior, and introducing new incentives.

This is a success story, one from which many lessons can be learned at the sharp end of the business – research and development – where the value creation story usually begins.

The pharmaceutical industry depends on investment in R&D for its future. But in recent years, R&D productivity has generally declined owing to increasing competition, regulation, and rising cost. Fewer and fewer blockbusters are coming to market. And the R&D functions of the big pharmaceutical companies – known as "big pharma" – have become slow, risk averse, and *input-* rather than *output*-oriented organizations.

In Figure 6.1, we show that the process from drug discovery to launch can take nine years or more, and that the cumulative cost per drug can grow exponentially to anywhere between $800 million to $1.7 billion.

For every million compounds screened, approximately only 250 make it to pre-clinical testing, ten advance to clinical trials, and only one is approved for patient use. If you're going to terminate a compound, it's better to do it earlier rather than later! With these odds, the company's R&D must be fast and accurate in its screening, identification, development, and testing of new quality compounds.

GSK is the second largest pharmaceutical company in the world, with more than £20 billion in annual revenue, £6 billion annual profit and some 110,000 employees worldwide. The company spends approximately £3 billion annually on R&D – 16% of turnover. With 140 projects in clini-

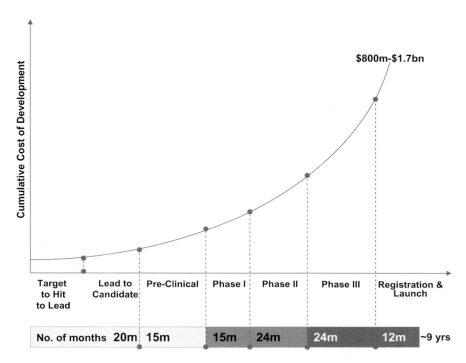

Figure 6.1 *Drug development duration and cost*

cal development, it has one of the largest and most promising product pipelines in the pharmaceutical industry.

The company has developed a flexible and innovative structure for R&D, allowing it to concentrate resources for maximum impact. The company has divided its R&D employees into eight Centers of Excellence for Drug Discovery (CEDDs) – each CEDD focused on a specific disease area. Each CEDD contains up to 350 GSK employees – an attempt to make the company's traditional *big pharma* research skills mimic smaller and nimbler biotechnology companies. Because of their smaller scale and focus, the CEDDs are able to make rapid and informed decisions about whether to progress a compound to mid- and late-stage development.

Based on the successful CEDD structure, GSK went one stage further and introduced six Medicine Development Centers (MDCs). Their agenda is to streamline decision-making and maximize global development opportunities for each product. The MDCs manage compounds from the proof of concept stage, through mid- and late-stage development to manufacturing and marketing. They collaborate at an early stage with the CEDDs. By integrating technical development and manufacturing, GSK helps ensure the rapid and effective launch and delivery of products to the patients who need them.

Jeff Baxter, SVP of Finance for R&D and Paul Fry, VP of Finance Drug Discovery, talk about the role of the finance function at GSK in making the organizational changes, introducing improvements in accountability, and creating performance measures and incentives.

BOOSTING THE PIPELINE
Jeff Baxter, SVP Finance R&D and Paul Fry, VP Finance Drug Discovery, GlaxoSmithKline

We have no future as a company without R&D – it's at the heart of our growth in terms of new, innovative medicines for patients. A few years ago, our CEO, J.P. Garnier, challenged us to improve the economics of pharmaceutical R&D. The cost of bringing a drug to market today can be anywhere between US$1 billion and US$1.4 billion. The level of R&D cost in our industry is simply too high for the level of productivity achieved. At these levels, many companies will find it difficult to return a positive NPV for the drugs in their portfolio that are in late-stage development. At GSK, like other companies, we had to significantly and rapidly increase the numbers of new medicines we were discovering, and become more cost-effective in their development.

Today, a much higher proportion of our shareholder value (SHV) is seen as being driven by the potential of R&D. Just a few years ago, R&D accounted for approximately 12% of our SHV; today it's nearer 30%!

Restructuring and delayering
We saw accountability as a key driver for increasing R&D productivity. We introduced CEDDs five years ago and MDCs two years ago to address this. We've got more than 14,000 people working in R&D, and traditionally there were lots of places for them to hide! We've successfully broken down our traditional global scientific hierarchies and organized R&D on a more business-like footing. This approach is part of a much broader organizational delayering instigated by our CEO – he believes

there should be no more than seven layers between the top and the bottom of the organization.

There are some aspects of R&D that benefit from scale – for example, high through-put screening, or executing large-scale clinical trials. We have global organizations for these services to get efficiency. But the task of discovering new chemical entities is more creative and innovative, and a smaller scale works best. The relation of our eight CEDDs to our global-scale services is shown in Figure 6.2.

The CEDD structure is designed to optimize our resources – ensuring that our scientists have clear objectives and report to managers who are clearly account-able for results. The CEDD and MDC initiatives have been a tremendous success; the metrics speak for themselves. The growth in the number of medicines, called New Chemical Entities (NCEs), is shown in Figure 6.3 for the various drug development phases I, II, and III.

Compared with our competitors, our pipeline is generating substantially more product for the cost incurred. Yes, we've benefited from in-licensing, but we've also invested more in the front-end of R&D – where the starting points for new discover-ies are generated – including our very ambitious £250 million screening automation program.

R&D accountability for performance

The performance of CEDD heads is now visible and truly transparent in terms of out-puts. They are measured at the beginning of the R&D process on the number of drug candidates selected for initial development; the number of times candidates first go into human testing; and then at the end of drug development phase 2A – clinical proof of concept – based on the number of positive proofs of concept (POCs) in the clinic. This is the drug transition point between the CEDDs and into the MDCs, and therefore a critical measure of CEDD head performance.

When comparing our approach with that of other companies, we prefer to meas-ure physical outputs rather than financial values. Of course, you can attribute NPVs to drugs in development, but these are based on estimated probabilities and finan-cial assumptions, and as such are open to question. Our CEO prefers just one final measure – actual POC numbers compared with target. If you combine that with focusing on areas of real patient need, you won't go far wrong in making sound investment choices.

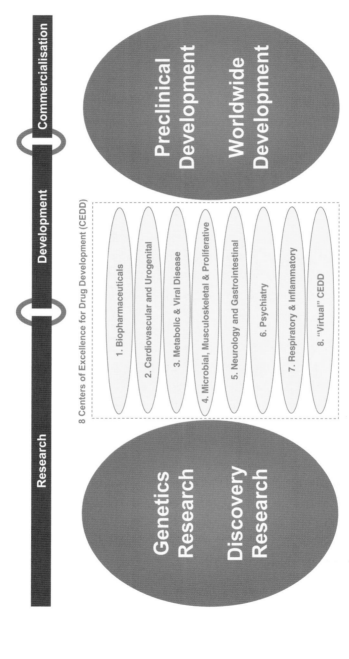

Figure 6.2 *GSK R&D structure: Centers of excellence for drug discovery*

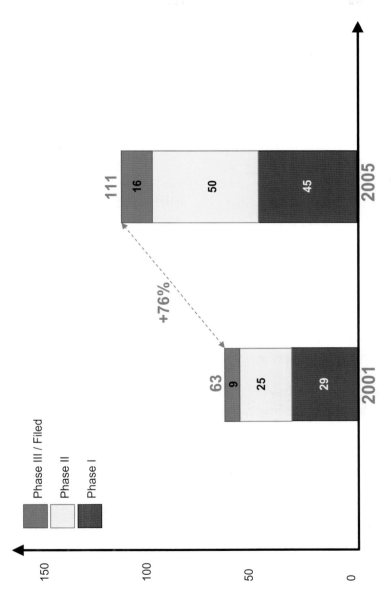

Figure 6.3 *GSK: Number of new chemical entities (2001–2005)*

We have a quarterly process where we report by CEDD, and in total as well, these key scorecard metrics to the corporate executive team. We're looking at our cumulative quarterly outputs in rolling three-year cycles because actual numbers of proofs of concept can vary widely from one year to the next – and R&D is a long-term business.

Of course, we have to evaluate the quality of this POC metric. The MDC has to receive quality drug development candidates. We have a heavyweight Portfolio Management Board – co-chaired by top executives from R&D and Commercial, with representation from finance as well as the Presidents of the three regional sales and marketing organizations – which examines the quality of POCs and approves them.

Motivation and incentives

We have a series of awards for scientists. Bench-scientists receive stock option grants for great science on an ad hoc basis – these can often be a welcome surprise to the successful candidates!

In addition, every two years we make a few truly exceptional and major awards at our senior management conference. These are our internal equivalent of "Nobel" prizes. We award a very substantial stock option to those scientists, champions, or relevant decision makers, at any level in the organization, who have found a key scientific and commercially viable breakthrough. These awards result from a rigorous selection and review process, and are signed off by the board.

Flexible sourcing: a new way of working

CEDD heads need some discretion and influence in the way they get things done to achieve their objectives. In the past, they had to deal with internal departments, such as safety assessment and chemical development, to get things done.

In these cases, another internal department's timetable or priorities could slow down R&D progress. Now the CEDD heads can make their own decisions on what gets done when – and are given access to external services if the services aren't available internally.

So, the CEDDs and MDCs are now fully accountable for milestone delivery and financial performance. The interaction between the CEDDs, the MDCs, the projects on which they're working and the other services provided – such as chemical development and clinical operations – is shown for each phase of a project in Figure 6.4.

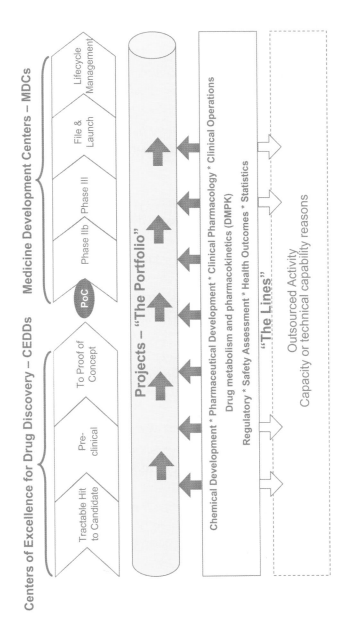

Figure 6.4 *Flexible sourcing for drug development*

Resources are now flexed, based on fluctuations in pipeline volume and project phase reached. CEDDs can determine the pace and priority of projects. They can attract more funds if they create more ideas – funds flow to CEDDs with the best portfolios.

Overall, finance has to ensure that it optimizes and balances the cost invested in internal platforms with costs invested outside, which can be up to 50% of project resources. So, we're less concerned with how much an R&D project is costing per se, and more concerned with whether or not the outputs are both valuable and delivered quickly. Time-to-market is the end game. Time is money!

Structural flexibility

We're still concerned with making our internal processes more cost efficient. Approximately 40% of our pharma R&D cost budget is on internal staffing, 40% on external clinical project costs, and about 20% on internal facilities – laboratories and pilot plants. We've reduced our headcount significantly since our merger, mainly in non-scientific functions. We've reinvested the savings in project expenditure – but on variable, not fixed costs – making our structure more flexible.

Over the last couple of years we've achieved other cost efficiencies in our R&D budget – over $100 million – for example, by off-shoring to low-cost countries the patient sourcing for clinical trials and by automating the back-end capture of clinical data.

Role of finance

A senior finance person is designated to work with each CEDD. This is a major investment. All of our finance staff in R&D are what we call "embedded" in the business. It's a balance between independence and objectivity on the one hand, and being closely involved on the other.

Our finance staff have to walk this tightrope. Our mantra: no surprises! This motto really does help finance directors in the front line. Of course, it works both ways – you can't have surprises coming from the CEDDs to headquarters, but equally, headquarters shouldn't be surprising the CEDDs, for example, with new harder targets out-of-the-blue.

In addition to core financial processes and governance, the roles of the finance directors in CEDDs include:

- *Putting the "business" into R&D:*
  - *ROI mindset, balancing investment, value and risk*
  - *Keeping teams focused on objectives*
  - *Developing robust business plans*
  - *Productivity*

- *Management of project resources and cost:*
  - *Presenting investment choices to management*
  - *Developing investment cases for new projects*
  - *Ensuring consensus on financial forecasts*
  - *Balancing internal and external sourcing levels*

In setting up the CEDDs, we weren't really sure what running a small business meant inside GSK. The finance directors played a particularly vital role in shaping the business model and introducing a commercial mindset.

Finance also drove the business planning process, which provided valuable strategic focus not only on the particular disease areas, but also on splitting and allocating resources. Our head of R&D overall credited the finance director appointments as being some of the most important in ensuring the success of the MDCs.

Maybe the biggest financial challenge in R&D in pharmaceuticals is attrition – those projects that have to be abandoned or suffer delay. Attrition is hard to predict and so are the resource implications. Finance people have to be well networked with project teams and line functions and not afraid to make the necessary hard judgments.

Scientists and medics may sometimes place greater value on the pursuit of knowledge than the commercial issues such as cost or return. They demand people who have high expertise in their fields. For GSK's finance directors on the R&D front line, there is constant tension between the financial realities of commercial business and almost infinite investment options available in pharmaceutical R&D.

Ultimately the test is in how the business perceives finance as a function. To quote one GSK CEDD head: "CEDD productivity has been helped by the fact that each CEDD has its own finance director to provide guidance and plan for our budget. This makes a huge difference – we now feel like a small successful business rather than a giant drug discovery organization."

The business and financial planning process for R&D at GSK starts with the R&D Executive, known as RADEX. Meetings are held twice a year off site for strategic review and plan updates. This process is overviewed in Figure 6.5.

In GSK, R&D strategy is directly linked with the reality of performance and delivery on the ground. Finance is involved in every step – and is critical to the building of the medium-term capability that fuels long-term shareholder value.

OPTIMIZING VALUE THROUGH INTEGRATION

Some companies bring relevant information on innovation together on an innovation scorecard. Such scorecards show the relative potential value of projects, their probability of success, their likely market launch timing, and future costs. Not only can the CFO and the finance function *measure* value, they can now *optimize* value too!

The approach to value optimization leads to a deeper understanding of what's driving value at each stage in the value chain – from initial R&D to manufacturing, to sales. But, as we've seen, it also requires a cultural change within the organization. Quite often we find that finance and those managers internally responsible for investment do not agree on investment assumptions. Data quality is often questioned. And frequently there is cynicism that the numbers are "cooked" to get the results required.

A full and frank exchange of views and documented assumptions promote transparency. Consistent value *measurement* can generate quick wins; value *creation* requires a cultural shift towards transparency; but value *optimization* can only be achieved by working across functional silos.

An integrated approach to managing projects – across the value chain – should pervade the culture of the enterprise. This means moving away from an array of different systems such as spreadsheets, planning tools, access databases, and accounting-based timesheet applications. What's required is an integrated all-in-one database with one set of flexible business processes.

Integrated solutions do exist for linking financial management processes for the early stages of the value chain – for example, for new product development. Such solutions exist for integrating, for example, portfolio and pipeline analysis, budgeting, and project NPV management. They also cover parametric estimation, multi-level scheduling, and resource allocation.

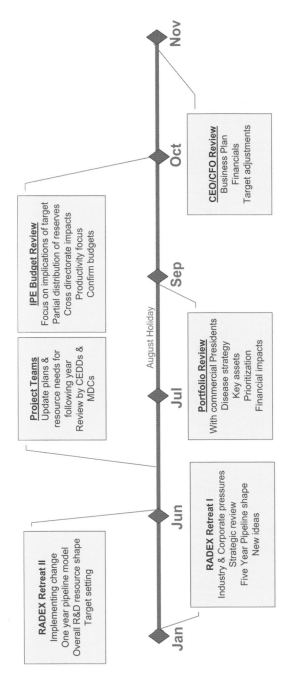

Figure 6.5 *GSK R&D Business and financial planning process*

Continuing with the pharmaceutical example, transformational improvements in R&D productivity can be achieved by integrating operations and business planning through four key capabilities, each with a strong finance component:

1 Portfolio management – defining strategic positions and priorities among portfolio products.

2 Resource management – matching demand with resource capacity.

3 Project management – aligning capacity and strategic timelines with day-to-day project activities and delivery.

4 Financial management – matching costs and revenues with project activities.

These are some of the new financial disciplines. Best-practice organizations integrate, yet distinguish clearly between, those processes involved in planning strategy and those for operational delivery. Figure 6.6 shows how strategic and operational processes link objectives and results together.

Having put the necessary financial management disciplines in place to link strategic initiatives with operations, companies are finding that they want to go one stage further. At a higher level than just projects and initiatives, they want to see how the bigger picture of the business fits together from a value perspective. How one business component works with another. How to value the value chain!

To quote one CFO: "The management gurus gave us the value chain, but they didn't tell us how to value it." The case study that follows is taken from a fast-moving consumer goods manufacturing company. It provides a good example of how to *value the value chain.*

VALUING THE VALUE CHAIN
A multinational consumer goods company

This multinational was developing its finance function in the field of decision support. It was keen to create a lean and agile value chain based on networks with suppliers and partnerships with retailing customers. Driven by the need to increase

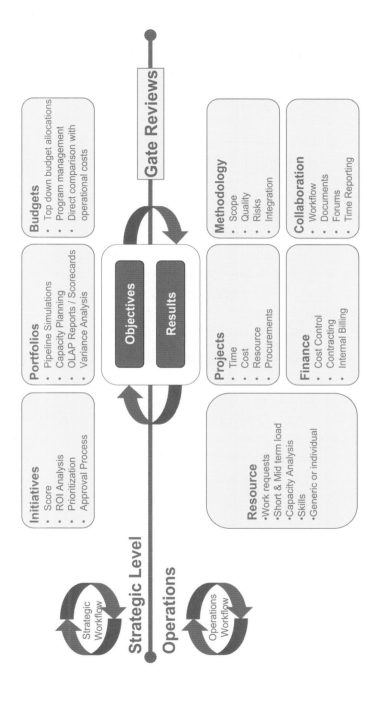

Figure 6.6   *Linking strategy & operational processes*

competitiveness across the value chain, it wanted to exploit core capabilities and scalability. The company also faced pressure from customers who were demanding increased collaboration and integration in processes and systems.

The CFO decided to focus on a value chain analysis pilot. Finance chose one product category in one emerging market that was under heavy competitive pressure. It was eager to try out new ideas about analyzing the value chain and "who" was contributing "what" to the overall profit pool in the market.

A preliminary study revealed some key issues. A competitor posed a threat in an emerging market where its product was rapidly gaining market share. Analysis suggested that the market was growing strongly in volume, but falling in value due to price cutting. Local management believed that the competitor had a high-quality product but was selling it at a price that was not making a commercial return.

So the company was interested in the strategic implications: would it experience this same problem in launching its product in other new developing territories? What are the implications in other more developed markets where discounters were increasing their penetration? To help answer these questions, the company set up a value chain analysis team with the following mission:

1. **Project brief:** *To identify sources of competitive advantage and competitive threats for a product category in an emerging market.*
2. **The issues:** *The market was growing in volume, but profitability appeared to be declining rapidly. A competitor was rapidly gaining market share, while the company's brand performance had flattened.*
3. **Objectives:** *To test the effectiveness of value chain analysis tools; analyze available data; identify underlying causes of market behavior; frame possible competitive responses and assess their long-term implications.*

Initial findings: the company found that while its product had increased market share slightly, one competitor had shown spectacular growth. This growth appeared to be driven by an aggressive pricing strategy that had depressed retail prices for all category suppliers. The target market was growing significantly in volume, but the company's gross margins had fallen.

The study team went on to raise the following questions:

- *Does the competitor's value chain provide any obvious advantages that allow it to maintain reasonable margins at a lower price?*

- *Is the competitor simply willing to trade at a lower total return?*
- *Is there any evidence that we will eventually lose market share?*

Next, the team mapped its own value chain, along with that of its suppliers and the retailer. The team identified KPIs in each of the three supply chains and looked at the "cause and effect" relationships among the KPIs to understand the value impact.

Figure 6.7 shows how the producer's value chain was extended into that of its suppliers and the retailer.

The symptoms of the problem experienced by the company manifested themselves through falling revenues – but the root causes and potential solutions were found in other parts of the value chain. A simple systems dynamics model simulated the effect of marketing on consumer behavior. The team carried out real-time simulations allowing it to test key relationships, refine theories, and recreate observed behavior.

These value chain analysis and modelling tools proved valuable in scenario planning, identifying KPIs, and understanding complex non-linear relationships.

The results of the exercise were translated into a profit-pool analysis that offered a holistic view of the market and the relative value contributions of each component of the extended value chain. Profit-pools help to identify where, and by whom, profits were being made and how this could change in the future.

The team concluded that the complexity of the market environment could be masking the true economic picture. A number of factors were potentially distorting data, including inflation and currency fluctuations, and standard rather than actual supply chain costs.

The team put together an "economic P&L" using true costs. It then went on to study the following issues in more depth:

- *The long-term attractiveness of the market.*
- *The levels of advertising required for a "price-follower" strategy.*
- *The levels of trade discounts and promotions consistent with brand leadership.*
- *The optimization of the current supply chain.*
- *The potential to reduce supply chain costs and alter product formulation to improve margins.*

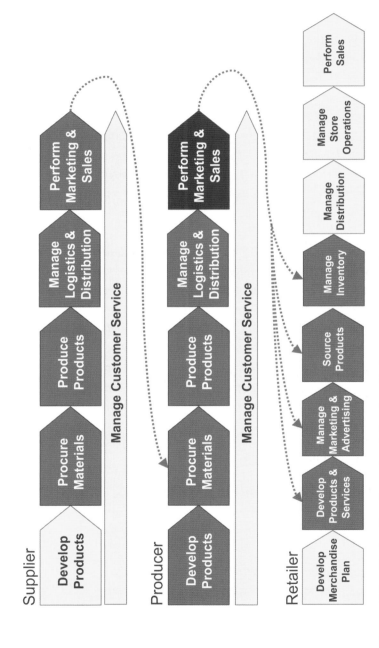

Figure 6.7 *Evaluating the extended value chain*

Most finance executives interviewed for this book felt that managing the value chain was important to their business. However, we found wide-ranging definitions of what a value chain actually is. They vary by industry. Large organizations like the one described in the case study above have multiple value chains with some common links.

Most organizations seem to value their value chains instinctively, without the use of predetermined process or terminology. However, all those surveyed felt that there was significant value in defining and optimizing the *extended* value chain.

Moving from the financial disciplines associated with strategy, planning, and optimizing value, we now focus on forecasting.

ROLLING FORECASTS

Why do organizations spend so much time and money on trying to predict the future? First and foremost, the process of forecasting can be a valuable aid to making decisions.

The ability to recognize and exploit changing business conditions is the driving force behind the current trend for rolling forecasts. However, forecasting is the one process that CFOs today – no matter what industry they're in – would like to learn more about.

To quote a recent CFO survey:

- 60% are dissatisfied with the alignment between strategy and budgets, and say budgets take too long to prepare.

- 52% are dissatisfied with the speed and accuracy of reforecasts.

- 60% plan to make major changes in their corporate performance management systems in the next 18 months.[2]

The increased volatility and speed of business have made annual, quarterly, and even monthly business reviews obsolete as a means of managing performance. Organizations sometimes must respond in days, hours – or even minutes – if they are to take advantage of short windows of opportunity or avoid taking a major hit.

Consider the comments of one CFO:

> "We forecast at a global and regional level. Our long-range forecasts have multiple scenarios – typically four – based on key sensitivities and consisting of a base case overlaid with upper

and lower ranges. These ranges depend on various probabilities, which determine our upside and downside forecasts.

"Our business is driven by our new product development pipeline, the outcome of which is uncertain. There's much more certainty in sales from current products than new ones. So our scenarios are heavily affected by potential internal pipeline performance, and by possible external events – for example, competitors bringing new products to market and changing their pricing strategies. We are continually retesting and validating our forecast assumptions.

"When you provide earnings commitments and guidance to the 'Street,' you need to be pretty sure you can deliver! However, the future is inherently uncertain. My first rule of forecasting – you may be correct, but you're just as likely to be wrong! As a CFO, you need a degree of humility when dealing with forecasts. Rather than being exactly right, you need to be confident that the actuals will turn out to be in the forecast range.

"Over time, you learn to focus on forecast assumptions rather than the outcomes. You need to consider: what are, say, the six key critical drivers and assumptions that influence results? Where are the 'mines' that could explode unexpectedly? You need a coherent system that links the predictions you make at the top with the expectations of the rest of the organization.

"When we go 'off course' with our forecasts, my job as CFO is to identify the impact on the principal components of the business, to assess what action is needed internally to correct the performance trend. Speed of communication both to management and to the 'Street' is vital."

Many companies fail to understand the crucial point that the real value of a forecast is not in the accuracy of the answer, but the insight it offers into how future events may interact to shape performance – and affect current decisions.

Most organizations develop multiple forecasts. Marketing, sales, operations, and finance develop their own independent forecasts – each of which use different assumptions and use different tools, information, and time horizons. Subsequently, significant time is spent reconciling the different forecasts on which the organization has to rely.

One of the more valuable aspects of forecasting is the ability to monitor the changes that occur over time. This is possible only if there is a high degree of consistency in the assumptions used in the forecasting process. Best-practice[3] companies:

- Base forecasts on the same goals and drivers used in their strategy and financial planning processes – *the forecast is not treated simply as an extrapolation of the financial plan.*

- Ensure that forecasts are based on a common set of assumptions to provide comparability over time. R&D, marketing, sales, production, and financial forecasts are developed using these same assumptions.

- Routine forecasts are prepared on a rolling basis – typically over, say, six to eight quarters – giving consistent visibility into the future.

Forecasting is a collaborative process that seeks to gather the richest possible insight into future performance regardless of the source. Forecasts are revised only on an exception basis and only when projected results differ from plan by a predetermined range.

So why is forecasting so difficult across a large multinational? In many companies, the very dominance of detailed centralized planning tends to drive a commensurate level of unnecessary detail into the forecast itself. The forecast cycle time lengthens as organizations struggle with too much detail. One group controller of a major corporation comments:

> "If you talk to any of our peer group competitors, the number one pressure is a relentless demand for performance and ever greater expectations. But I have yet to come across any organization that believes they are really good at forecasting. What we need is reliable forecasts to maximize the opportunities for adding value; to provoke the business into a mindset shift to identify and take advantage of such opportunities; and to continuously drive out more performance.

> "We've already cut down unnecessary work in budgeting. Should we spend the huge amount of time on forecasting that we do? I'm not sure that this investment is as productive as it could be. We are now focused on measuring progress through KPIs in our scorecards. How do we get the combined benefits from our forecasts and performance processes?"

The average company can take up to 14 days to develop a financial forecast. Forecast cycle times are lengthy because:

- It can be difficult to get timely information, particularly if there is a long accounting close process.
- The level of detail required in the forecast is so great that managers require significant time to develop estimates for each line item.
- The tools available to create the forecast are limited to a series of disconnected spreadsheet models.

Consistency and simplicity are the hallmarks of a good forecasting process. Forecasts have to be action oriented. They should not merely identify problems, but should help explain why the problems exist in the first place – and also explore the options for fixing them.

As cycle times for forecasting lengthen, some companies are moving away from set-frequency updates to event-driven forecasts. This means that forecasts are triggered by, for example, material external events that affect business performance, or by a competitive or regulatory change.

Best-practice organizations are in fact *increasing* the frequency of forecasting, reducing detail, and enhancing quality. The emergence of tools and technologies to support real-time information and rapid forecasting continues to accelerate this trend.

MONITORING REALITY

The effectiveness of an organization's performance management is a major contributor to achieving its commercial and financial objectives. A recent Gartner report said *"high performing organizations follow best practices in corporate performance management including:*

- *Displaying a strong sense of purpose – sharing their values inside the organization (employees) and outside (customers, suppliers, and other stakeholders).*
- *Setting consistent, ambitious targets and continuously achieving them.*
- *Have a strategic focus and alignment, so employees know how they're contributing to results."*

One CFO we interviewed stressed the importance of not only linking performance management to incentives, but also of taking advantage of non-financial drivers to motivate the right behaviors:

> "We use a corporate scorecard, covering non-financial measures such as progress in R&D, number of product recalls, and out-of-stock situations. Of course, as CFO, I am accountable along with the other members of the executive team for overall business performance.

> "When we monitor performance during the year using management's estimated outturn quarterly updates, we are asking for upper and lower ranges, as well as point estimates. We're particularly interested in how management determines these ranges – this in itself is a valuable learning exercise for us all. The middle-point estimate may not be exactly in the middle of the range and this, too, can tell a story about management's relative optimism, or indeed, conservatism.

> "We have a full array of incentives covering basic salary, bonus, ordinary share options, and 'restricted' share grants. Normally, these are awarded for exceptional performance. Everyone on the commercial side of the company benefits from a bonus and, undoubtedly, company-wide variable compensation is generally based on making budget. Hitting the number is the driver!

> "However, there are exceptions. For example, in one part of our business we're experimenting with non-financial incentive drivers such as market share. We're looking at opportunities for this approach elsewhere in our organization. We want to use the bonus to influence the correct behaviors."

In many companies, planning and reporting has become something of a juggernaut exercise, driven more often by cost and control than by value enhancement. Cumbersome, bottom-up planning and budgeting exercises are undertaken to meet important deadlines rather than provide effective management information.

Significant finance time and effort is applied to compiling data, much of which rarely gets delivered in the form required by senior management. KPIs are often out of alignment with business strategy, and decisions are made outside the context of budgets. Skepticism creeps in and the integrity of the overall performance management process comes into question.

To recap, the real challenges to achieving an effective performance management model in most organizations are twofold:

1 **The structural challenge** – shaping the performance management processes to focus on decision-making, on driving value creation, and on efficiency.

2 **The behavioral challenge** – getting the business to effectively deploy the model.

Some leading organizations, have successfully addressed these challenges. Figure 6.8 shows how such organizations integrate the performance management components – from shareholder value and strategy to forecasting and reporting.

There are a number of issues for the CFO and finance function to resolve in deploying their approach to performance management:

1 **Delivering information that provides a single version of the truth.** Many companies draw information from non-financial sources as well as the general ledger. Additionally, legal entity complexities and associated statutory reporting requirements create significant variations between data generated for management information and that for statutory reporting.

2 **Structuring efficient data models and system architectures.** Recent acquisitions can lead to systems proliferation. Most companies want to standardize around a common chart of accounts. Their accounting systems require significant modification to adjust for changes in statutory reporting as well. IFRS is a case in point. Consider embedding statutory reporting standards into the underlying systems and reporting processes.

3 **Applying relevant planning and budgeting models.** Different organizations at different stages in their economic development require different approaches. For example, financial institutions typically operate to targets for growth in their balance sheet. Other types of organizations focus on earnings and cash-flow targets.

4 **Managing external stakeholder communities.** The ability to quickly compile, explain, and present concise financial and non-financial data to the external market has proven to be a significant factor influencing external stakeholder confidence and supporting share price.

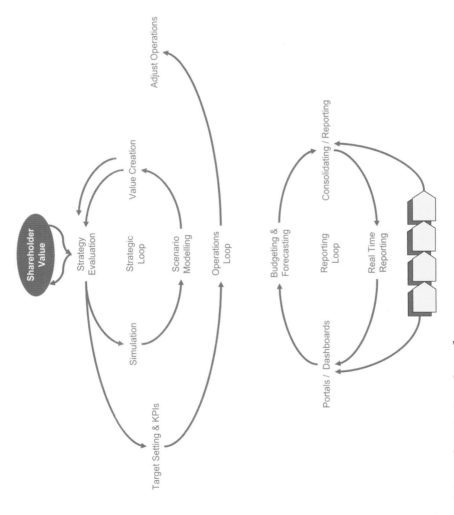

Figure 6.8 *Integrating strategy & performance*

5 **Ensuring performance management is applied, but differently, to** *both* **transformation and operating activities.** Traditionally, a company's planning and reporting framework is geared to ongoing operations. However, the transformation agenda can be a major focus of the business. Transformation activities need to be planned and reported in appropriate time buckets and as discrete projects.

Traditionally, corporate performance management has encompassed all processes, methodologies, metrics and technologies that organizations use to measure, monitor, and manage their performance.

Today, there are many things that a company has to do to achieve, and also *protect,* value. Performance management, as a discipline, has necessarily broadened to include governance, risk management, and compliance:

- **Governance** – determining risk appetite, establishing cultures and values, developing internal policies, and monitoring performance.

- **Risk management** – assessing risks, applying risk management to gain competitive advantage, determining risk response strategies and controls.

- **Compliance** – adhering to laws and regulations, internal policies and procedures, and stakeholder directives.

CONNECTING THE DOTS THROUGH SYSTEMS

Governance, risk, and compliance as a systems issue is still an emerging field. Nevertheless, the processes and systems involved have to be aligned, and in some cases integrated, with those already existing for performance management – *from strategy all the way through to execution.*

CFOs invest significant time and money in systems for planning and reporting. Are they getting adequate return on investment? Consider what one CFO said about his systems:

> "In a perfect world, we would have just one instance of SAP across the globe. Sitting at the center, it would be great to be able to drill down without lengthy, time-consuming ad-hoc investigations. As in so many companies, the reality for us is very different.
>
> "Here, it's the consolidation systems that bring the information

to the center. But they don't provide direct access to the data source. You have to go out and get the detailed information you want. There is an additional cost for this.

"Fully integrated systems for planning, forecasting, consolidation, and risk would be desirable. As we switch systems to one version of ERP, we're evolving gradually onto a harmonized and common platform – not a 'Big Bang' approach, but a sensible, relatively low-risk solution."

Companies that are considered to be best practice in strategic financial management systems have four major characteristics:

1 **Integration** – employing a well-defined process and methodology for linking strategic plans with forecasts, and for linking forecasts with KPIs.

2 **Focus** – concentrating on a small number of KPIs, budgeting on a relatively small number of line items, forecasting only the major variables, and reporting by exception.

3 **Speed** – closing their books in three or four days, completing their annual plans and budgets in fewer than 90, and reforecasting across the enterprise in less than a week.

4 **Technology** – leveraging a single integrated system, providing access to a broad spectrum of users.

In most organizations, solutions for planning, budgeting, forecasting, and reporting are treated as disconnected processes and supported by different technologies. This lack of integration creates problems:

- *In making changes* – most existing management systems do not allow changes to be made easily – such as altering structures, accounts, and assumptions – so that management can quickly see their impact.

- *In reporting flexibility* – systems tend to report from one perspective only: the accounts code or cost center. Viewing data by product, turnover, geography, or any other business perspective – such as strategy or tactic – is extremely difficult.

- *In disseminating information enterprise-wide* – many systems require a great deal of effort to disseminate the actuals, the latest forecasts, and information on strategy implementation.

- *In managing file data* – many organizations still rely on spreadsheets for budgets, forecasts, and reporting results. While spreadsheets are great personal productivity tools, they can become a nightmare for corporate planning and reporting. Version control is a huge issue: multiple files have to be maintained, relinked and then redistributed. This is time consuming and error prone!

Extensity is a global enterprise software company that has business performance management solutions which deal with these issues. Donna De Winter, previously CFO of GEAC (recently acquired by Extensity), explains how.

 ## SOLUTIONS FOR THE FUTURE
Donna De Winter

We address the needs of CFOs in strategy management, planning, and forecasting. We are integrating several of our product lines into more comprehensive suites of solutions across the financial value chain – linking back-end transactional activities such as accounting, procurement, and inventory through processes of expense management and compliance to performance measurement.

Integrating the organization
We used to be managed as a conglomerate – a portfolio of different product-based companies. Our products used to be presented to customers as stand-alone solutions, rather than as an integrated solution covering both the back office and the front office. We're slowly moving away from the portfolio approach and running the company more as one global combined entity. I'm very much involved in working with the CEO and the board on strategy.

Not unlike our customers, we too have a strategy gap! This gap existed between our corporate expectations of an overall market competitive return for all our assets, and the goals when added together for our business units, which were operated in silos. Our strategy has been to link together our previously separate product-based business units into more of a market-led organization.

Dealing with the unexpected
Just recently, we encountered a challenge with a dissident shareholder – an activist hedge fund. The shareholder had 5% of our equity and demanded two positions

on the board – a 25% board coverage for a 5% shareholding! Its intentions were unclear, but we suspected they wanted to break up and sell elements of the product portfolio. We felt this would destroy value. Fortunately, we were able to fend off the unsolicited approach.

Nevertheless, this unexpected event did consume an inordinate amount of management attention during a critical month. At the time, two of our biggest competitors were coming out with new products.

These unexpected events can disrupt your management focus and business rhythm. As you're responding, management's eye is taken "off the ball," customers play a waiting game, and business generation suffers. So, your planning and forecasting processes have to be sufficiently flexible to cope.

Benefiting from rolling forecasts
You need flexibility not only to deal with unwelcome events, but also to seize unexpected opportunities such as an acquisition. In such circumstances, budgets and compensation plans have to be flexed. Incremental investments have to be measured on a stand-alone ROI. Incremental adjustments are made to ongoing targets and our 15-month rolling forecast. We have now moved to reforecasting our revenues monthly, and our costs quarterly.

My advice on forecasting?

- *Understand the lines on the financial statement that truly impact business decisions.*
- *Understand the relationships between key numbers and their associated variables. That's where forecasting efforts should be spent.*
- *Keep it at a high level; see the "wood for the trees" – don't get dragged down by unnecessary detail.*

Annual budgets are only a snapshot based on the best assumptions you have available at the time. As with most software companies, most of our software revenue is contracted right at the end of a financial quarter. You have to be very focused on the key drivers of the business to understand what the financial outcome may be – the budgets won't help.

A rolling forecast combined with a fixed annual budget gives you the necessary balance of dynamism and control.

Decisions relating to return on investment – be they related to people assets, intellectual property, physical assets, or services – are critical to the modern CFO. New products are vital to our growth coming from both existing and new customers. To track corporate returns, we've developed key benchmarks across the company – for profit margins, license/services revenue mix, and most interestingly we now have an "innovation index." This index monitors the performance of new products in generating new licenses and future revenue.

Integrating the "financial" value chain

We work closely with our customers to understand their challenges and to deliver the necessary ROI on their investment in our products. I believe the CFO is responsible for the entire financial value chain as in Figure 6.9.

Through Extensity's "Build, Buy and Partner" initiative, customers can benefit from integrating parts of the financial value chain.

Next, we use two of our customers as examples of how the financial value chain can be integrated.

CASE STUDY 1: UNIVERSAL STUDIOS, HOLLYWOOD
Dan Aptor, Director of Finance at NBC Universal, Hollywood, says:

We're very much a daily business – one of the world's largest movie studios and theme parks. We need to reforecast our numbers every few weeks, know how we're tracking, and where we're going to land! We take our annual target and break it down to a daily level, down even to the individual hot-dog stand!

The challenges we faced:

- *Eliminating non-value-added work and transforming our finance function into an 80% analysis–20% data gathering model.*
- *Delivering real-time visibility on KPIs.*
- *Improving data integrity.*

We needed to integrate our performance management to gain greater insight into operational results and help meet strategic objectives. Managers now conduct "what if" analyses that allow them to plan, predict, and take corrective action as needed. As a result, they have become more proactive and accurate in their decision-making.

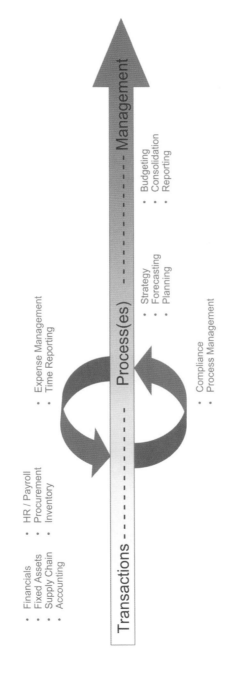

Figure 6.9 *Integrating the financial value chain*

So, with Extensity we built an integrated scorecard, modelling, consolidation and reporting capability, which:

- *Improved the close process from 5+ days to a "virtual close."*
- *Enabled self-service reporting, which included more timely and frequent forecasts.*
- *Moved us from fragmented applications to a coherent financial and operational solution.*

We've cut down our budgeting cycle time by about 50%. More important, we've created some value. We've implemented an integrated suite of tools, leveraging best practices to provide timely information to key stakeholders.

Looking forward, I expect our systems to take more advantage of the web, and of mobile devices for monitoring actual performance. Maybe the future is personal "mini-dashboards," 24/7!

CASE STUDY 2: RSA SECURITY

Dave Stack, Director of Financial Planning and Analysis

RSA security, a leading provider of data identity and access management, has integrated the financial processes for budgeting, forecasting, long-term strategic planning, and more.

The company is now enhancing its system to enable consolidated product line P&Ls that capture actual results and compare them with forecast and plan. We're integrating product line P&L forecasts into our three-year models so that we can make resource investment decisions based on projected product and market growth.

The ROI we achieved:

- *Budgeting efficiency increased by 58%*
- *Product P&L forecasting efficiency increased by 95%*
- *Monthly forecasting cycle times fell from 13 days to 4 days*

We now spend a minimal amount of money on system maintenance, get more efficient every year, and generate more information from our performance management system. It just gets better and better!

Donna De Winter goes on to talk about the regulatory pressures brought about by Sarbanes-Oxley and the growing need for enterprise-wide risk management.

RISK MANAGEMENT
Donna De Winter

We've got more to do in the risk area. Over the next three quarters we'll be developing an enterprise risk program for the company. We're currently very involved with implementation of SOX – in fact, achieving our SOX certification objectives is part of the incentive plan for every one of our executives.

We get a written risk assessment from every business unit every quarter, setting out how the business is doing, noting changes in the competitive landscape, and highlighting any new developments that could affect performance. We now also have an electronic roll-up certification of the quarterly results – not just for SOX 302 (everything that should be disclosed is disclosed), but for our purposes as well (the numbers have been recorded the way the business has been "done").

You've got to consider risk at a higher level than internal controls. For example, we need to reconcile what we'd like to do strategically – say in Asia Pacific – with the realities of what we actually achieve in revenue. So we'll need key risk indicators (KRIs) to go hand in hand with our KPIs. No doubt we'll be looking for joined-up processes and systems to bring the performance and risk picture together.

Extensity uses its own systems
Companies tend to think they're unique in terms of business process – but I've always contended that there are great similarities between the ways that many businesses relate to and contract with their customers, and their linkage to financial systems.

In Figure 6.10, we show how Extensity connects initially with customers, contracts, and invoices, and then links transactions to the financial routines and to performance monitoring.

Worldwide, I've visibility on what's happening in each of our three shared service centers. We've one set of GL account codes, one set of cost centers, and one system mapped one way across the world. It's been a challenging journey.

What are the benefits of all this systems integration investment? Greater visibility, at all levels in the organization, and a quicker "time to decision." We're now in a

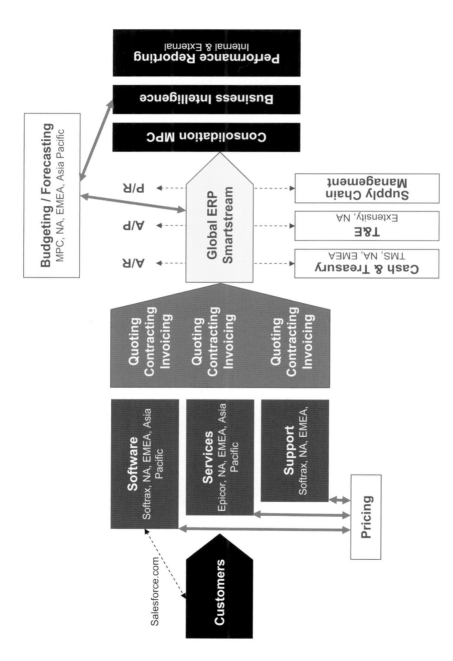

Figure 6.10   *Linking Extensity's financial processes & systems*

much better position to know whether we need to cut costs or not, to hire or not to hire – and to determine whether or not everything is going to plan. Our next move will be to make the connections with business intelligence and human resources.

For our customers, the CFOs of the world's leading organizations, I would like to be able to offer them our strategy product on "steroids" – predictive planning and analysis!

Prediction

In the next five years, the systems used for developing, resourcing, and monitoring strategic and operational plans will change beyond all recognition. They'll be focused on supporting strategy; be dynamic and continuous in operation; show the "cause and effect" of one KPI on another, and the impact of one end-user's activity on another.

STRAIGHT FROM THE CFO

- **Look forward, not backward**

  Abandon formal strategic planning. Debate possible outcomes based on forecasts with multiple scenarios. Secure accountability and commitment to your future plans. Align incentives. Prepare for the unexpected!

- **Close your strategy gap**

  Identify what's missing. Build medium-term capability to deliver. Like GSK, restructure to improve accountability for performance in the innovation and development areas of the business. Measure by output, rather than input. Create incentives accordingly.

- **Optimize value**

  Don't just measure value; understand what's driving it at each stage in the value chain. Integrate business planning with operations. Value the extended value chain. Choose the right methods and tools to model value – above all, be realistic!

- **Roll the forecasts**

  Focus on assumptions rather than outcomes. Base forecasts on strategic goals and drivers. Use forecasts to capture insight into how current decisions and future events interact to shape performance. Ideally, consolidate your forecasts automatically through a single common tool.

- **Integrate performance components**

  High-performing organizations have strategic focus and alignment; employees know how they're contributing to the results. Link strategy to performance; link performance to incentives and the non-financial drivers to foster the right behaviors. Include governance, risk, and compliance in your performance framework.

- **Connect the dots!**

  Consider embedding statutory reporting standards into systems. Integrate back-end transactional systems with front-end strategic planning, forecasting, and performance management.

REFERENCES

1 Michael Coveney (2003) *The Strategy Gap*, Wiley.

2 GEAC, CFO Research Services (2004) *Finance Seeks a Seat at the Strategy Table*, CFO Executive Programs.

3 David A.J. Axson (2003) *Best Practices in Planning and Management Reporting*, Wiley.

CHAPTER 7

Innovative Business Partnering

Dealing with uncertainty is a fact of life! World-class finance functions are increasingly focused on providing decision support in uncertain times. Finance is no longer viewed as a precise discipline and its traditional focus on historical cost accounting and book-keeping can no longer keep pace with today's business demands.

The foundations for finance's new decision support discipline – intangibles, growth and innovation, and an orientation toward the future, not the past – have been covered in the previous three chapters. In this chapter, we show how one company, Unilever, brings together all these strands of the new finance discipline into one cohesive strategy, "Finance of the Future."

Through interviews and case studies with leading Unilever finance executives, we show how its Innovative Business Partnering (IBP) program has accelerated Unilever's finance capabilities in building brand value and identifying new options for growth. We also describe how, in parallel with its IBP initiative, the company has implemented another innovative approach: *dynamic* performance management (DPM). The chapter concludes with a look at Unilever's Finance Academy – a unique resource for formulating and sharing best practice.

FINANCE OF THE FUTURE

Unilever is best known for its leading brands, such as Dove, Knorr, and Lipton. As a world leader in both foods and home & personal care, the company employs more than 200,000 people in 100 countries. Its portfolio has been dramatically streamlined in recent years to give center stage to brands with the highest shareholder value potential.

The path to growth has not been easy. One of Unilever's characteristic strengths has always been its geographic reach. Ironically, that strength has also been the source of one of its key challenges: making things happen consistently around the world. This requires a complex balancing act for Unilever: harnessing the power that comes from nurturing strong local roots while realizing the benefits of scale.

At the heart of Unilever's transformation program is its intention to turn the company from what most investors perceive as a dependable generator of profits and cash into a more dynamic and entrepreneurial enterprise. The finance function is playing its part with a substantial change program of its own. John Ripley, Deputy CFO and Head of Financial Group at Unilever, describes how its finance development agenda has evolved.

FINANCE OF THE FUTURE: THE JOURNEY SO FAR
John Ripley, Deputy CFO and Head of Financial Group, Unilever

The starting point for finance was a conference in Brighton six years ago. This set a new mission for Unilever's finance team: becoming partners in value creation. However, we recognized that some basic building blocks had to be put in place before we could make significant headway with our transformation.

These building block initiatives were in the areas of transaction processing (harmonization and shared services), planning, global information supply, balanced scorecard implementation, and people development. However, it was clear that these initiatives alone would not deliver the leading-edge capability the business would need from its finance partners in the future.

We needed a broader agenda – one that could motivate and energize the whole finance team. We wanted a vision of the finance role to which our best and most ambitious people could aspire. So we started the task of planning the future beyond the relatively limited horizons of the Brighton initiatives. Ultimately, we developed a visionary blueprint, which we call "Finance of the Future."

We focused some of our younger and most promising executives on what the finance function would look like ten years into the future. Our goal was a new comprehensive business strategy for the group. The starting point for the small team we created was a survey of internal stakeholders – about 70 key managers in the business. After a period of research and a process of filtering of new ideas, a structured migration plan and implementation approach were developed. These were subsequently agreed to by our CFO and his finance leadership team.

The "Finance of the Future" program was formally adopted at a major meeting of our 200 top finance people. The mission of this project remains relevant to this day and was reconfirmed at our most recent conference where we updated our five key initiatives.

To put our finance excellence program into context, it's important to understand that Unilever has a history of running all its different businesses separately, albeit under the one Unilever umbrella. As a consequence, we have traditionally not extracted the full synergies of our combined scale and scope.

As a company, the cultural shift we've made has moved us away from a purely collaborative effort to a more centralized, directive approach. This shift, prompted by our overall organizational change strategy, affects not just finance but functions all across the company.

On this journey, we've seen a clear correlation between the dedication of full-time resources and leadership on priority initiatives and our progress in achieving them. This has been especially noticeable in our finance business partnering program, where a relatively small global team has had a disproportionately strong impact throughout the business.

Companies like Unilever are combining their finance change initiatives into "finance of the future" strategies designed to create the distinctive capabilities and the environment for adding value to the business. Such initiatives fall into two clear groupings for development and implementation:

1 **Routine processes** – the pursuit of *world-class finance*. Typically, this involves the simplification, standardization, and up-scaling (either through shared services or outsourcing) of business processes such as payables, receivables, and financial accounting. It can also be extended to areas such as information management and analysis. Invariably, this type of major structural change is accompanied by global or regional rollouts of ERP systems, such as SAP.

2 **Business partnering and decision support** – the upgrading of finance capabilities to enable them to add direct value to the business. Change initiatives in this category include processes, such as decision support and resource allocation, underpinned by appropriate analytics and aligned with fit-for-purpose planning, budgeting, forecasting, and performance management systems.

Most global companies today have extensive experience in implementing the transaction processing initiatives described above. Furthermore, there is a wealth of relevant external benchmarking material for use in calibrating potential benefits.

However, while most companies recognize the importance of developing business partnering and decision support capability, little knowledge is available in this area for understanding and sharing best practices. Unilever's strategy map, as shown in Figure 7.1, offers some helpful guidelines.

This strategy map translates the high-level stakeholder objectives – such as increasing total shareholder return (TSR) – into the needs of internal customers. These high-level objectives range from investing financial and other resources for growth and value to the co-invention of new ways of doing things. This mapping approach enables Unilever to validate and demonstrate the relevance of its finance strategy to its business objectives.

The critical finance objectives, as shown in Figure 7.1, are divided into two levels:

1 **The upper level**: those finance activities that require a *step-change* in capabilities – in Unilever's case, innovative business partnering, dynamic performance management, and world-class finance processes.

2 **The lower level**: those finance activities that require only *continuous improvement* – such as M&A, corporate finance, investor interaction, and risk management.

Unilever's "Finance of the Future" change agenda is structured into five "strategic thrusts" derived from these critical finance objectives:

1 **Innovative business partnering** – developing, embedding, and sharing best practice decision analysis and support. The focus is on the core value-creating areas, principally brands, innovation, and customers.

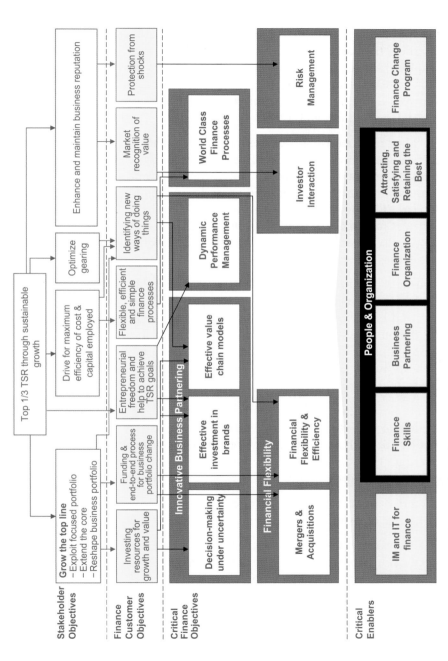

Figure 7.1 *Unilever's finance of the future strategy map*

2 **Dynamic performance management** – moving from a world of "predict and control," based on fixed performance contracts negotiated in advance, through an often labyrinthine budgeting process to a more adaptive "sense and respond" model. This new dynamic model features relative performance targets, rolling forecasting, and trend reporting. Internally, it supports real-time resource allocation across the brand/product/geography matrix.

3 **World-class finance processes** – covering the areas of transaction processing, accounting, and information management. This strategic thrust is intended to leverage the powers of improved connectivity, automation, simplification, and shared services to provide processes that are flexible, cost competitive, and easy for internal and external partners to work with. This in itself results in substantial value creation; it also frees both resources and management time to concentrate on business partnering activities.

4 **Financial flexibility** – providing ready and cost-effective access to funds for growth. These initiatives deal with optimizing finance, tax, and legal structures. They also encompass processes for reshaping the business portfolios, such as M&A transactions. They focus on improving the effectiveness and transparency of external dialogues with investors and internal dialogues with management around value creation.

5 **People and organization** – developing the leading-edge finance team needed to deliver on this agenda. This thrust focuses on changes required in behavior, technical skills, and corporate culture. It also leverages the opportunity of "Finance of the Future" to provide a compelling career proposition and attract the best talent.

Says Paul Baumann, leader of Unilever's Finance of the Future project and Director of its Finance Academy:

> "The reason for getting involved in a finance transformation is very simple – none of us has any choice. On the one hand, we have to be successful in automating and streamlining our core processes for accounting and information management. On the other, more than ever before, we in finance need to add real value through insightful engagement with the business.
>
> "Our internal customers will judge us on the quality of those insights – this is a challenge for which we need to be well pre-

pared. Since we are now equipped and freed from other distractions, there are no longer any excuses for not delivering.

"Much of our influence in finance stems from our role as guardians of the value-based management models by which we run the business – and, more specifically, from our ability to bring them to life in strategy, decision-making, and performance management. The financial 'mafia,' as it is often known with varying degrees of affection, is respected for its professionalism, envied for its uniquely strong network across the business, and trusted as the stewards of business control and ethics.

"But with ever-greater emphasis on growth and the uncertainty that it implies, we needed to take a fresh look at the core governance and decision-support approaches on which we have prided ourselves in the past. We needed to question many of our instinctive behaviors to ensure that we accelerated progress along the path to growth rather than blocking it."

Having set out the strategy for developing the finance function of the future, Paul and his project team soon realized just how enormous the transformation was going to be. Paul notes:

"One of Unilever's great assets is its global reach, but you can imagine the issues this creates in terms of rolling out a consistent, but locally relevant, transformation process. Our push for accelerated growth requires us to 'up our game.' How do you get to the hearts and minds of 9,000 people in 150 countries? And how do you tell whether more than 20 separate promotion evaluation tools in use around the world are a healthy reflection of genuinely different business models or a prime example of reinventing the wheel many times over?"

Unilever's Finance Academy was specifically created to equip its large and far-flung finance team to cope successfully with transformation. Its creation was approved on the same day that its ambitious change strategy was adopted by the Finance Leadership Team.

Next in this chapter, we explore Unilever's "Innovative Business Partnering" in more detail. We also show its impact on the effective brand investment and growth initiatives.

WORKING IN PARTNERSHIP

Paul Baumann introduces the IBP concept:

> "With Innovative Business Partnering we come, for me at least, to the very heart of the finance role of the future. It provides the capabilities and processes by which we are 'operationalizing' value creation in our core business decisions about where and how to invest for growth. It helps us deepen our interaction with our business partners in developing successful solutions so that value creation is maximized. Today, our involvement spans all stages of an opportunity's evolution, from initial concept to implementation."

Unilever's vision for innovative business partnering focuses on maximizing brand potential through improved decision analysis. Finance works in *partnership* with the marketing, customer development, and supply chain functions to develop, embed, and share best-practice decision analysis in:

- Brand launch and communication.
- Customer development.
- Extended supply chain.
- Innovation and strategy.

Why is this important? With nearly €10 billion invested in brands each year, it is critical that Unilever maximizes its returns on this enormous investment. Furthermore, from an external perspective, investors are demanding more rigor in this area. They are rewarding companies that use "fact-based" analysis in determining brand investment – and this has become a major source of competitive advantage.

The finance function can make a huge difference in brand value creation. It is uniquely positioned within the business to integrate information, improve analysis, and ensure links between strategy and business results. Like most companies, Unilever often "reinvents the wheel" with its analysis. When the company benchmarked its finance function, it found that its finance function had enough decision-support people worldwide, but that they needed to shift their focus.

The heart of the IBP program is the application of designated best practices. Unilever differentiates between what it considers *good* practices and *best* practices. A good practice adds value to the business and can be built upon by other functions. A best practice is one that Unilever has formally adopted based on its broad applicability and significant impact on decision-making quality. These practices are fully documented and shared through the company's finance learning program.

Each best practice includes:

- An overview of the business process.
- The role of finance.
- Relevant case studies, tools, and templates.

The development and implementation of these best practices is a long-term process and one that Unilever treats in the same way as product innovation. One of the key challenges is balancing the flow of new concepts with the capacity of the organization to absorb them.

An "innovation funnel" has been developed by the IBP team. Concepts progress through the funnel from the "ideas stage" through a series of validation gates to launch as a certified best practice. Best practices vary, from new roles for finance in existing processes to the development of entirely new cutting-edge approaches.

Examples of best practice processes from the first wave of development:

- **Brand launch and communication** – investing for brand development, advertising budget, and quality guidelines, marketing mix optimization.
- **Customer development** – sales promotion evaluation.
- **Innovation** – a "decision-making under uncertainty" toolkit for probability analysis, and decision framing and structuring.

In addition, there are best-practice guidelines for effective business partnering.

IBP activities are divided into a number of work streams with annual goals. Outlined below are the targets for the first year of IBP's initiatives:

1 **Embed best practices in the business.** Implement and integrate best practices throughout Unilever. Goal: embed at least two best practices in 15 out of 30 target units. Successfully introduce pilot toolkit for "decision-making under uncertainty" in at least five major innovation projects.

2 **Develop new best practices.** Continually design and launch new best-practice decision support frameworks. Goal: launch four new best practices with focus on customer.

3 **Share and leverage good practices.** Continually share good practices and foster a "steal with pride" culture. Goal: capture at least 20 good practices.

4 **Communicate and activate.** Ensure awareness and nurture progress throughout finance and among business partners. Run learning programs and coach implementation teams. Issue quarterly IBP newsletters. Goal: run learning program for 200+ people and launch "IBP in Action" recognition program.

An IBP development cycle has been implemented. It focuses on the role of decision-support people in operating companies, brand categories, and geographic regions. It also encompasses the role of the central development function – the Finance Academy. The IBP development cycle is captured in Figure 7.2.

David Calle, previously Unilever's first IBP Program Leader and now Director of Customer Development Finance for Unilever USA, talks about some of the successes achieved to date:

 ## INNOVATIVE BUSINESS PARTNERING

David Calle, Director of Customer Development Finance, Unilever USA

My role was primarily to kick-start the business partnering initiative which has now been under way for several years. I'm passionate about finance playing a lead role in the business. We are moving from just being controllers and scorekeepers to being finance people who play a key part in driving the business forward. For me, this is not about second-guessing the job of marketing. It is about having access to information and leveraging it throughout the business so that we truly understand the impact of business decisions on value creation.

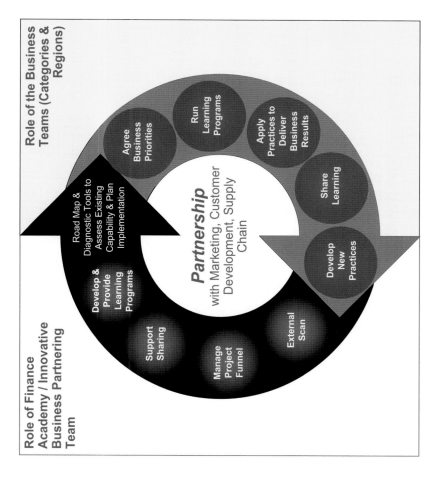

Figure 7.2 *The innovative business partnering cycle*

Unilever had pockets of excellence. But IBP is about raising both the "floor" and the "ceiling" of finance excellence. We have to bring the entire business up to the highest standard while also bringing our most advanced operating companies to the cutting edge as measured by reference to our best peer companies.

IBP example 1

In India, our finance people had worked in a cross-functional team in the area of brand health. They integrated traditional measures of brand health, such as attitudinal measures, with executional measures of financial performance. This allows the business to understand in a consistent way where a brand is in terms of opportunities for further growth or issues that need to be resolved. From a business execution viewpoint, this allows us to focus on the actions that promised to have the biggest impact.

Part of my job has been to make this best practice from India visible across the globe. In this case it was quickly picked up by a number of businesses, including our foods company in the USA. What's really exciting for me is to see the teams working together on brands in a truly cross-functional way.

IBP example 2

In our Lipton side-dishes, such as mashed potato and noodles, the team had developed a really wonderful advertising campaign and was ready to launch it. The brand health scorecard which had been developed in India, when applied to the project as a pilot, provided additional insight: the brand health discriminators regarding product variety showed that more product development work was needed before the advertising campaign could be launched.

As a result, the team re-prioritized its activities, sorted through flavor insights, and postponed the advertising campaign until the flavor product mix issue was resolved. The role of finance: to ensure alignment between investment decisions and the brand health insights.

IBP example 3

In our Latin American business, our finance folks and our media channel planning group worked together on guidelines for advertising and brand support. The guidelines involved three levels of analysis:

1 *Investment relative to competition.*
2 *Investment relative to the "clutter" of other market campaigns.*
3 *Activity-based budgeting.*

Our Latin America businesses faced a number of challenges, especially multiple exchange rates and vast geographic distances making face-to-face meetings difficult. The integrated IBP team found a way to share relevant learning using a regionally accessible database coupled with training programs. In Latin America, one of our most successful business regions, best-practice guidelines have given us a couple of wins:

1 *Annually, we make trade-offs across brands to ensure that they are appropriately funded to meet their goals.*
2 *For the longer term, we ensure that our brand aspirations are properly funded – that investment funds are available to support our long-term brand strategy.*

This practice, which started in Latin America, is now moving to various countries around the globe. I am very excited that we now are having much more fact-based discussions about the brand investments we are making and about properly aligning those investments with our growth targets.

Launching best practices
Launching best practices is, of course, an important first step. But without a comprehensive program of learning to support them, these practices would never have taken root. So we developed an IBP learning program which has at its core three modules:

1 *A residential workshop where the practitioners learn best practices and get to work with experts.*
2 *A 12/14 week action learning project – where practitioners use their new business learning, applying best practices to a specific business issue.*
3 *A "share" workshop where we bring everyone back together again so they can discuss what they've learned and analyze the challenges and successes they experienced in bringing new practices to their respective businesses.*

The output of the "share" workshop is reported back to the senior management of the units concerned. The IBP team provides one-on-one coaching and networking opportunities to support the implementation of the relevant best practice.

Finally, but very important, I come to the way we celebrate progress and achievement. Annually, individual practitioners are recognized for their successful contributions. The "IBP In Action Awards" celebrate successes nominated by the practitioners themselves. In our first year, we had 23 submissions, the best of which were recognized with awards presented by our CFO at our global management conference.

IBP Vision

What is Unilever's vision for IBP? Well, looking back several years from now, we would like to feel that we've achieved the following aspirations set by John Ripley:

1 *We do things according to the "One Way" culture in Unilever and innovative business partnering has become an established way of life for our finance people.*
2 *Our ROI on incremental investments is competitive; all plans are based on our embedded understanding of marketing mix dynamics.*
3 *We understand our share of industry profit pools – particularly our customers' profitability and the returns on our promotions.*
4 *We embrace risk and manage it effectively to realize its full value potential.*
5 *We understand the competition and know how to beat it!*

To achieve these aspirations, Unilever is devoting significant effort to revamping the way that finance leverages management information. To generalize a caricature: historically, finance has spent far too much time gathering information and correcting it, too little time analyzing it, and even less time acting on it. In best practice companies, this profile is almost reversed.

After designing a more dynamic approach to management information, finance conducted "pulse checks" to assess the difference that its new approach was making to the business. In the region that has shown the most progress, this development work now really "lives." Both financial and non-financial people have incorporated the partnering approach into their "strategy into action" program and their personal plan objectives. It's not just the quality of the thinking upfront that's made this a success, it's the passion for the execution.

Of course, there is still more to do to widen and deepen the scope of the implementation. Despite significant progress in some of the biggest business units, finance is still rolling out the partnering initiative to others. IBP training has been given to over 700 of Unilever's key decision-support people. It's clear that making such a profound change will require ongoing coaching and support. It's also clear that not all of the existing finance resources will make the "business partners of the future" transition. IBP is encouraging the finance members of the multifunctional decision support teams to play a more proactive role and to adopt a greater external focus – for example, in their interactions with retailers such as Tesco.

John Ripley summarizes the progress made:

> "We've had a lot of success with IBP. The finance function has embraced the business partnering initiative in a way that I wouldn't have thought possible – moving it from just being a project involving tools and techniques to something more fundamental. Truly integrated business partnering is becoming part of our daily working lives. IBP is the aspect of our future vision that our best people find most motivating. It's bringing us closer to becoming the leading-edge company that we aspire to be."

EFFECTIVE INVESTMENT IN BRANDS

This Unilever initiative is focusing finance on partnering with marketing and sales to ensure that the return on investments in brand building and support is maximized. The critical success factors for Unilever are as follows:

- Full involvement in the assessment of projected and actual impact of marketing/sales investments on growth and value creation. *This requires cooperation between functions in developing, piloting, and deploying an integrated approach to investment return management.*

- Managing trade-offs between long-term brand building/value creation and short-term profit delivery. *This requires developing a brand valuation methodology.*

- Tracking brand valuation movements over time and through portfolio transformations. *This requires a dynamic approach to gathering and analyzing management information.*

Nick Rose, CFO of Diageo, was an inspiring keynote speaker at Unilever's Finance of the Future launch conference. Unilever has interviewed Diageo finance executives extensively to benchmark their best practices in this area.

To quote Nick:

> "The question of how you measure marketing effectiveness is the Holy Grail for most consumer goods companies. Diageo effectively manages the health of its key brands through a brand monitor scorecard utilizing finance-based measures. These scorecard measures are based on economic profit as well as advertising promotion spend, market share, share of voice, brand penetration/awareness.

> "At Diageo, both the marketing and finance people are trained in the managing for value initiative. The finance function is now taking a lead role in this important area. The results are encouraging: economic profits at Diageo provide a clear line of sight between brand performance and shareholder value – and are supported by applying measurement systems to prioritize brands."

Effective brand investment is as much about finance and sales/marketing working together in new ways as it is about specific tools and techniques. At Unilever, the brand investment partnership between the finance and sales/marketing functions is shown in Figure 7.3.

Here are three examples of best practice in brand decision support.

 ## BRAND BEST PRACTICE 1: HEALTH MONITORING

Brand health monitoring is a common approach to understanding brand strength. It can be used to compare brand categories and brands across different countries. This "health check" evaluates three brand value criteria:

1 *Executional strength: measured by operational factors – such as relative price, distribution, share of advertising, share of market, and promotional pressure.*

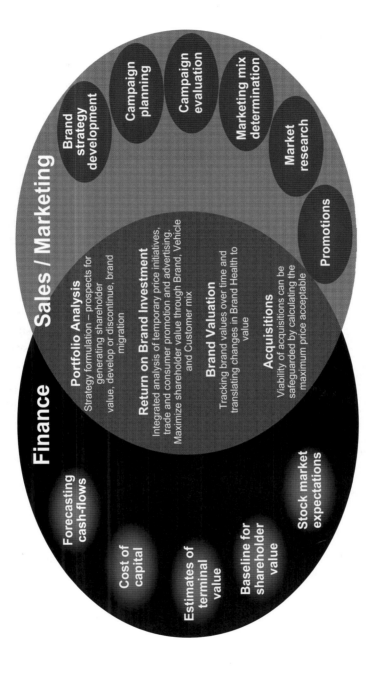

Figure 7.3   *Effective brand investment – finance in partnership with sales/marketing*

2   *Behavioral strength: measured by purchasing behavior factors – such as value share and penetration.*

3   *Attitudinal strength: measured by consumer preference and quality factors – such as consumer brand endorsement, brand strength, and brand potential.*

A healthy brand is resilient and responsive to market changes. Consumers will pay more for it and the healthier it is, the more profitable it is. The finance function can add value by improving understanding of the brand health check:

- *Supporting brand management in setting targets and monitoring progress by focusing on measures that have the greatest brand impact.*
- *Ensuring alignment between brand health insights and investment decisions within a brand and across the brand portfolio. This alignment can help identify which brands are facing the toughest challenges and which activities offer the best investment potential.*

Brand Health Scorecard	
Market Performance	**Brand Proposition**
• Category volume and value	• Brand differentiation
• Brand volume and value	• Brand loyalty
• Market share	– Conviction
• Customer behaviour	– Advantage
– Penetration	– Performance
– Volume per buyer	– Relevance
– Share of requirements	– Presence
Financial Performance	**Brand Promotion**
• Turnover	• Spontaneous awareness
• Profitability	• Media spend
• Price	• Advertising quality
– Relative price	• Placement
– Value for money	– Distribution quality
	– Out of stocks
	• Product
	– Product quality
	– Pack attribute

Figure 7.4   *Brand health scorecard*

- *Validating brand growth plans – annual and longer term – by identifying key opportunities and risks.*
- *Assessing brand strength both internally and as part of an external scan to determine how brands' strengths compare to their category peers.*

Figure 7.4 shows an example of a scorecard linking a brand's health to its operational and financial performance.

BRAND BEST PRACTICE 2: ADVERTISING GUIDELINES

In a company with significant investments in advertising, it is important to assess the right level of expenditure on brands. Finance can work together with marketing to ensure that there is a logical framework for making trade-offs in advertising investment so that fact-based decisions can be made regarding advertising spend levels. In this area, there are two key best practice opportunities:

1 **Budget setting:** *Budget setting tools can provide different perspectives on the right level of brand advertising. Such tools can put advertising in the right competitive context by considering factors such as strategic importance, brand size, innovation, brand profitability, competitive spends, and future activities. Ultimately, this should support decisions on how much money is required to do the job in terms of target audience, activity level, and cost.*

2 **Advertising quality:** *Companies like Unilever routinely test the quality of advertising before proceeding with a campaign. Finance should help factor these test insights into decisions on spend allocation.*

The role of finance in this best practice area is to assist decision-making by:

- *Providing an unbiased view on investment options and performance – keeping the business focused on the ultimate goal of value creation.*
- *Aligning investment levels with brand strategy and corporate objectives.*
- *Ensuring that measurable objectives are set and agreed actions taken if objectives are exceeded or missed during the year.*
- *Monitoring progress against budgets and marketplace objectives, and reassessing investment decisions during the year.*

BRAND BEST PRACTICE 3: MARKETING MIX MODELLING

Marketing mix models deploy statistical or econometric techniques. These use historical data to disaggregate total brand volume by marketing activity/investment and associate such investments with sales results. The outputs of these models provide investment return data on each element of the marketing mix, price elasticity, and sources of brand volume. The role of the finance function in applying marketing mix techniques is to:

- *Provide input into marketing models and translate sales uplift into profitability.*
- *Evaluate the portfolio of investment options available.*
- *Link marketing mix decisions to business planning.*

Companies like Unilever can track the impact of different marketing channel investments – be they TV or special promotions – on brand volumes over time. These marketing mix models can be regularly refreshed and reconfigured on an as-needed basis. The effects of various marketing channel investments on brand volumes over time are illustrated in Figure 7.5.

There are several aspects of the budgeting/planning process where close cooperation is required between marketing and finance. In particular, the two functions need to jointly determine the best use of funds – incorporating insights on marginal spending effectiveness by advertising medium. Working together, advertising and marketing must also ensure that these decisions are accurately reflected in the monthly forecast cycle.

The best consumer goods companies take a very rigorous approach to evaluating their advertising and promotional investments. For example, Diageo has a highly structured process in which all advertising and promotions expenditures above a certain threshold must be reviewed by representatives of sales, marketing, and finance before approval. Projects are reassessed to check on achievement against projection. The learnings and results are shared via a central intranet site.

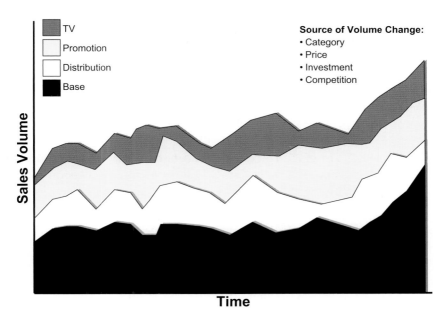

Figure 7.5 *Impact of marketing channel investment*

DECISION MAKING UNDER UNCERTAINTY

Finance has a tendency to be risk averse. Quite often finance executives equate uncertainty with risk. As a result they may miss some of the best opportunities to create value. Traditionally, finance has been reluctant to support uncertain projects, perhaps failing to appreciate that they could offer more opportunity than risk. If companies are to outstrip their competitors in growth, their finance functions must change their attitude to uncertainty. The world of venture capital and private equity offers some valuable best practice advice:

- Follow a rigorous assessment process to evaluate risks and opportunities with the goal of influencing possibilities.

- Focus on building flexibility and options – these become increasingly valuable in making decisions where uncertainty is high.

- Dedicate the resources needed for quick action in order to exercise options at the best possible time.

At Unilever, the finance function has defined "Decision Making Under Uncertainty" (DMUU) as a disciplined and structured approach. Probabilistic analysis is at the heart of this discipline.

Unilever has developed a DMUU toolkit as part of its IBP initiative. Figure 7.6 illustrates some of the tools it employs.

DMUU's toolkit is not prescriptive; the choice of approaches depends on the decision under consideration. The toolkit contains:

1 Tools designed to clarify decisions and ensure that all possible outcomes are considered – using stakeholder mapping, decision hierarchies, de-biasing techniques, and influence diagrams.

2 Tools designed to model, analyze and visualize uncertainty – for example, Monte Carlo simulation, Tornado charts, risk matrixes, and decision trees.

When applied effectively, this toolkit enables finance to identify the full value of *growth options* owned by the business and to play a major role in the decision-making process by which this growth is realized. Unilever has identified the following critical success factors for decision making under uncertainty:

- **Probabilistic evaluation of options for growth**: This involves developing, piloting, and rolling out valuation tools and techniques appropriate to each decision-making layer.

- **Making the right choices on total resource allocation:** This involves structured, regular appraisal of options for intangibles investment and their linkage to internal market processes.

- **Involving finance as a full partner:** Finance takes part in every phase of the decision-making process, from incubating and improving ideas through initial generation to "post-mortem" reviews. Perhaps the most important challenge is getting relatively diverse groups to apply their combined knowledge when choosing the right options to pursue.

The ultimate objective of DMUU is high-quality decisions. Finance executives normally equate good quality decisions with good, solid analysis. But a high-quality decision has many elements. It has a comprehensive framework for analysis and goal-setting and is based on evaluation of the full array of realistic options. It also reflects a broad view of informa-

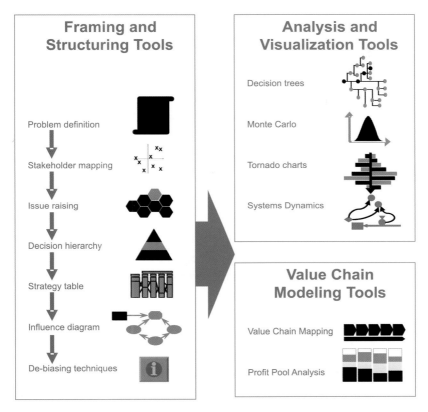

Figure 7.6 *Decision making under uncertainty tools and techniques*

tion management and employs a rigorous approach to trade-off analysis. Finally, it uses a formal value creation model with the goal of turning analysis into action.

Without a proper framework for decision making, unnecessary scenarios will be generated. Too many scenarios can confuse, rather than clarify! As much emphasis should be placed on framing decisions as on analyzing them. Surprisingly, Unilever found the analysis phase to be easier than establishing a framework to decision making.

Unilever's DMUU program enables participants to gain practical experience in structuring decision-making scenarios in complex, highly uncertain situations. Using probabilistic analysis instead of single-point estimates means that the finance function has to adopt a fundamentally different approach to valuation. It must move away from traditional *assumed precision* and become more comfortable with *ranges of potential outcomes* associated with varying confidence levels.

In decisions where there are many variables and the quality of available information is not guaranteed – the "most likely" outcome is but one of many. Hundreds, perhaps thousands, of permutations exist. Building in flexibility – instead of relying on pin-point accuracy – is one of the hallmarks of the finance function of the future.

 ## DMUU BEST PRACTICE: SOURCING STUDY

DMUU was applied to a complex sourcing study by a factory in Unilever's Home and Personal Care business in Latin America. The finance executives involved wanted to define the optimal sourcing configuration for all products manufactured there.

The project involved teams and resources from various functions, including planning, manufacturing, and supply management, as well as finance. The project team used many of the tools in Unilever's DMUU toolkit, including "issue raising," the decision hierarchy, stakeholder plotting, and Monte Carlo analysis. The project resulted in a sourcing proposal that was approved by management.

The project proved to be a great learning experience. The DMUU approach allowed the team to address a highly complex and sensitive project with robust analysis. This was a major factor in creating a smooth decision process and gaining strong consensus among the team about its recommendations.

The tools and approaches used for the analysis promoted confidence in the results and the recommendations – for example, the decision-framing process helped build trust among stakeholders. This led to highly strategic discussions and insights. In conclusion, the project leader said: "DMUU allows us to compare different scenarios, and to understand the risks and rewards of each option – a win–win opportunity for both us and our sourcing partners."

FINANCE AND INNOVATION

Many CFOs ask the question: how does finance support innovation? Unilever has developed a "Finance Innovation Guide" for tracking new product introductions – from initial portfolio decisions through monitoring in the crucial weeks after launch.

The benefits of finance being involved in innovation include:

- Improving the quality and completeness of the financial evaluation.

- Enabling better, more informed, and more consistent decisions.

- Increasing the speed with which decisions are made.

A generic, cross-industry, best practice process for involving finance in innovation tracking is illustrated in Figure 7.7.

The role of finance during the key phases of the innovation process is as follows:

1 **Ideas phase (charter gate):** Provide a basic financial analysis of project potential and financial action standards to force early choices.

2 **Feasibility phase (contract gate):** Ensure that all assumptions – including those about speed to market (STM) – are carefully defined and realistic. Complete full financial analysis.

3 **Capability phase (launch gate):** Use STM results to evaluate the potential of the project based on different price positioning and marketing plans. Update the financials with agreed assumptions. Identify critical success factors.

4 **Launch preparation (launch):** Ensure that key assumptions made in the capability phase are still valid. Establish key performance metrics.

5 **Post-launch:** Provide an early assessment of innovation performance and potential for roll out.

 ## INNOVATION BEST PRACTICE: MODELLING THE INNOVATION THRESHOLD

The Unilever Foods Retail business in Canada developed an innovation threshold model for every project that is submitted for "innovation gate" approval. The model was created by executives drawn from marketing, sales, and finance. The model helps financial analysts on business teams to become better business partners – asking

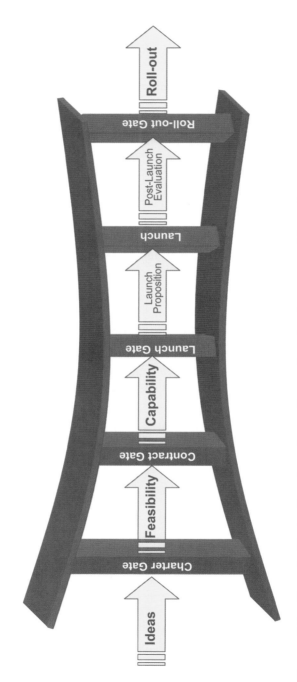

Figure 7.7   *Generic illustration: key phases for product development and launch*

insightful questions, and providing useful evaluations of the current business, marketing and sales strategies, and the innovation project itself.

The innovation threshold process encompasses three key decision-support elements. First, it involves modelling P&L sensitivities to identify business contingencies associated with the innovation and to reduce project approval times. Second, it requires determining minimum sales levels for payback on product launch during the idea phase, when product-cost information is generally not available. Finally, the innovation threshold model requires data on consumer demand, opportunity size, financial measures, and other relevant issues.

The rigor of decision support by business teams has increased since they now consider margin improvement and sensitivities before they seek gate approval. The Retail Foods business in Unilever Canada has evaluated 33 projects since this model was first introduced and rejected five of them based on the model's recommendations and strategic considerations.

DYNAMIC PERFORMANCE MANAGEMENT

Each year, the vast majority of businesses in the world launch budgeting processes, which involve the negotiation and fixing of targets, rewards, and plans. They then measure and manage business performance against these plans. This approach has three main defects. First, it is inflexible. Second, it encourages dysfunctional "gaming" behavior. Finally, it is complex and bureaucratic – and therefore costly.

These defects typically result from the fact that current performance management processes are based on the concept of a *fixed* financial performance contract. This creates a *fixed* performance management system designed to meet internally negotiated annual targets.

However, the world is unpredictable! The fixed performance management system, which ties activity to predictions about the future, does not match the dynamic business environment in which companies like Unilever operate. In constraining action, rather than guiding or stimulating it, this system has limited value. It does not acknowledge that the fundamental business objective is to be successful competitively rather than just to meet internally negotiated targets.

Unilever has chosen not to tinker with existing practices but to rethink the way that the whole process works. What's new is their approach to tackling the problem. They have done this by exploiting ideas derived from the "Beyond Budgeting Round Table" – a cross-industry research collaborative whose insights into the way that performance management processes work have been attracting increasing attention over the last few years.

This approach has been christened "Dynamic Performance Management" to reflect the fact that it is a holistic approach.[1] It takes its cue from the environment – which is unpredictable and ever changing. As a result, it is far more wide-ranging than "financial planning" or performance measurement.

Paul Baumann explains what Unilever means by Dynamic Performance Management (DPM):

> "DPM enables us to respond quickly to growth and value creation opportunities as they arise, rather than having our hands tied behind our backs through self-imposed constraints. It can also free up resources – in Unilever's case, the equivalent of a staggering potential 1,300 man years, which we invest in plans each year. This time is spent in creating these plans, and then meticulously reporting against them even when, in many cases, they had become obsolete!"

Dynamic Performance Management is holistic – providing a *flexible* management system based on continuous improvement relative to the competition. There are six key process principles for Dynamic Performance Management:

1 **Adaptive target setting** – setting aspirational goals aimed at relative improvement. Targets can be set flexibly from a "threshold" to a "ceiling."

2 **Adaptive rewards** – rewarding shared success "after the event." The reward range moves from merely *meeting* targets to *beating* the competition.

3 **Adaptive planning** – planning becomes an inclusive and continuous process. The goal of a plan is not to predict and control, but to *project* the consequences of marketplace trends as the basis for *action*.

4 **Adaptive measurement and control** – controls are based on relative performance indicators. Performance is not gauged by plan compliance but by interpreting external and internal indicators to separate *signals* (which need to be acted upon) from *noise* (which should be ignored).

5 **Adaptive investment management** – making resources available as required. Investment resources are not an *entitlement* enshrined in a budget but something that must be earned based on the quality of business proposals.

6 **Adaptive coordination** – coordinating cross-company interactions dynamically. From a management *push* philosophy, where management focuses on local compliance to central commands, to a *pull* approach, in which the center empowers the local execution of strategy by providing the right support (resources, advice, and shared knowledge from across the organization).

Adopting these principles helps create a simpler and more agile business – and fosters a healthier workplace culture. It also promotes business partnering by creating a culture of "stretch targets" built on winning. Beyond this, it provides a flexible management framework for responding to the insights offered by IBP tools. The impact of moving from a fixed performance contract approach – "predict and control" – to a more adaptive "sense and respond" model is highlighted in Figure 7.8.

 ## DPM BEST PRACTICE: UNILEVER POLAND

Over a period of a few months, Unilever's Polish foods business moved from a traditional top-down "budget driven" management process to a dynamic process built on the creation of nine entrepreneurial cross-functional "Brand Teams."

This required Brand Teams to set their own targets within the context of a strategic framework. These targets ranged from "good," representing adequate performance, to "great" – a "dream" of what could be achieved, the ultimate goal of collective endeavour.

This way of working is driven by tightly coupling the brand management team to its local market and underpinned by a transparent, continuously updated forecasting process. This process provides management with a guide as to how much money

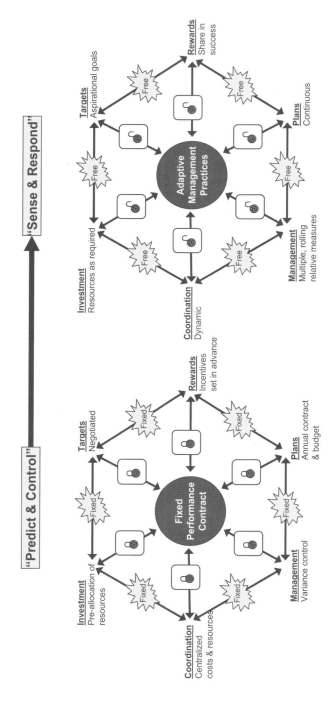

Figure 7.8 *From fixed contractual performance to free dynamic performance*

is potentially available to support the brand teams; a view of the inherent risks; and a set of options for managing those risks.

Within months, this new approach enabled the business to move from low, unstable performance to continuous growth. In the process, it has significantly outperformed the market, moving from 10th in a local growth "league table" to consistently ranking in the top three.

In summary, Unilever's DPM initiative provides it with "business relevant" information and dynamic performance management processes. The results: realistic targets aligned with total shareholder return objectives.

John Ripley comments on the more dynamic approach that Unilever now uses for budgeting and forecasting:

> "If you're going to manage the business dynamically, you have to see the company more fully in its external competitive context. The aspiration cannot just be a growth target of, say, 3.7% in the budget: it's a broader objective – growing faster than the market as a whole.

> "We now have a much better and more formal understanding of what's happening in our markets and with our competitors. This information is more available and ready to use. We are moving the business from fixed annual budgets to rolling forecasts: depending on where we are in the annual financial cycle, we roll our forecasts forward between nine and eighteen months.

> "Our monthly reports on business unit results describe our outcome against the same period of the previous year and how we feel we performed against our current forecast. Reporting against budgets is a thing of the past! The key document for top management review is now the forecast. We're increasingly looking to the future to influence the business outcome, not the rear-view mirror.

> "The forecast is now receiving more and more attention. When we looked at what constitutes best-practice forecasting, we realized that it's more behavioral than 'process-related.' So, we give feedback on forecast accuracy in our monthly pack. We also

use forecasting bandwidths – rather than predicting precise outcomes. We rely on a mid-point forecast, a moving annual total, and a top-and-bottom forecast range. We also distinguish between the granularity required for short-term planning and the broader view required for the longer term.

"We've also made major changes to our targeting and reward processes to reduce the incentive to 'manage' performance, rather than optimizing it. The result? Greater transparency."

THE FINANCE ACADEMY

John Ripley goes on to comment on Unilever's Finance Academy:

"Many people see finance as the most 'joined up' function in Unilever and our academy has taken this cohesiveness and net-working to the next level. Our finance academy was formed to provide a center of expertise. This combination of thought leaders, best-practice propagators, and learning providers helped create the push needed to get initiatives under way. Now we're gearing up to cope with the strong pull coming from the business.

"The academy has also been successful in developing the individuals who work within it. It is now time for some of those involved in business partnering to move on within the company to senior line positions. So we will experience some turnover. This process of refreshment should re-energize and invigorate."

The Unilever Finance Academy is seen as a key enabler of the "Finance of the Future" agenda. The academy's mission is to:

- Help finance professionals by being *influential business partners.*

- Equip them with *world-class capabilities* in business and finance.

- Enable Unilever Finance to deliver *consistently outstanding perform-ance* and become an employer of choice.

The academy's objective is to translate external trends into internal initiatives. Its work also includes identifying the competencies, skills, and tools required – and providing "cradle to grave" learning opportunities.

Most important, its job is to promote a learning-and-coaching culture by stimulating best practice creation and sharing. The academy is becoming the focus of a cohesive and externally networked global Finance community across Unilever.

The Finance Academy has set up an internal website for sharing knowledge and personal development. A specially designated area of this website houses documentation for best practices. The website also features information on:

- Overviews of IBP and the latest news about what is happening around the world.
- The "IBP in Action Award."
- Links to resources and websites that provide an external perspective (for example – the Working Council of CFOs).
- IBP learning programs and online support materials.

CONCLUSION

Paul Baumann comments on the challenges of driving such a significant transformation through the finance function:

> "Even with an attractive agenda like IBP, we've found it takes many more iterations than we expected before people get the message. The temptation to revert to old behaviors when under workload pressure or meeting resistance is enormous! Just one example – over a year after we abolished detailed budgets, we found that 45% of businesses were still doing them 'just in case.' It was no great surprise that those businesses didn't have the time to get on with the new agenda. We need to get people to take the plunge and throw away their old comfort blankets.

> "My advice to companies embarking on a new finance development strategy: be clear and disciplined about your priorities related to strategy and other business initiatives. Invest in creating and activating powerful and visible change agents to stimulate action and give confidence. Measure success by rigorous scorecarding and use 'war stories' to help people connect.

We've also found from experience that it's important to learn quickly from failures and celebrate success loudly! Above all, we found that you can't ever rest – this is a sustained change program.

"The bottom line: it is taking time for the substantial business benefits we have promised to be fully visible – to us and to our partners. However, our results so far have created a new mood of confidence and energy."

One of the most exciting recent developments at Unilever has been the growing partnership between the Finance Academy and its counterpart academies in Marketing and Customer Development. All new capabilities under the IBP program are now being developed and rolled out jointly. There is, for the first time, the prospect of combined learning programs for team members from all three functions. This cooperation sets a clear signal about what's expected of business partners at all levels. It has significantly speeded up the process of getting the new practices embedded in core business decision-making processes.

STRAIGHT FROM THE CFO

- **Take the plunge, throw away the comfort blanket!**

  Map *your* "finance of the future" strategy. Establish building blocks – for the pursuit of world-class finance, and business partnering and decision support.

- **Learn from outside, and inside**

  Try not to reinvent the wheel. Borrow as much as you can from others. Take care – build and share your corporate knowledge with pride. This approach is in itself a best practice!

- **Create a business partnering culture**

  Establish innovative partnering as a way of life – make it the heart of finance. Change the profile of how your finance staff spends its time. Move them away from processing and reconciliation – and towards value creation.

- **Build a decision-making toolkit**

  Introduce a structured approach and rigorous tools for assessing and optimizing ROI on brand and customer investments. Embrace uncertainty, but follow a structured process in understanding and influencing possibilities. Build *in* the flexibilities and options, and dedicate resources. Embed in the business your *corporate* decision analysis. Support best practice tools and techniques.

- **Develop dynamic performance management processes**

  Create a fast-moving enterprise culture – respond quickly to growth and value creation opportunities. Abolish complexity and detail inherent in a fixed performance culture. Don't tie your organization's hands behind its back! Go for the *adaptive* processes.

- **Invest in creative and powerful change agents!**

  Raise the *floor* and the *ceiling* of finance excellence. Question many of finance's instinctive behaviors. Ensure that your finance function accelerates progress, rather than blocks it! Select the best and brightest.

- **Be disciplined about implementation**

  Balance the flow of new concepts with the capacity of your organization to absorb them. Distinguish between *good* and *best* practices. Establish "pulse checks" to see how you're doing.

- **Take other disciplines with you**

  Don't see finance transformation as an end in itself. Solutions and programs that are jointly owned with other functions will have longer lasting impact.

- **Celebrate successes and war stories**

  Allow your internal customers to judge the quality of finance insights. Recognition programs really do work – especially when visibly sponsored by top leadership.

> ● **Institute a finance academy**
>
> Coach finance professionals in becoming influential business partners. Equip them with world-class capabilities – provide "cradle to grave" learning opportunities. Work with counterparts in other functions, such as marketing and sales, to roll out joint learning programs.

REFERENCES

1 Steve Morlidge (2004) *Dynamic Performance Management,* MTP Publishing and Unilever.

CHAPTER 8

Promoting Global Connectivity

Thomas Friedman, New York Times columnist and author of the book *The World is Flat*, believes globalization has reached a whole new level.[1] The dynamic force driving global integration has been multinational companies in industries ranging from the traditional manufacturing giants of yesterday to the titans of the consumer goods, energy, and technology industries of today.

These *multinationals* went global to find new markets and labor resources. We saw the birth and maturation of the global economy, creation of a global marketplace, and global arbitrage of products and labor. Because the world is shrinking – flattening the playing field – new companies are emerging in countries like India and China and individuals from around the world are now empowered to participate, to plug and play!

We started this book on the premise that CFOs and their finance functions of the world's leading companies have a twofold agenda: first, improving control, consolidating the current round of regulatory and accounting standard changes, and moving beyond them to seize the benefits; and, second, helping their companies to innovate and grow.

We focus in this chapter on what we refer to as "the next wave" – the recent rapid escalation in globalization, the trend towards off-shoring, and the extension of regional, single-functional shared services to ones which are:

- Multi-functional
- Truly global

How do companies build global capability? What is the learning from past experience of shared service implementations, ranging from Europe to Asia? And how does the CFO set about building a truly global shared service capability? How does technology support global connectivity?

The chapter begins with an interview with the CFO of Renault, who makes the case for globalization in the context of its joint alliance with Nissan. Next we look at shared services and how these have expanded regionally and globally to functions beyond finance. Finally, we draw upon the experience of companies like Microsoft in using technology to promote connectivity – *proving that the world really is flat!*

BUILDING GLOBAL PARTNERSHIPS

The Renault-Nissan Alliance is a unique partnership bringing together two global companies linked by cross-shareholdings. The goal of this alliance, now in its sixth year of operation, is to become one of the top three automotive groups in the world – in terms of quality, technology, and profitability.

Collaborative ventures in the alliance range from manufacturing and sales to R&D, purchasing and logistics. Thierry Moulonguet was appointed CFO of the Renault group some two years ago and comments on the challenges facing a CFO in a major global joint venture.

SHARING GLOBAL OPERATING PRINCIPLES
Thierry Moulonguet, EVP and CFO, Renault Group

Renault continues to implement successfully its strategy for profitable growth. It is the number one brand in Europe, and with a 2004 operating margin of 5.2% under IFRS, Renault is also one of Europe's most profitable vehicle manufacturers. The Group's strategy is structured around five fundamental goals:

- *Building brand recognition.*
- *Becoming the most competitive manufacturer in their markets.*
- *Extending our international reach.*
- *Promoting Renault's core values.*
- *Translating our performance into financial success.*

Outside of Western Europe, our domestic market, our sales were up over 16% last year. For example, Renault has a major subsidiary in South Korea (Renault Samsung Motors), often cited as a success in a country normally closed to foreign investment. Other regions where substantial recent progress has been made include Central and Eastern Europe, with the successful takeover of Dacia in Romania, and Mexico. But it is the Renault-Nissan Alliance which attracts the most attention. This type of business model, unusual in the automotive industry – in which independent companies work together, each retaining its own identity – is particularly suited to the twenty-first century as markets become increasingly international, fast moving, and fiercely competitive.

After its first six years the alliance is proposing a new initiative to the two companies, called "Vision/Destination." Not only do we want to be recognized by customers as one of the three best automotive groups in the world in terms of product and service quality, we also aim to be among the best three in terms of key technologies. We intend to do all this while maintaining high operating profit margin (once again among the top three) and pursuing growth. Renault and Nissan will be extending cooperation, dividing up the research workload – for example, in fuel cells and hybrid vehicles. Each partner is a leader in different domains of technology excellence.

The main focus of our finance agenda across the group:

- *Renault in the world economy – how we can move speedily to be a really effective global player. We face a big challenge in developing our presence in emerging markets.*
- *Governance and regulation – responding to the latest legislation at a global and country level; identifying best practice and putting it into operation, particularly in terms of risk management.*
- *Excellence in the finance function – specifically looking into what we can do in the alliance to achieve process and system improvements. Quality of partnerships, for example, is very high on our agenda and I personally put a lot of effort behind the concept of "co-opetition" – stressing the role of finance in facilitating and ensuring that we maximize value in a win–win relationship with our external business partners. These partners range from the vehicle dealers in our network to suppliers to joint ventures across the world. This is one of the keys to high performance in a global economy.*

The finance attributes we need to be high performers through co-opetition include having an open mind, the ability to listen, and benchmarking continuously by sharing best practices. In Europe, Renault shares services with Nissan for back-office processes in several countries. In the developing economies, this partnership approach is even more important because we don't necessarily have the experience on the ground and we need to get it right the first time. For example, in India, with our latest joint venture partner, MahindraMahindra, we share our business best practices in finance – we learn from them; they learn from us.

We are trying to standardize as much as possible on an IT and systems platform worldwide. In my role as EVP, I'm also responsible for information systems and I'm pushing very hard, not only for standardization, but also for global business partnerships.

Like other automotive companies, we see financial services as a way of retaining more value. RCI bank, the financing arm of the Renault group, provides a full range of financial products and services for its three main customer segments: retail customers; fleet customers; and the Renault, Nissan Europe, and Dacia brand dealer networks.

The finance function has been innovative in supporting RCI and other business activities, such as service and parts/accessories. We also take a proactive role in identifying and managing risk – for example, in the new and emerging economies.

We also negotiate with external business partners, identifying relevant financing structures, sharing best practices, and playing our part in sustaining ongoing relationships. For example, we give a lot of attention to the partnership balance sheets – especially working capital and the management of inventories – keeping a close eye on ratios like ROIC (return on invested capital).

The International Financial Reporting Standards (IFRS) and corporate governance regulations are tending to move in the right direction – particularly as they lead towards greater transparency. I am also open to the idea of market value in the accounts, unless such valuations lead to unnecessary earnings volatility. If it can contribute to convergence between IFRS and US GAAP then it is a good move. However, a market value approach to the balance sheet should not detract from a clear view of the reality of the operating results – the focus of reporting should be on the way we deliver real operating performance.

In our scorecards, we benchmark performance against our competitors, and we monitor the relationship between capital investment and returns. We also highlight and track progress on our strategic initiatives – how we're doing in improving our performance. We use key performance indicators (KPIs) extensively in Renault to report on performance. Externally, we report these KPIs at a summary level.

Our future plans for the finance function? To spread balance sheet awareness and culture across the organization. To develop a strong finance network around the world. To link finance departments in individual countries, and between Nissan and Renault. And to connect all these with the finance departments and processes of our extended network of external business partners.

Above all, we in finance aim to be an internal business partner – supporting our business colleagues and sharing with them action plans to innovate and grow. We in finance want to be involved at the beginning of business decisions, not at the end!

Most companies, like Renault, want to extend their global reach, standardize their business processes, and integrate their finance departments across the world. The end goals of multinational companies are similar, but their starting points vary considerably.

Figure 8.1 illustrates the varying depths to which global standardization can be taken.

Not all companies want to go *all* the way. Some want to standardize processes but leave some flexibility on systems, for example. Many companies, however, do want to standardize systems, data, and organization as well as processes and controls. It's important to standardize only where the benefits outweigh the costs. Standardization is not just about cost control, it's about service effectiveness and responsiveness – freeing up expert resources to concentrate on where they're needed the most.

Shared service centers are more than just a trend. It's estimated that 50% of multinationals either have, or are planning to set up, a shared service center.

Most companies use shared service centers as the mechanisms for introducing standardization in both processes and systems. The issue for them today is how far to take this organizational concept.

Deciding on the scope of shared services tends to be an ongoing process. Figure 8.2 shows how finance processes can be divided into four quadrants – transaction, specialist, decision support, reporting and con-

Standardization	Process / Controls	Systems	Data	Organization
High Level	Standard Policies	Common Platform	Top Level Reporting	Common Functions
Mid Level	Consistent Process Maps	Standard Implementations	Common Chart of Accounts	Roles & Grading Structures
Low Level	Common Procedures	Common Procedures	Common Data Dictionaries	Job Descriptions

Figure 8.1   *Degrees of standardization*

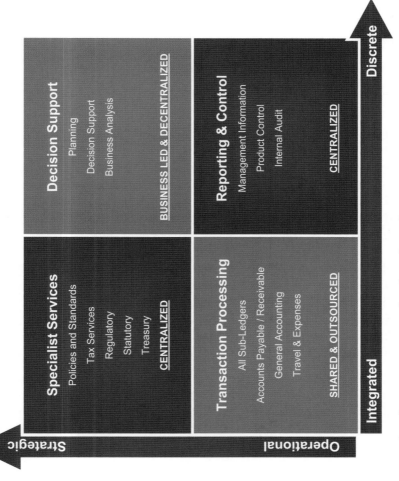

Figure 8.2 *Segmenting finance processes for shared services*

trol – to identify those processes that lend themselves more readily to shared services because they are more operational and integrated.

There are a number of prerequisites for a successful finance shared services implementation:

1 Clearly defined business processes.

2 A robust IT platform.

3 Clarity of organization and management structure.

4 Defined service levels for SSC customers.

5 Quality – "right first time," controls, data, and service delivery.

INTEGRATING SHARED SERVICES BY REGION

The world today broadly breaks down into three regions for shared services – the Americas; Europe, Middle East, and Africa (EMEA); and Asia Pacific. Geography, time zones, and language have, in the past, been some of the key criteria for deciding how best to group shared services into regional centers. However, the picture is changing:

- **The Americas** – North America is a relatively homogeneous market with few barriers and, therefore, the implementation of shared services has been relatively straightforward. Today, the trend is for North American shared services to go either near-shore, for example, to South America, Costa Rica or even off-shore to the Philippines. The rationale: labor arbitrage, increased language capabilities, and technology.

- **EMEA** – Language, political, fiscal, and cultural barriers have traditionally impeded the evolution of shared services in Europe. Today, many of these obstacles have been overcome and the trend is towards the re-siting of European shared service locations from western to central and eastern Europe. Some are even relocating to Africa, India, China, and other parts of the East.

- **Asia Pacific** – Arguably the most culturally and politically diverse of the three regions, there has been a recent explosion in shared services here as globalization takes root in traditionally conservative countries such as Japan; barriers come down in countries such as China, and multinationals push for consistent standards in the way they do business across the region.

Undoubtedly, there is tremendous value still to be created from further developments in the shared services field. Not only is the world becoming smaller geographically, but companies are taking a much broader view of what should be included in their shared service operations. They are also becoming more confident with experience in operating across the regulatory and fiscal regimes, which still differ from one country to another. Nevertheless, there seems to an inexorable trend towards consistent global business practices and standards as capital flows from one part of the world to the other.

Consider the experience of SAP in Asia Pacific.

OUR SSC EXPERIENCE IN ASIA PACIFIC
Colin Sampson, SVP and COO Asia Pacific, SAP

Some five years ago, we decided that we needed to set up a regional shared service center for the Asia Pacific region of SAP. This was the first shared service center implemented in the company and effectively became a pilot for the rest of the organization, providing us with the experience and knowledge for the rollout of shared services elsewhere in the world.

At the time, this initiative was not driven predominantly by cost savings, since Singapore is a relatively high-cost location, and the various Asian countries we operated in were for us relatively small. But we did need to establish a standard operating model with the appropriate level of quality and skill across the region.

Location choice
We chose Singapore as our SSC location for the following reasons:

- *As our regional headquarters, it offered us management overview and support.*
- *It provided access to IT – we already had the infrastructure and system support in place.*
- *There was a strong country infrastructure – good communications, transport, and education facilities.*
- *Skilled labor was available.*

- *It was politically and economically stable.*

Initially the roll out covered some 12 countries in Asia Pacific, ranging from China and Korea in the North to Australia and New Zealand in the South. It was later extended to include Japan.

The objective of the SSC was to perform the following processes for the 12 subsidiaries covered by the region:

- *Finance and administration.*
- *Software contracts administration.*
- *Human resources and payroll.*
- *Education and consulting administration.*
- *Partner services.*

Being a subsidiary of the SAP group, which is headquartered in Germany, we in the Asia Pacific region are mainly concerned with local marketing, license sales and support, and consulting. The scope and coverage of the Singapore SSC today is shown in the 2005 organization chart in Figure 8.3.

Freeing up local CFOs

By moving finance transactional services to the new SSC, we were keen to "free up" the local CFOs – and their finance and administration organizations – in the individual countries, so they could focus on providing decision support to local country management. The impact of the SSC implementation and the new role for CFOs in the field is reflected in the following comments:

Hiroshi Fujiwara, CFO and COO SAP Japan talks about the broadening of his role: "CFOs in Japan increasingly wear two hats: managing regulation and risk on the one hand, and management of the business on the other. As COO, I can influence much of what is happening in the field, better understand our contractual exposures, and feel more empowered to support our sales organization in dealing with external customers."

Jae Sam Lee, CFO of SAP Korea, comments on the specific benefits of this change in his country: "Generally in Korea, middle management tends to follow senior management's direction: the power in Korean companies comes directly from the top; corporate governance does not necessarily flow easily down through the management tiers. As a country CFO in SAP, I have to both support local management but

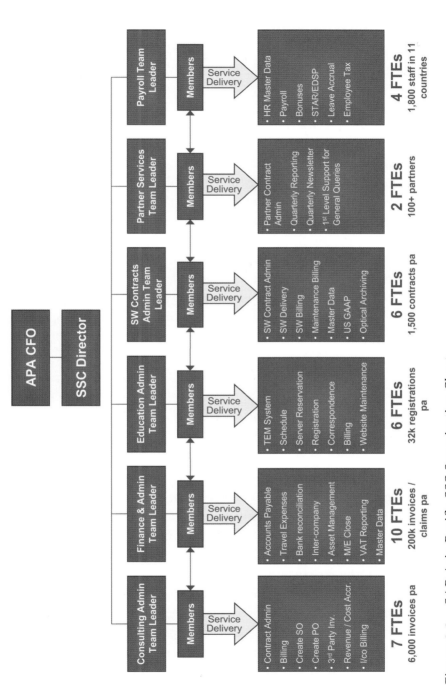

Figure 8.3 *SAP Asia Pacific SSC Organization Chart*

also follow global direction. As a result of the SSC implementation in Singapore, I can now rest easily that we fully comply with global corporate governance guidelines. Instead of dealing with transactions and documentation, I now spend more than 50% of my time visiting with sales people and external customers."

Chan KK, CFO of SAP Hong Kong, takes up the story on the SSC implementation itself: *"We've been working with the Singapore center for more than two years. During the implementation, we needed to pay attention to the human issues because people the world over are naturally resistant to change, and Hong Kong was no exception! We had to make it clear that the SSC initiatives were designed to transform the roles of individuals, not to eliminate their jobs entirely, and that the process would open up new career development opportunities."*

At the country level the CFOs can now focus on decision support and performance management, as well as being strategic business partners to the CEO.

Colin Sampson continues from the regional headquarters perspective:
We started the implementation process with a feasibility study by external consultants, then we established our process improvement and cost benchmarks, and settled on Singapore as our choice of location. Our subsequent approach to implementation planning was as follows:

- *Not "big bang"!*
- *Start with "bite sizes," and learn from experiences along the way.*
- *Get quick wins.*

Benefits

We took a phased approach, starting with the HR processes country by country then moving onto finance and administrative support. Some five years on – have we achieved our objectives? Well, we've achieved a 40% reduction in cost, and a similar reduction in head count. So it has been cost effective. We've also managed to contain our administrative costs in preparation for our next wave of rapid growth, for example, in China. We're now doing more work than ever before, but we're doing it with less staff than we had because we're more efficient. A double benefit!

But perhaps the biggest benefit has been improved corporate governance and in establishing best-practice processes across the region. We have consistency across our systems and transactions, we have improved our controls for the independent "checks and balances," and have levers we can pull at the center – for example, in complying with SOX 404 and US GAAP.

We also find we have greater transparency in terms of the quality and timeliness of financial and management information. Our CFOs in the region are able to work with me more efficiently and effectively, particularly in relation to risk management. There was also one unexpected benefit – the SSC in Singapore is used as a showcase for our new prospects and existing customers, and provides a centerpiece for customer dialog and briefings.

Inside the SAP finance function we use our own software! We run one global system and have only one database, so we have one version of the truth, with real-time data update and access all over the SAP world. Not only do we use the SAP financials modules, but also those for customer and supply chain management. So we now have the management information available to us in finance for fully integrated decision support, including the budgeting and forecasting processes.

Implementation challenges

With hindsight, Singapore was certainly the right choice. Nevertheless, we still faced many challenges owing to the diverse cultures of the countries we serve, and the differing legal and tax requirements. Another issue: the relatively long travel distances from one part of the region to another, and the variation in time zones – up to 7.5 hours!

Some of the challenges we faced at the outset:

- *Resistance to change – a lack of cooperation from some countries; the required information not given to the SSC; insufficient knowledge transfer of local requirements and regulations.*
- *Business processes not in place – those in-country processes which were supposed to be in place, and in fact were not!*
- *Local culture – so many different cultures were involved that this could affect the business processes being implemented; there was some resistance to reduction in headcount and ownership conflicts.*
- *Local legal requirement – the SSC needed to have knowledge of the local direct and indirect taxes in all 12 countries.*
- *Lack of resources –dedicated people were required.*

Nevertheless, the implementation has been successful and one of the first jobs was to set up a service-level agreement that was acceptable to all parties with an appropriate charging mechanism.

Learning points
So what have been the implementation learning points? Well, change management and communication are at the top of my list. You have to get top-level management buy-in early, build the case for change up front with accurate base lines, and communicate to death! Plan well and engage line managers affected from the start. Be transparent in your dealings with all concerned, particularly in terms of the hard objectives of the SSC implementation and the likely realities of rollout. Don't forget to change the compensation, rewards, and recognition systems for both the SSC staff and the finance teams remaining in-country.

Finally, it's important to think big: the bigger the scope the better. Set aggressive targets and don't get stuck with small issues. Keep the implementation momentum going and don't lose focus, since true transformation can take a number of years to deliver fully. Shared services is all about process redesign, not just operational consolidation and cost cutting!

What was unique about doing this in Asia Pacific? Building strong rapport and mutual understanding with our subsidiaries in the various countries; minimizing, where we could the impact of the cultural and language barriers; and most importantly, recognizing that all this takes time.

As SAP's experience in Asia Pacific shows, shared services are not about steady-state service delivery; they are about constant evolution spanning many years. As such, they represent one of the most challenging and unique environments in which to operate. Change comes quickly and in many forms as you navigate your way to powerful results. Along the way, the most common pitfalls you'll face are:

1 People do not understand the pressure to change.

2 Executives are not equipped to manage the process of change.

3 Lack of a coherent vision undermines long-term benefits.

4 Underestimating the enormous communication required.

5 Too narrow a focus, obscuring obstacles from executive line-of-sight.

6 Long-term goals shift focus away from short-term wins.

7 Changes are not assimilated into the corporate culture.

8 Victory is declared too soon!

Consider further what's happening elsewhere in the world of SAP: Europe is following quickly on the heels of the Asian experience!

SHARED SERVICES IN EUROPE
Peter David, CFO Germany, SAP

In the Europe, Middle East and Africa (EMEA) region, we also needed to address the cost issue since we are operating in a number of large, mature country-based markets with high labor costs, for example, Germany. But also, like Asia, we wanted to address the issue of standardization and highly comparable quality since we also operate in a number of immature markets such as Africa and Central and Eastern Europe.

Initially, we had to survey the potential countries where we could site our EMEA SSC. We chose Prague, based on the factors of proximity, language and culture, and cost. Our primary focus was to improve process efficiency and quality by automating wherever possible – for example, in electronic self-billing, using web services, and automating payment of purchase invoices. We also used process benchmarks to evaluate the potential opportunities for process cost improvement and to drive towards standard best practices.

We're still at an early stage, having launched our SSC implementation in Switzerland, and then moved to our German subsidiary and SAP AG headquarters, and some other selected countries. The European-wide rollout should be complete by 2008. Depending on the size of the subsidiaries, we're using either a process-by-process migration or a one-time approach. One of the main learnings from the first wave of the SSC implementation in Europe has been to ensure that a number of key best-practice processes are in place first in the individual countries, prior to migration to the SSC.

As a first step, our approach to finance shared services so far in Germany has been to transfer the purchase-to-pay and travel and entertainment expense accounting processes to the SSC. Subsequently, this will be extended to a wide range of transactional processes. Fortunately, we've been able to redeploy most of the staff affected by the first wave of the SSC migration to other jobs. But we work very closely on people issues with the Workers Council and employ a very sophisticated approach to change management, staff consultation, and HR support.

The next step for us in Germany is to migrate the order-to-cash, training and consulting billing, and general accounting. In addition to finance, the scope also includes specific HR and payroll processes.

The financial skills now required in the German subsidiary have changed and will continue to change as a result of the SSC implementation. My vision is to have more people capable of providing decision support to marketing and sales. For example, my role with external customers, as the local country CFO, is growing to include decision support, customer contract negotiations, internal revenue recognition issues, and presenting to customers our own software as used internally as an example of best practice.

Although finance shared services begins, as in the case of SAP, with the handing over to a shared services organization factory-like processes such as invoice matching, it's now moving up the value chain, and in some cases migrating to an outsource supplier. A recent survey[2] from the Shared Services and BPO (Business Process Outsourcing) Association reveals, based on a survey of 170 large companies worldwide, that corporations plan to expand their routine finance shared services and outsourcing to include more technical activities. Survey results are shown in Figure 8.4.

In late 2003, for example, GlaxoSmithKline (GSK) uprooted its UK financial shared services center and moved it to India. In 2005, it handed over off-shore operations – including processes such as accounts payable, inter-company and financial reporting, payroll, and travel expenses – to Genpact, GE's BPO unit in India. GSK decided that these services could be provided at a lower cost while maintaining current service standards.

Compliance is one of the key factors influencing the trend towards the expansion of shared services and outsourcing. To achieve global compliance, companies seek to take advantage of an outsourcer's methodolo-

Function	Shared Services (%)		Outsourcing (%)	
	Now	In 12 Months	Now	In 12 Months
Accounts payable	50	55	11	19
Accounts receivable	42	51	9	15
Budgeting	14	16	2	3
Cost accounting	21	29	2	8
Collections	36	42	9	15
Credit	32	39	3	10
Customer Billing	29	36	7	10
External reporting	20	25	5	9
Fixed assets	40	44	3	13
Strategic planning support	13	17	1	5
Tax accounting	29	34	8	15
Tax planning	18	23	7	11

Number of companies surveyed

Figure 8.4 *Finance shared services & outsourcing trends survey*

gies, to have processes, controls and systems better documented, and to have services such as management of the general ledger and inter-company reporting within a specialist shared service center.

However, for many finance chiefs, the idea of relinquishing control of even low-level finance processes is one with which they struggle – mostly because of the perceived difficulty of achieving suitable management oversight and control from a distance. Add to that the fear of valuable data falling into competitors' hands, the erosion of in-house knowledge, and the possible degradation of service levels during the handover – and the whole proposition can seem too risky.

CREATING A WORLDWIDE CENTER

In helping companies make the shift to shared services, we've found that implementation usually follows one of three paths:

1 Shared services are implemented within a *country* or a single business unit.

2 Some SSCs, like SAPs, are *regional* – processes are shared for all business units across a continental theater.

3 Some companies are even more adventurous – they go *global*, establishing a single shared service center for all business units in all regional locations.

Finance processes in most organizations remain part of a spider's web of connections between different departments, and there are practical difficulties in decoupling even repetitive transactional processes, such as accounts receivable. Nevertheless, world-class companies are constantly looking afresh at the options open to them, delving into the process metrics and the economics of off-shoring and outsourcing, and asking the questions: is this process of competitive advantage to me? What's the best way to do it? Should it be done within a business unit, in corporate headquarters, in shared service centers on-shore or off-shore or outsourced?

Consider next how Diageo is developing its finance shared services by going truly global, with one shared service center worldwide. Consider also its decisions on what to insource, what to outsource, and where to locate activities.

GOING TRULY GLOBAL
Ray Joy, Global Head of Finance Shared Services, Diageo

The biggest change in our recent history took place in the late 1990s when we merged the old Guinness business with that of Grand Metropolitan to form Diageo, a truly global premium alcoholic drinks business with brands in just about every country in the world. Since then, we've made selective acquisitions of drinks brands from companies such as Seagrams.

Following the formation of Diageo, we found that, although we had great brands and people, we also had inherited a legacy of woefully inadequate processes and systems. To operate effectively, on a global scale, we invested in new processes and systems, specifically a global SAP platform, to drive our brands forward, cut costs, and improve control. Organizationally, we took some back-office functions, particularly finance, and set up shared services. But shared services were only going to work when we had common processes and systems, along with simplified business models.

Moving to shared services has also required conviction and commitment from the whole organization, from the top to the bottom! We've been fortunate to have the full support of senior management, led by the Chief Executive and the CFO, for our global agenda. So it's not been a question of "if" we move processes from a certain location, but a question of "when."

We chose Budapest as the site for what has become our global shared services center. Why? At the time, labor costs were relatively low and there was a strong financial case based on the labor arbitrage. But even more important, we were impressed by the caliber of the young and relatively highly skilled workforce and we have not been disappointed with the results. We are a big employer now in Budapest; we benefit significantly in having the critical mass and local reputation to attract the best people, and from the Hungarian government's support for training and development.

Process scope
We migrated our first country-based finance operation, the UK, into this center in 2002. We moved the accounts payable, order-to-cash, and reporting processes to Budapest at the same time as we implemented SAP – a major step for us.

In the shared service center (SSC), we've started by including the following four core finance processes:

- *Purchase-to-pay:* paying the bills.
- *Order-to-cash:* order entry, invoicing, and collections.
- *Record-to-report:* general ledger and accounting.
- *Data management:* definitions and control.

This process coverage has been extended to budgeting and forecasting. In the next year, it will also cover large parts of our centralized accounts consolidation and financial reporting. Today, we have 430 people in the Budapest SSC.

The critical success factor in making the SSC concept work was to build confidence and form the right relationships in the country-based marketing and sales organizations. On the one hand, it's an attractive proposition to have taken off their hands routine finance processes, which are an administrative burden; on the other hand, the business managers in the markets do not want to put their relationships with customers and suppliers at risk.

We now have a more sustainable approach for our finance interactions with key customers. The underlying business process framework is now more robust, as it is standardized on SAP, and uses best practices and one global SSC platform.

We've also managed to get hard cash benefits, not only with salary savings but also in improving process effectiveness – for example, in the order-to-cash process we've reduced our average days sales outstanding (DSO) in the GB market to 24 days.

There have also been benefits in terms of internal control – in complying with SOX, in bringing together accounting responsibilities under one SSC "roof," in reducing the number of process "hand-offs" between locations, and in reducing the amount of inter-company accounts reconciliation. The external auditors and the audit committee prefer dealing with one SSC on a number of issues too.

Management model
As far as corporate governance is concerned, we have an SSC operating committee that includes not only myself and the SSC manager, but also the representative leaders of the country markets affected and key finance executives from our London headquarters.

Our staff in the Budapest center have strong linguistic skills – they speak over 24 different languages. We've also been able to recruit a Hungarian general manager to run it and he brings many local leadership and management advantages.

Of course, running an SSC such as this is quite a management challenge. The SSC manager is not a finance expert, but has quite a broad and relevant background in our industry, and is very experienced in negotiating, managing, and handling staffing issues. He has the necessary industry experience to deal successfully with the country-based marketing and sales teams – and to "liberate" them from routine financials, freeing them to concentrate on what they do best – driving the brands and enhancing the top-line.

We're quite proud of the fact that out of the total of more than 400 employees in the SSC only five are ex-pats from other countries. The rest are Hungarians. Terms and conditions of employment are consistent across the group and the SSC staff is fully incorporated into Diageo's corporate-wide people development agenda. I am delighted to note that at least ten of our SSC Hungarian employees have now moved out of Budapest to take on other more personally challenging roles elsewhere in the world of Diageo – making this a great example of how the SSC fits into the company as a whole.

Going truly global

Once you're established in a proven, successful SSC location, as we are in Budapest, you're in a much stronger position to move shared services from other parts of the world. When you can rely on the available pool of talent, and when the control environment is stable, then it's only a matter of dealing with time zone differences.

Not only have we focused our European shared services in the Budapest location, we've also transferred our North American processes there, as well as parts of our business from Africa and Asia Pacific, including all of Australia. We operate an afternoon/evening shift to service the North American time zone. This makes it a truly global SSC.

This migration from North America also happened quite conveniently at a time when we were making other organizational changes there, such as relocating our head offices. The shift has proven remarkably successful.

We're actively exploring extending the scope of the SSC to processes such as HR, supply chain, and logistics. We're also considering moving in our Central and Latin

American operations. The benefits case cannot always be justified in labor cost savings – for example, from Mexico to Budapest – but it can be justified in terms of improved internal controls, particularly for our smaller countries.

The SSC journey doesn't just stop in Budapest. Ultimately, for example, with certain Asian countries such as Japan, we are going to experience language skill limitations. So we're always open to new ideas on where to go and how to get there, and ever mindful of the risks we're taking.

As companies fine-tune their approaches, feedback about what works and what doesn't is accumulating. Today, some trends[3] are emerging:

Shared services are increasing in scope

- Economies of scale are achieved by bringing more countries and business units into the fold.
- More processes are included, such as IT, finance, human resource management, procurement, and customer relationship management (CRM).

Shared service centers are shrinking in size

- Better technology, less human intervention, and greater speed are close to making "lights-out processing" a reality.
- Collaborative relationships, like the Renault–Nissan alliance, are increasing as process specialists move beyond corporate boundaries.

Businesses are being pushed toward greater flexibility

- Companies are being driven to quickly decide whether to perform services internally or to outsource them.
- Companies have to move faster to absorb new acquisitions and handle disposals.

Businesses are working hard to drive down investment and operating costs

- Using new technology to process transactions in lowest-cost locations.

- Partnering with suppliers, customers, and possibly competitors, to share non-strategic support services.

To exploit the full opportunities offered by global scale and labor arbitrage, should companies outsource their finance processes or not? In the US, more than 75% of the Fortune 500 have initiatives under way to outsource a broad range of business support services. But outsourcing generally works well only for carefully selected non-core processes. We find that companies often hesitate to run the risks associated with outsourcing. They fear losing control or getting locked into using a single supplier, particularly for critical areas such as finance.

Outsourcing experiences vary enormously – when it works well, it works wonders! Firms typically reap cost reductions of 30% or more, along with improved service. No wonder the outsourcing industry has doubled in size in less than five years. What's more, outsourcing is expected to continue growing as firms outsource not just information technology, but also entire business processes.

However, only very few take the outsourcing plunge. Most companies, like Diageo, prefer to operate their own shared service centers, and realize the benefits for themselves of siting their shared service centers in strategic, low-cost locations.

SEAMLESS SUPPORT: NEAR-SHORE OR OFF-SHORE?

Choosing where to go can be quite a daunting proposition. Over the past few years, various locations, such as Budapest and Prague in the Diageo and SAP examples and more recently, China and India, have become favorites. Why, exactly, are near-shore and off-shore locations becoming more popular for shared services and outsourcing? Among the most critical factors[4] are:

- **Skilled manpower availability:** India, for example, has the second largest English-speaking workforce and the largest higher education system in the world.

- **Multilingual proficiency:** Diageo's service center in Budapest, for example, offers 24 languages. In Shanghai, one service center offers 17 languages.

- **Highly motivated employees:** Labor arbitrage, surging productivity, and higher quality levels are all having a profound impact. Centers are attracting better educated, strongly motivated employees who, as in Diageo's case, see outsourcing as a career path.

- **Favorable government policies:** These include tax concessions, telecom deregulation, patent protection, and better policing of software and intellectual property piracy.

- **Improvements in telecom infrastructure:** Bandwidth is increasing and costs are plummeting; cheaper, more efficient internet technologies are now available.

The results of a survey showing sample countries' relative location attractiveness against local cost and capabilities are highlighted in Figure 8.5.

As results indicate, India's abundant skilled manpower is making it increasingly attractive as a target destination for many multinationals. A cautionary note: care should always be exercised when evaluating location studies, given the rapidly evolving shared services and outsourcing landscape. Factors to consider should include not only prevailing labor cost, skills, and business environment, but also the socio-geopolitical risk, time zone displacement, and local culture.

Consider next the shared services location experience of a senior finance executive of a leading multi-national corporation, who wished to remain anonymous, headquartered in North America.

SEAMLESS SUPPORT
The world is flat

In the context of our company the world truly is flat! Today, we are able to move a transaction seamlessly to any part of the globe. Technology provides you with the opportunity to create a platform where work can be handled, more cheaply and efficiently than ever before, from anywhere in the world. The components of a trading transaction may be disaggregated, analyzed, delivered, distributed, produced,

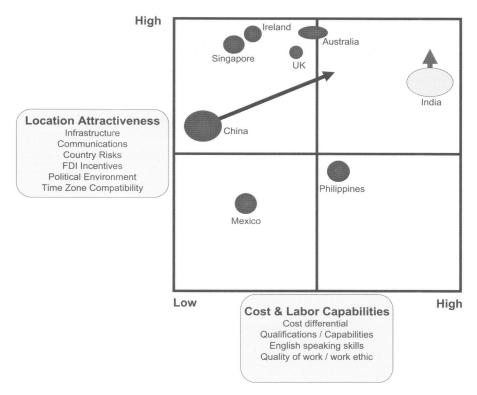

Figure 8.5 *Country attractiveness matrix*

and put back together again simultaneously across Europe, the Americas, and Asia Pacific.

Take, for example, a supplier's transaction. The goods will be entered in the system as having been received by one of our European factories; the payment is rendered from a different location – one of our off-shore shared service centers handling global supply transactions; the payroll for the people involved will be paid from a different location that specializes in payroll accounting; the support for the contract administration will be provided by a third facility; and the price paid will be validated in yet another country across the Atlantic! All the different pieces of this particular transaction are splintered all over the world and integrated quickly, seam-

lessly, and accurately utilising our global technology capability. And for the parties to the transaction all would be completely transparent!

Shared services network

Several years ago, we set out our strategy to leverage our enterprise systems, mainly on an Oracle platform, with fewer large global instances of Oracle in our shared service centers (SSCs) around the world. Recently, we've consolidated virtually all of our transaction processing into these shared service centers – which also include customer service, IT, and support.

We have a network of these off-shore center locations – the key ones being strategically located in the major world time corridors. The key criteria we used for selecting the right off-shore location were: labor cost, quality and availability, language skills, political risk, communications infrastructure, telecommunications, and office facilities. And I'm pleased to say that the talent pools in our chosen SSC locations have been more than adequate in providing staff of the requisite quality.

Most of the efficiencies come from moving from a relatively decentralized environment to one that is modularized around the key processes in the enterprise. At the same time, similar to other firms with overseas operations, we've benefited from the labor cost arbitrage between locations.

Some of these new SSC locations were "green field" sites for us. We had very little in the way of pre-existing company operations there – not much existing capability and knowledge to leverage. So it was quite a challenge during the initial set-up of the infrastructure. Asia was particularly challenging for us in terms of change management – we had more than 15 accounting and finance support offices, all in different locales, which we consolidated into the SSCs. Despite having Oracle across Asia, there are also business model and statutory considerations that hinder full commonality and uniform standards.

Progress on standardization

The next challenge is standardizing our processes across geographies, across and within our various business units. It was a huge chore initially just getting everything consolidated in the SSCs, and we've still not completed 100% of that program. As we approach the point of having everything under the one "SSC roof," we have to capitalize on the opportunity to simplify our processes and really benefit from the increased scale.

So, we made the decision we were going to run the finance function on a global process basis and this process development effort for putting our accounting under a common umbrella continues today and into the future. Increasingly, we are looking at the differences in what we do and selecting the best practices.

Where to cut the process?

On a global process, we have process lead directors – for fixed assets, inter-company accounting, banking and cash, cost and account management, general ledger, and financial. Each has a small number of staff that provide a pool of expertise. The directors' job is to provide process leadership across the network – setting the standards, ensuring compliance, and providing expert support on a worldwide basis.

When deciding how to delineate the accounting processes for SSC inclusion purposes, we carried out a portability analysis. One of the criteria for selection was the need for proximity to the frontline business operations – the elements of the processes that could be physically distant from the business operations were relocated in the SSCs. Time zone changes and their consequential impact on operations and transactions were another major consideration.

At the end of the day, the critical decisions on what to put in the off-shore service centers boiled down to risk assessment. A major part of this risk consideration was the retention of institutional knowledge transfer. For example, we had a lot of institutional knowledge built up in North America in our Toronto and Phoenix centers. If the knowledge transfer challenge was too great we left the process where it was, therefore avoiding unnecessary disruption to our business support continuity.

Decision support

*As a result, from an accounting process standpoint, what we have **inside** the SSCs are generic corporate accounting and related transaction processing – that which resides in the general ledger, and everything up to and including production of the financial statements. **Outside** the SSCs are the decision support and analysis functions needed on the ground on a daily basis.*

We thought it more important from a "value-add" viewpoint to co-locate the decision support where it provides the in-country sales and manufacturing units with a unique and tailored service for the individual product lines. For example, the nature of management information analysis and interpretation required for the foods business, covering our domestic client, is so specialized that the detailed decision support has to be embedded in the business. So management reporting, budgeting, forecasting, and performance monitoring are carried out locally and reports through the local business controllers to the group business controllers.

At the same time, these decision support activities also offer opportunities for standardization and process improvements. Ongoing efforts continue to transfer "portable" activities into the SSCs so that financial analysts who are co-located with operations can focus on developments that are higher value-added to management. These analysts – multi-disciplinary, not just finance but manufacturing and marketing skilled too – remain in-country and are expected to broaden and deepen their skills base around core business processes.

The virtual business

We treat our SSC network as a virtual business – the finance function effectively rents its space in the SSC locations, along with other functions such as HR, procurement, customer service, and IT. Every function, such as headquarters finance services, has its own budgets, performance metrics, and account responsibilities. We charge out each function's costs to the business lines according to service level agreements.

Arguably, the creation of this shared services organization was one of the largest single change management endeavours that our corporation has recently undertaken. Today approximately 40% of our total finance staff worldwide and ultimately >15% of the entire company's workforce will be employed in our SSCs. We've replenished hundreds of jobs with new people with different demographics and skills. When we started, I said to my people that we needed to think of it as building a new enterprise. We had to put in place all the building blocks that you would normally need for a new, successful, and growing financial services sector in our group portfolio.

We did have the advantage, of course, that most start-ups don't have, of leveraging the parent organization – our company's core values, policy and procedural frameworks, group financing, and our sheer scale. Aside from this, from the beginning I tried to inculcate an entrepreneurial business mindset to the set-up of the infrastructure – finding the facilities, recruiting, training, and assimilating the workforce – to a commercial, structured, methodological approach to the ongoing support services management.

What are the learning points? We've benefited from very disciplined and strong project management. Sufficiently long lead times for planning the implementation and comprehensive, well planned change management programs are also distinguishing characteristics of a successful shared services implementation. At no point were we willing to compromise our traditionally very high standards of accounting integrity and control – or indeed, the corporate values and culture.

If at any time we felt we were about to take short cuts that were going to compromise us, we said: "Stop! Slow down! Let's do this properly." And we made mid-course adjustments.

We've also been flexible in taking advantage of unexpected opportunities as they've presented themselves when relocating a process into a SSC. How much further could we go down the process continuum? We continue to learn each day as the components of our business are broken down and analyzed through process mapping. The correlation and number of interface dependencies that we've identified with our core accounting processes have been amazing. As a result, we continue to discover new opportunities for repositioning and capitalizing on the scale and efficiencies of the SSCs.

Controls and compliance

The evolution of shared services has the added benefit of generally improving overall controls. From an enterprise-wide viewpoint, process standardization undoubtedly makes control easier and we've seen evidence of that already in our own assessments and audit work. The capability to implement systemic improvements across the enterprise has been enhanced with the maturing of the SSCs.

There are also some benefits from a compliance testing viewpoint – for example, SOX 404. With global processes, the number of test points is minimized, and a higher reliance on process design vs. transaction testing can result. Simply stated, you minimize your exposures to variability, thereby improving adherence to compliance standards and statutory requirements.

New skills

All this change has meant a re-focusing of the skills we require for the finance function, especially in accounting. A global orientation is paramount – in the past you would be responsible for a finance process, such as purchase ledger, for a specific country or a region within a business line. Today, you would take a cross-business line, multi-national viewpoint. The implications of any process or system changes now have to be thought through on an enterprise basis and this requires a very different mind-set. Oracle is a highly integrated platform and the implications of any changes often transcend several modules and many locations.

Process thinking – cross-functional, end-to-end – is also very different from the finance activity-based approach we used to take. The bank accounting process today, for example, impacts not only what we do in treasury for cash forecasting, but with customer service and the customers themselves, for monitoring credit and accounts receivable, and also with the banks themselves.

The ability to network has also become very important. Our senior finance executives quite often have to work off the formal organization chart through informal networks to influence on the case for change and to get things done. IT plays a significant part in making this networking happen – not only have we standardized on the one Oracle platform, but we're also investing heavily in "middleware" with tools for collaboration, instant messaging, net meetings, and portals.

The people management skills are changing too – because we've replenished our human capital stock with younger, technologically savvy staff, their motivation and career aspirations are different. The leadership of this new workforce must keep the staff "challenged and engaged," creating multiple career opportunities with substantial lateral personal development, thereby improving retention. Bringing more functions into the shared services unit also creates such new opportunities – moving people seamlessly between accounting and the other functions.

A personal viewpoint on the future

Increasingly we are seeing the potential in a number of "interface" points between the functions resident in the SSCs. Such "interface" points exist in the overlap of the business processes, the functions involved, and the supporting Oracle systems; for example, between finance and procurement, between finance and HR, and between finance and customer service. There are also "interface" points in the co-ordination and career development of the people working in the physical centers.

One can view the shared service center as a free-standing line of business. From my past experience in this and other companies, there seem to me to be four key major business segments that lend themselves to this concept:

1 *Transaction processing*
2 *Customer service*
3 *IT support*
4 *Speciality services.*

I would call the four potential aggregations the next generation of shared services – new seamless support functions and disciplines. Each demands a high degree of process integration, standard system enablers and platforms, customer orientation, and common skill sets.

In transaction processing, for example, there are enough synergies and commonalities in the management of finance, procurement, HR, and IT to run it as one business function. You could optimize on process efficiency, staff costs, training, and system platform enhancements. Similarly there are sizeable potential benefits of bringing external customer service activities under one umbrella organization – common processes, skills, and customer relationship executives. IT support, in this context, would include IT helpdesk, maintenance, telecommunications, and property management services. Speciality services – for example, product configuration and manufacturing support – are also candidates for shared services and other companies related to our industry sector are quite a way down this path. Standardization of speciality and basic support activities on a worldwide basis is bound to yield sizeable economic benefits.

CONNECTIVITY THROUGH TECHNOLOGY

In his book *The World is Flat*, Thomas Friedman summarizes ten forces that are reshaping the world including outsourcing, open sourcing, insourcing, and wireless technology. The net result of these ten flattening forces: the creation of a global, web-enabled playing field that enables multiple forms of collaboration – the sharing of knowledge and work – in real time, without regard to geography, distance or language.

Friedman refers to a triple convergence:

1 **A new playing field** (global web-enabled platform).

2 **New ways of doing business** (processes and habits for horizontal collaboration).

3 **New players** (China, India, and Russia and Central Europe).

All this is likely to naturally foster new business practices that are less about command and control and more about connecting and collaborating horizontally. As a result, we are likely to see further growth in shared services and *the trend towards a truly global, multidisciplinary support service.*

At the most recent World Economic Forum in Davos, the theme of Governance and Globalization for the 21st century was debated by Thomas Friedman and Bill Gates, Chairman of Microsoft. Among the issues they discussed were the connectivity between innovation and technology as well as the rapid growth of the economies in India and China.

Clearly, technology has the power to transform industries and the way that business is done around the globe. Leading companies are already tapping that power: *rethinking* business strategies, processes, and management practices; *reshaping* companies and cultures; *recasting* infrastructures and product portfolios – and, most importantly, achieving exceptional business results.

We conclude this chapter by looking at how Microsoft is using technology to innovate and make change happen inside its business – and how it plays its part in *flattening the world*. In his book *Business @ the Speed of Thought*,[5] Bill Gates talks about the power of technology *inside* Microsoft:

> "Our internal tools have two goals: to use software to do routine tasks, eliminating wasted time and energy for our knowledge workers; and to free people up to do more difficult work and handle exceptions. The successful companies of the next decade will be the ones that use digital tools to reinvent the way they work."

Paul Hart, the UK CFO of Microsoft, talks about how the company is using its own technology in its finance processes.

SHOWCASING OUR SELF-SERVICE AND CONNECTIVITY
Paul Hart, UK CFO, Microsoft

Microsoft maximizes the efficient use of technology in running our organization. In fact, we effectively "eat our own dog-food" – everything we do inside Microsoft, every day, incorporates the technology we sell to the outside world. We like to think we're the first and most extensive users of the company's products.

Over the last decade or so, we've had our fair share of business challenges:

- *Our business model is constantly evolving – we work in a world where technologies, markets, and competitors are constantly changing.*
- *We've experienced rapid growth, and made numerous acquisitions.*
- *We work in an increasingly global business environment.*
- *And yet, like so many other companies with numerous diverse and non integrated legacy systems, we want to take advantage of rapidly changing technologies – always a moving target!*

Over the years, our finance function has evolved in the face of constant pressures to increase efficiency and reduce cost. In the past, we had disparate business systems, a general lack of worldwide revenue information, and were hampered by an inability to track people and positions. We also had hundreds of paper forms, far too many hard-copy financial reports, and excessive resources focused on transaction processing.

Today, Microsoft has a single financial transaction system worldwide. We have consistent business policies and processes, and key financial and operating metrics are available in real time, including:

- *revenue and inventory by product, customer, location, channel;*
- *headcount and personnel details worldwide; and*
- *transaction cost details.*

All financial reports are distributed electronically and are available four days following the month-end. Virtually all our procurement is processed electronically and all employee services are web based.

We've configured our finance organization, people, and processes to take advantage of best practices in areas such as online collaboration, employee self-service, portals, and query tools. This approach has enabled our company to implement shared services on a standardized process and technology platform, freeing up finance resources for business partnering and adding value.

Greater empowerment, less detail

Microsoft is a pretty complex business with a matrix organization – global product divisions on one dimension and country-based subsidiaries focused on specific customer segments on the other.

Three main product divisions – Platforms and Server Division, Microsoft Business Division, and Entertainments and Devices Division – are, in turn, divided into seven business groups as illustrated in Figure 8.6.

All these divisions have very different strategic and operating characteristics, but they share one standard P&L format, use the same general ledger, and have one set of account codes. Additionally, we follow standard processes for measuring revenue, analyzing costs, and monitoring headcount.

My own role as UK CFO has also broadened over the last few years. In some respects, the role is more of a COO because of my involvement in advising the UK General Manager on strategic decisions concerning our business model, resource deployment, and discretionary investment.

The processes for resource allocation have also changed. In the past, subsidiaries around the world submitted to headquarters their budget proposals and investments for the forthcoming year. Now, because we are more centralized, our targets are set by the center and are cascaded down to the subsidiaries.

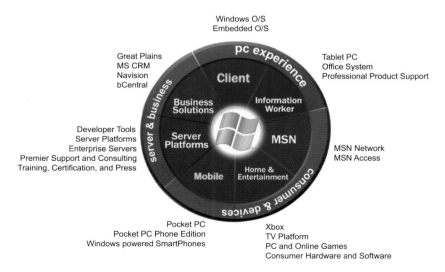

Figure 8.6 *Microsoft's seven business groups*

At the same time, today, we are much more empowered locally – our top-line and bottom-line targets are agreed with headquarters, but what happens in between is down to local discretion. During the year, subsidiaries are empowered to invest in manpower and marketing campaigns, subject to meeting – or beating – our hard overall revenue and profit-margin targets. We have considerable discretion now in what we spend to drive both top-line growth and bottom-line profitability.

Decision support in the subsidiaries is therefore more strategic and much less tactical. This imposes far greater responsibility on the finance function to control, understand, and interpret the numbers. Today, I spend 80% of my time on revenues and only 20% on costs.

Consequently, the detailed budget is less important, but the forecast is king! The forecast is driving the business. We're measuring the business against it all the time and with ever-increasing granularity. We now have much greater intelligence around the levers driving our forecasting.

Whilst we continue to provide a forecast every month, there is far greater detail and scrutiny of our quarterly forecast. Our goal is two-fold: first, to focus our dialogue with the center on the bigger financial picture and second, to synchronize more effectively with Wall Street's expectations. We maintain a regular rhythm of interaction between business units and headquarters – we call it "rhythm of the business." Through a series of structured conference calls across the breadth and depth of the organization, the people at our headquarters are kept in touch with the people on the ground.

In the UK, our finance function is very concerned with providing decision support on revenues. We're known as the "custodians of data," not just in terms of the way we report accounting results, but in our forward-looking view of the revenue pipeline, and in our real-time forecasting and analysis of our revenue position. We've substantially increased our finance headcount in the revenue area because of the positive impact we have had on field decision-making.

Freeing up our people

In our country subsidiaries, only a small proportion of employees are directly involved in the finance function. In the UK, for example, we employ approximately 2,000 Microsoft employees and only 22 of them are directly involved in the finance function. With the rollout of shared service centers and outsourcing of low value add activities, local finance employees are free to focus on the higher value aspects of providing finance advice and support. I believe we have now reached a stage in the UK where members of our finance staff are seen as true business partners.

ERPs have a reputation for being difficult to use. At Microsoft, we've overcome this problem by developing our own systems and using our own tool-kit. In particular, three key state-of-the-art self-service applications – Headtrax, MS Market, and MS Expense.

These unique front-end tools really do leverage the full power of our ERP investment, making the systems exceptionally user-friendly and virtually paperless. The result: the worldwide cost of Microsoft's finance function is in the upper quartile of the benchmarks set by other high-performing companies – substantially less than 1% of revenue. Figure 8.7 shows the cost of processing transactions and savings achieved.

Each of the three key finance applications, the heart of our finance controls and operations, are described briefly below:

- *Headtrax is our tool for tracking headcount and managing personnel data real time. This intranet application displays headcount information around the Microsoft world and around the clock – providing full analysis of the status of employees. Direct integration with our ERP systems eliminates redundant data entry, ensures data integrity, and consolidates different databases.*
- *MS Market is the procurement tool we use for placing and approving orders, and, when linked with MS Invoice, for processing purchase invoices. This enables employees to place orders via the intranet and facilitates online approvals. Purchase invoices are either scanned into the system or received directly from suppliers in electronic form. Figure 8.8 illustrates the Microsoft procurement process.*
- *MS Expense is our system for online processing of employee expense claims, providing real-time employee validation and error checking upon claim submission. This application has achieved significant annual cost savings and reduced employee reimbursement turnaround times.*

We've empowered our employees with these and other self-service applications, so they can focus on the jobs they're really paid to do. If a self-service process can't be achieved in less than three minutes – we call it "the 3 minute rule" – then we go back

Metric (Worldwide)	Purchases (MS Market)	Invoices (MS Invoice)	Expense Reports (MS Expense)
Cost per Transaction Impact	$15 to $5 per order ($60 to $17 per PO)	$8 to $2 per invoice ($30 to $5, excluding EI)	$21 to $10 per expense report
Savings – Annual	$7.3 million	$9.6 million	$3.3 million
Savings – Cumulative	$18 million	$20 million	$9 million
Transaction Volume (annually)	400,000 orders	1,100,000 invoices	200,000 expense reports
Transaction Value (annually)	$5 billion	$3.3 billion	$220 million
# of Users (monthly)	11,000	7,000	14,000
# of Countries	48	9	37
% Electronic (US & UK only)	99.8%	90% total	98%

Figure 8.7 *Microsoft finance process productivity metrics*

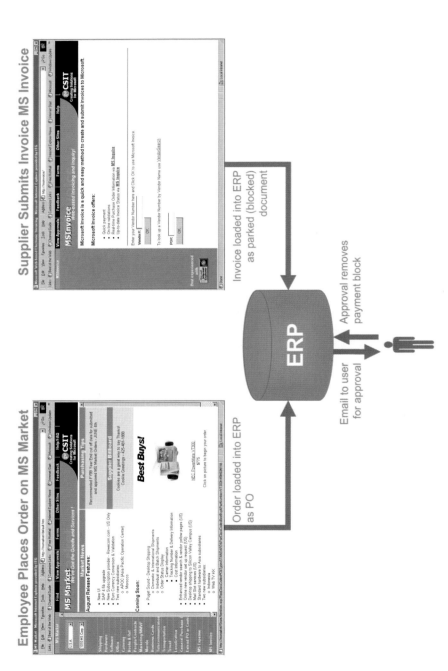

Figure 8.8 *Microsoft procurement process*

and see how we can improve the process further.

Our shared service centers contribute to this efficiency as well. We have one in Dublin for Europe, and two others serving the US and Asia. These centers handle billing, purchase invoicing, expense payment, and the partner rebate process. For example, in the UK we have 35,000 invoices and expenses being processed every year by four people in Dublin with expenses being paid weekly and invoices every month.

Technology showcase

Now we are in a position to showcase to external customers how we use our own technology in our finance function. Every week I am asked to make at least one presentation to external customers – our sales force really recognizes the external value of how we operate internally. Customers are interested in how we maximize the use of technology, our efficiency, and our relatively low-cost business processes.

What they like to see is our tools in action, through live demonstrations. Suddenly, the light bulbs go on! Customers realize that it's not just theory: you can draw upon the data in your ERP and see what's happening in real time.

At Microsoft, we embrace the latest technology and use it wherever we can. Over the last three years or so, personal productivity has massively increased due to the latest round of technologies. We provide our employees with Smartphones, tablet PCs, and broadband at home. It's the inter-connectivity – how we use all these technologies in conjunction with each other – that makes us more productive. For example, I use my Smartphone to check email any time of the day from anywhere in the world. It holds my Outlook diary schedule, my contacts, and email – it duplicates what's on my PC. The beauty of it is in the synchronization: I am always connected to all the material I need to support me for urgent interaction at any time of the day, or night for that matter!

When I come into the office in the morning, I dock my tablet PC and deal with emails like everybody else. I then go to my first meeting, taking my PC with me, and will use One Note – it's the equivalent of carrying a pad of paper with you – to take notes and to refer to notes I've made. From my machine, I can access all my files wherever I am on any of the company's premises since we operate a comprehensive corporate wireless network. Whenever I am working with another Microsoft employee, we're always connected to the same data and working off the same page.

We provide all employees with free broadband access at home and we're now moving to wideband. This will quadruple the speed and capacity of our internet interactions. We will also be introducing 3G Smartphones for use by our employees and this will connect us even more! The benefit of all this technology to the finance function at Microsoft is the flexibility of being able to work away from the office, or elsewhere in the office – not just at your desk.

We test our own technology on ourselves before it's released to customers. By experiencing our own product, not only can we iron out problems in advance, but we have the advantage of operating not only at the edge of technology, but sometimes "over the edge"!

Working for Microsoft means that you have a lot more empowerment and responsibility for decisions as an individual than you would in most other companies. There is a drive to get things done that comes with increased personal autonomy. In finance, you're involved more in business decision-making and business partnering at a much earlier stage in your career. This is all part of our culture and the way we do things.

Undoubtedly all this technology makes us more effective in dealing with ever-increasing workloads and travel requirements. Today, work is always available on demand. But there is always a danger that you are over-connected: that you don't have the time to reflect, meet people physically, and sustain a satisfying work/life balance. Work/life balance is absolutely key to understanding how best to motivate your employees. The best way to do that is to lead, by personal example, with a change in behavior toward a more rewarding and balanced lifestyle.

The CFO would seem to be at the center of the business process revolution. For example, as we've seen from our interviews, CFOs are becoming more heavily involved in supply chain management. The reason: the globalization of supply chains not only builds on the finance executives' experience of shared services and technology, but also presents a dramatic increase in risk.

One survey carried out recently in the UK showed that the average company experiences more than one supply disruption or outage every month. Forward-thinking CFOs are incorporating supply chain strategy into their firms' broader risk management frameworks. Ultimately, successful supply chain management is all about trade-offs – striking a balance between the competing demands of marketing, operations, and the external customer; linking financial and non-financial metrics with the supply chain, tying things together and supporting the business from end to end.

In the past five years, Hewlett Packard has gone from having 87 supply chains – each managed vertically and independently, with its own hierarchy of managers and back-office support – to just 5 supply chains, with functions like accounting, billing, and HR handled through a company-wide system.

Frontline advice for coping with a flattening world:

- As a small company, learn to act big – take advantage of the new tools for collaboration to reach further, faster, wider and deeper. For example, use a global logistics company to get your products to market.

- As a large company, learn to act small – enable your customers to act big. For example, financial services and booksellers are doing business with customers over the Internet.

- Collaborate – the next layers of value creation, whether in technology, marketing, biomedicine or manufacturing, are becoming so complex that no single firm or department is able to master them alone. For example, pharmaceutical giants are now partnering with smaller bio-techs on R&D.

- Constantly reassess your company's strengths – outsource value chain elements that are non-core/non-differentiated.

- Outsource to win, not to shrink – use outsourcing to innovate faster and more cheaply, to grow larger, gain market share, and hire more and different specialists.

STRAIGHT FROM THE CFO

- **Develop global partnerships**

  Put quality of external business partnerships very high on your finance agenda – include them in your plans for shared services, off-shoring, and outsourcing. Stress the role of finance in facilitating win–win relationships and maximizing value for both parties. Share best practices. Standardize on one global set of operating principles, one set of processes and one global IT platform.

- **Stretch the shared service envelope**

  Start by connecting the simpler transaction processes – then go further. Take the quick wins, then move up the value chain. Go beyond your comfort zone, pull back if you have to. Why not include the routine aspects of management information, budgeting and forecasting, and general accounting – even corporate consolidation? Then consider how to expand the finance SSC to embrace other functions such as HR, supply chain and customer management.

- **Create value by outsourcing**

  Consider how you want to improve financial process costs, controls, and transparency. Test your own capabilities to make the change, then contrast with what outside suppliers can offer. Be realistic! Are you prepared to share the potential prize with an outsourcer? How fast do you want to move? How much control are you prepared to relinquish?

- **Go near-shore or off-shore**

  Consider skills and manpower availability, infrastructure, and country risk. Decide where to site your SSC and stick with it! Recruit your management locally, benefit from labor cost arbitrage, but also take the opportunity to standardize on one IT platform.

- **Build a worldwide center**

  Win commitment, from top to bottom! Build the right service-based relationships with your internal customers. Start with one pilot country, extend the SSC to include the first continental region, then take on the others and become *truly* global!

- **Create a new business**

  Set up your global shared services as a business in its own right. Introduce a separate SSC corporate governance and management model. Develop an SSC management discipline and career track. Go for "lights out" processing and make it a competitive advantage.

- Flatten *your world*

  Explore the opportunities for collaboration, reconfiguring your value chain and taking advantage of 1:2:1 connectivity potential across the world. Constantly reassess what should be insourced, what should be outsourced. As CFO, act more like a COO. Exploit opportunities for globally integrating other processes and move towards the seamless *support function of the future!*

REFERENCES

1 Thomas Friedman (2005) *The World is Flat*, Penguin.

2 Shared Services and BPO Association (2005) *Shared Services and Outsourcing Trends*.

3 Cedric Read, Hans-Dieter Scheuermann and the mySAP Financials Team (2003) *The CFO as Business Integrator*, Wiley.

4 Stewart Clements, Michael Donnellan, Cedric Read (2004) *CFO Insights – Achieving High Performance Through Finance Business Process Outsourcing*, Wiley.

5 Bill Gates (1999) *Business @ The Speed Of Thought*, Penguin.

CHAPTER 9

Leveraging Risk and Regulation

Top of the agenda of many CFOs today is the issue of regulation. As every year goes by there's more and more of it and it gets more complex! Changing accounting standards, new regulations for accounting control, industry specific and customer regulatory changes – all this adds up to massive responsibility. Factor in continuing uncertainty in the global economic and political environment, and the result is an ever-expanding risk agenda.

The challenge: how to implement the regulations without disrupting business as usual and at an acceptable level of cost. In some cases, regulation may actually benefit the business. However, the prevailing view is that it is a necessary evil.

Most CFOs dedicate substantial resources to the implementation of new accounting standards and specific legislation, such as Sarbanes-Oxley – and in the banking industry, Basel II. Even so, such regulatory demands often lead to major distortions to a company's published results. This, in turn, can consume even more resources on the presentation and explanation of these results.

The bottom line: top directors dedicate a huge amount of time to this non value-add issue.

Next, we interview CFOs from Spain, the UK, and the USA in the two sectors – telecommunications (telecoms) and financial services – where regulation seems to be particularly intensive. We capture their points of view on the regulatory impact and how they're coping with the additional workload. The case is made by a leading CFO in the insurance industry for dual accounting. The chapter concludes with a look at how some companies are expanding the function of risk management – going enterprise-wide.

THE MISERY OF REGULATION

LIFE BEYOND REGULATION
Santiago Fernandez-Valbuena, CFO Telefonica

Telefonica is lucky to have been based in Spain. Over the last 20 years, regulation hasn't been soft or cozy! Nevertheless, Spain has been a success story in terms of growth. Its leading companies – such as Endesa, Banco Santander, and ourselves – have been heavily involved in the global development of our industry sectors. Today, we're all part of the European mainstream.

In the European telecoms industry, Telefonica has established itself as one of the "big five" and a strong performer. We recently entered the Dow 50 – our market capitalization is US$90 billion. We have a private sector culture, having always been privately owned. We've avoided over-expansion and overstretching our capabilities – unlike some of our competitors in other countries who have a public-sector legacy.

In our industry, the pendulum swings to and fro between expansion (often into non-core businesses) and consolidation (back into our core telecom roots). Today, we have three core strategic pillars:

- *Fixed line telecommunications (Spain).*
- *Mobile telephony.*
- *Latin America.*

We've experienced growth in all our major business lines, except for content and media where we're divesting. We've found expansion abroad in our core businesses to be manageable.

Our very success in our three key core pillars has sometimes led to criticism. Regulators in countries like Argentina and Brazil may have felt that we were making excess profits and that these should be shared with customers and tax authorities. Our response has been that we've invested very heavily in making huge developments and inroads into local telecoms markets. We've had a significant risk appetite, albeit balanced with the rest of the portfolio, and we need the profits to service investors and for reinvestment.

Telecommunications regulation

Industry regulation is well intended, but badly executed. Regulation goes in one direction, the real competitive market in another. Everyone agrees that regulation can be positive and have a beneficial outcome. Unfortunately, if you take regulation in an industry like telecoms, the regulatory agencies can become bureaucratic over time and cease to be as effective as when they were first set up.

We've experienced so much change in technology, in our markets, and in consumer appetites. We now provide broadband services for information and communication. Mobile telephony has become a multi-trillion-dollar business. But regulation has not moved at the same pace, it can slow us down – that's why I call it the "misery of regulation"!

However, regulation has a legitimate role and can be a good thing. Regulations are essential, for example, in curbing the power of natural monopolies. As markets liberalize, there are barriers to entry. Competitors have to emulate the incumbents' market reputation, brand awareness, and service quality to compete successfully. Regulation is the price we have to pay for competitive industries in developed societies. So I'm in favor of it, but I don't think more regulation is necessarily better regulation.

Who regulates the regulators? We invest in other countries, not just Spain, such as Czech Republic and Brazil. Regulatory agencies are not all that different from one country to another. But in countries like Brazil, which is large and geographically segmented, there are extra layers of regulatory complexity – a maze of national, state, and local government regulators!

Multiple standards, multiple listings

In an ideal world, we would have one set of accounting standards and one principal stock exchange listing. But in the real world, we have a "spaghetti" of different standards and stock exchange regulations from country to country. Unfortunately, this does not necessarily mean useful information for investors. It creates additional complexity, which often leads to confusion, misunderstanding, and inefficiency in the world's capital markets.

IFRS is an opportunity missed. What's wrong with IFRS is that it has added to the complexity and the workload of the existing standards, rather than replacing them. There are just too many standards! One day this may change. One set of global standards may prevail, rather like English prevailing as the unofficial world business language. But getting every regulatory authority in every country to agree officially – that's a long way off!

However, I do not share the view that accounting standards get in the way of good business decisions. At the end of the day, IFRS and US GAAP are not that far apart. The change to IFRS has not been too traumatic for us at Telefonica because we've already gone through the reconciling of our accounts under local standards with US GAAP.

Underlying IFRS is a set of very sensible business principles – for example, market and fair value. The resulting business judgments and management decisions, far from damaging the business, can lead you to face up to realities.

Sarbanes-Oxley

I'm not a great fan of SOX. It's rather like a health check – it's something you only should need to do once in a while. Unfortunately we're saddled with a compulsory, onerous, and bureaucratic process which is way out of proportion to the issues it's trying to address. I believe that SOX has led to something of a bureaucratic "underclass" which carries out its work in the name of good regulation but doesn't really add value.

Value creation vs. value distribution

The tension between those who create value in an organization and those who want to extract value has always existed. Telefonica has a great track record in value creation. This has been due, in large part, to growth in our local economy. Stakeholders – be they government, regulators, customers, employees, or investors – all want to take their cut. This "entitlement" culture is all-pervasive.

Reconciling all these different stakeholder objectives can, in an organization like ours, be an industry in itself. It can turn your culture inwards on itself, with a self-serving preoccupation. This blunts the entrepreneurial sharpness of the management edge. If left unbridled, it can lead to value destruction.

One of the symptoms of such a culture is an excessive number of management layers. At Telefonica, with 180,000 employees, we're fighting the bureaucracy and streamlining our structure. Today, we only have 900 people at our corporate center, but there's still some way to go. We're a customer business and the closer we – our managers and staff – are to customers, the more likely we are to create real value.

Risk diversification

The CFO function at Telefonica has definitely shifted in emphasis from finance and administration to value creation, regulation, and risk. I devote less and less time to pure accounting and cash management issues. Of course, I do have specialists who handle these. But I spend most of my time on capital markets, investor relations, and bringing together the risk functions across the group.

With a group like Telefonica, investors often argue that the sum of the individual parts is greater than the combined value. Stock markets are quite fickle in this respect. On the one hand, having a balanced portfolio of assets is seen as beneficial in terms of risk diversification; on the other hand, an integrated company may be seen as not having management depth in all the individual businesses.

We believe in a focused portfolio with relatively low overall risk. We have different businesses in varying stages of development and various parts of the world. But they are all relatively mature and all benefit from scale.

I'm now much closer to our markets, investors, and opportunities. Unlike the role of controller, which is more risk averse and more about controls, my job as CFO is more forward-looking and strategic. I help the board define its risk appetite, optimize financial structure, and take advantage of opportunities as they present themselves and regulations allow – taking risk, but within our tolerance limits.

In summary, I have to instil the view that regulation is part of the company's landscape, so it's not to be avoided but managed. I also have to point out that there is life beyond regulation! CFOs have to encourage their organizations not only to work within regulatory frameworks, but also to think "out of the box" – how to compete in open, less-regulated markets.

Telecom companies like Telefonica face fierce competition in a rapidly changing environment. New products and new technologies are introduced at an increasingly fast pace. This implies a multitude of changes in their sector to network infrastructure, billing systems and revenue reporting. So what's the impact of regulation such as Sarbanes-Oxley (SOX) on the processes, controls and systems of a company like Telefonica? Are there any real benefits, or is it all downside?

LEVERAGING SARBANES-OXLEY

First, consider key aspects of the legislation. The Sarbanes-Oxley Act 2002 contained a number of requirements for issuers in the United States. The intent of the law was to prevent future corporate and accounting scandals, and to restore the public's confidence in corporate America. It established new rules governing the relationship among officers, the board, and both the internal and external auditors. Moreover, SOX requires additional disclosures by management and increases significantly the penalties for violations.

From a CFO viewpoint, two sections of the Act are having a significant impact on the role of finance in supporting the organization:

Section 302 implications

- Identify significant disclosures and evaluate the processes delivering this information.
- Establish a Disclosure Committee.
- Cascade the accountability for disclosure controls and procedures, and roll up the results.

Section 404 implications

- Document processes impacting financial reporting and the design of significant controls.
- Evaluate control, design, and effectiveness.
- Identify resulting control issues and monitor remediation.
- Ensure documentation reflects changes in processes and controls.
- Prepare internal control report.
- Attestation by external auditors.

Under 302, both the CEO and CFO must monitor the disclosure situation quarterly and produce annual report certifications. They are both individually responsible for ensuring that the requirements of the Act are met. They have to ensure that procedures are maintained and certify: disclosure controls, disclosure of control deficiencies and fraud, and the factual accuracy and completeness of quarterly and annual financial statements. They are personally liable for the results and face the threat of both a fine and a jail sentence if they fail!

Under section 404, management has to report on internal controls over financial reporting. Identifying the control gaps is one thing, fixing them permanently is another! Remediation requires a company to:

- Identify the root causes of control gaps.

- Take a holistic approach, considering the entire process, end to end.

- Focus on departmental interfaces and communication.

- Improve employee participation.

- Monitor the impact of further changes in the control environment.

A well-designed and executed SOX compliance program should pay for itself many times over in the years to come. Most companies are setting up a SOX compliance office and implementing necessary changes in technology. They support the program with training and ongoing communications. Most important, they embed ongoing periodic testing into business operations, and establish exception-reporting protocols to ensure a timely response from senior management.

So what are the benefits? Improving finance function efficiency to foster operational as well as financial effectiveness across the enterprise. "Trust but verify" is more formal, but also more effective.

Before SOX came along, many companies had already realized the value of re-engineering the financial close, consolidation, and reporting processes. Synchronizing these processes, along with others in the business, removes needless steps. And by formalizing accountabilities, companies can rely more on adherence to the systems in which they have invested.

The discipline and formality invested in SOX implementation infrastructure can also be used to address operational improvements. Best-practice methodologies – such as the one reproduced in Figure 9.1 – should improve internal management controls, while also supporting compliance with SOX 302 and 404.

Best-practice SOX compliance methodology has the following features:

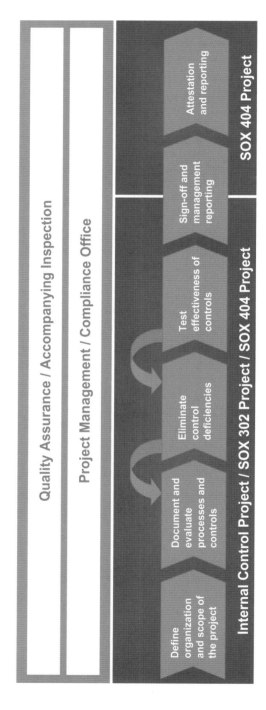

Figure 9.1 *Best-practice SOX compliance methodology*

- Internal control is assessed against consistent standards, such as those published in the COSO Control Framework (referred to later in this chapter).

- Control deficiencies are identified and evaluated.

- Measures to eliminate control deficiencies are defined and monitored.

- Management receives timely reporting on the effectiveness of internal controls.

In some industries, and telecoms is one, there have been some real benefits from SOX 404 compliance, particularly in the area of revenue assurance. CFOs in the telecom sector have to be confident that they can manage properly the risk of revenue leakage across the value chain. The challenges in the *end-to-end revenue cycle*, for example, include:

Order intake

- Are adequate controls in place to limit credit risk?

- Are products properly registered in systems upon activation?

Service provisioning

- Are customers and products properly provisioned in:
    - the network (switch, router)?
    - the billing systems (mediation, billing engine, interconnect application)?

Data collection and billing

- Does *every* customer get an invoice?

- Do customer invoices include *all* services rendered at the appropriate tariffs?

- Are customers billed in a timely manner?

Collection and "dunning"

- Is everything done that can be done to collect outstanding receivables?
- Are *only* authorized compensations and adjustments processed?

Accounting and reporting

- Are adequate controls in place to ensure the integrity of revenue data and associated KPIs?

So generally, across industry and continents, what are the lessons learned from SOX 404 projects so far? Communications between functions and departments within, and between, enterprises are not as good as they should be. Employees do not understand the full implications of controls and the extent to which enterprises rely upon process and systems integrity. SOX 404 has also led to companies discovering major gaps in their business processes – which, when plugged, truly add value!

Figure 9.2 illustrates results – both tangible and intangible – from a variety of initial "year 1 programs" of SOX compliance.

Clearly, many companies have established a positive momentum. The question is: How can you build value from that momentum?

Employees generally want to do the right thing – all the CFO and finance function has to do is to provide the right tools and harness their power! So, what are the key challenges for *future* compliance? Here is a checklist:

1 How to reap further benefits from the ongoing remediation of control deficiencies.

2 How to continue with the initial SOX implementation efforts and sustain ongoing programs of cost reduction and process efficiency improvement.

3 How to capitalize on the opportunities for streamlining fundamental business processes, investing in integrated systems and automating preventative controls.

4 How to go beyond SOX 404, and apply the financial control disciplines to *operational processes.*

Hard Output:

- Hundreds of end to end process flowcharts
- Hundreds of risk and control matrices
- Dozens of enhanced policies
- Thousands of testing plans
- Thousands of pages of test results
- Hundreds of individual control gaps
- Varying levels of training material for employees

Intangible Impact:

- Employees have begun to expand the understanding of their responsibilities
- A sense of discipline to documenting and evaluating processes and control activities
- Loose activities have been formalized
- Opportunities to streamline processes have been identified
- Work-arounds have been eliminated
- Accountabilities redefined
- Ownership firmly established

Figure 9.2   *Initial results from SOX compliance*

Next, we assess the impact of International Financial Reporting Standards (IFRS), and how the SOX implementation experience can be leveraged in other regulatory compliance areas.

MULTIPLE LISTINGS, MULTIPLE STANDARDS

Consider the point of view of one senior finance executive, based in Spain:

> "Most companies agree that standardization of global accounting is desirable. The point at issue – how to get there? It's going to take a long time.

> "How do you pick the right standards? European, and certainly Spanish, companies often differ in their views on standards from those in the US. For example, the presentation of performance – earnings and profit results – is seen by Spanish CFOs as being too American, too aggressive. We're looking for more conservatism.

> "Similarly, many European companies feel that accounting standards relating to market value – for example, IAS 39 on derivatives – lead to too much volatility in the reported results because of balance sheet revaluations. Such volatility is not necessarily good for business! The point of view I hear much in Spain – first take care of business, second take care of the distributions to shareholders. Market revaluations can often get in the way."

IFRS, known formerly as International Accounting Standards (IAS), represents the biggest change in financial reporting that most companies have ever seen. The impact on the financial results of a company can be enormous: profits may well be altered and the balance sheet could look very different. Conversion to the new standards can be complex and the technically demanding change process needs a carefully planned approach.

It's tempting for companies contemplating the adoption of IFRS to view the change simply as an accounting exercise – something that CFOs and their staff can do in their spare time! But just "changing the numbers" is dangerous. IFRS conversion is a change in primary GAAP, which means that everyone in the organization must learn a new language, a new way of working. The whole basis of reporting to the market will be different.

It's likely to take considerable time to plan and make the necessary changes – and to integrate them fully across the company. Perhaps the best way to tackle this is to think about the change to IFRS in three parallel work streams:

1 **Changing the numbers**: Collecting, collating, and fully understanding the IFRS numbers, disclosures, segment reports, and impairment tests. This work stream enables the CFO to produce IFRS financial statements that compare to, and eventually replace, current national reports. *But it's just as important to see how IFRS information will affect the perception of business performance.*

2 **Changing the business**: Anticipating and planning for the necessary changes to accounting policies and reporting procedures, to the information systems, and to the skills and knowledge of the finance organization. There should be opportunities for restructuring and streamlining. *Most important: communicating effectively with everyone who has an interest in the business.*

3 **Managing the change**: Defining roles, responsibilities, and resourcing needs and project planning to guide the transition and to manage progress. *But above all, it will be necessary to actively manage shareholder and market perceptions.*

As they deliver their IFRS implementations, most companies go through a sequence of technical analysis and impact scenarios – assessing the quantitative business impacts. They go on to look at the changes required in processes, controls, and systems. A sample work plan for IFRS implementation, taken from a company in the banking sector, is reproduced in Figure 9.3.

The biggest differences between the numbers, pre- and post-IFRS, are expected to be in: *accounting for financial instruments, deferred taxation, business combinations, and employee benefits.* For example, transition to IFRS can affect:

● **Product viability** – product managers in financial services companies, such as banks, need to recognize that IFRS fair value requirements can reveal volatility in certain products, unsettling investor confidence.

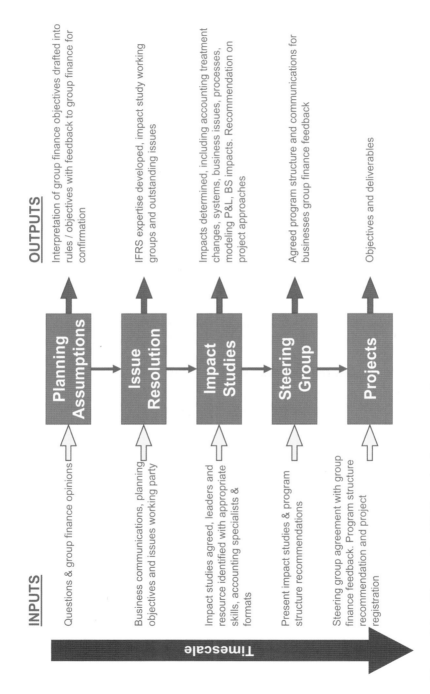

Figure 9.3 *Illustrative IFRS work plan approach*

- **Capital instruments** – IFRS has complex rules governing what constitutes debt and equity. These rules can result in equity-type instruments being reclassified as debt.

- **Derivatives and hedging** – IFRS can significantly increase income volatility because all derivatives must be recorded on the balance sheet at fair value. Some companies may be forced to re-examine the way they do business; they may spot "embedded" derivatives for the first time.

- **Employee benefits** – IFRS accounting for pensions and the new treatment of stock options may precipitate a significant change in company policy that affects all employees. This will need very careful management by both finance and HR.

The list of changes prompted by IFRS goes on to include fair valuations, capital allocation, leasing, segment reporting, revenue recognition, and impairment. Actions the CFO can expect to take:

- Adapting annual reports and accounting manuals.

- Adapting systems and redesigning group reporting packages.

- Integrating and embedding internal and external reporting standards.

IMPLEMENTATION OVERLOAD

When you take the impact of IFRS and SOX in a UK bank, and combine this with the new capital regulatory controls in the banking industry known as Basel II, and you add in specific customer regulation – it all becomes a potential nightmare! Consider next what Helen Weir, the CFO of Lloyds TSB, has to say:

KEEP IT SIMPLE!
Helen Weir, Group Finance Director, Lloyds TSB

I've been at the bank for over 18 months now – my previous role as Group FD was in retailing. Fundamentally, the challenges for the CFO are the same whatever industry you're in. Banks can be considered retail businesses, too. The questions you ask in the businesses are the same: *How do we make our money? Are we pulling the right levers? What can we do for our customers? How can we do it better than anyone else?*

We all have to address our constraints and the needs of our stakeholders. We all need to create value and sustainable top-line growth and we all do this by building customer relationships. And there are always opportunities for better managing the costs.

But the answers to such questions may be fundamentally different. For a start, the business models differ. In retailing, your sales very quickly turn into cash. However, in banking, much of the profits we make today are from new business first generated many years ago. Banking is inherently more complex – even within our wholesale bank we have ten or so business models.

But what differs the most is the regulatory environment – how we manage our capital, our investment, and our risks.

Customer regulation

The way a bank, or any other financial services organization for that matter, transacts business with its customers is very heavily regulated. Of course, the purpose of most regulation is to ensure the customers are treated fairly, and that's clearly a worthwhile objective. Financial services products are inherently complicated; it's not like selling a tin of paint! It is clearly important to have standards to which everyone in the industry adheres and which make product and sales processes as transparent as possible. However, it is clear that, as always, regulation can have unintended consequences – which are sometimes not in the interests of the customer.

For example, in the very worthy cause of eliminating money laundering, banks were required to request several different pieces of identification when a customer opened an account – sometimes even when the customer had been banking with a particular organization for a number of years. This seemed nonsensical to customers and also resulted in a much more lengthy and difficult account opening process – which was not necessarily appreciated by customers.

International accounting standards

The objective of IAS is consistency and transparency in financial reporting for businesses across the world. This is the right way to go. However, despite the "Big Bang" approach this will not be achieved overnight. The norms established under existing *country-based standards – such as the UK GAAP – have been developed over a long period of time. This all gets thrown up in the air when things change.*

A number of the international standards have yet to be finalized – and there are differing views on how to interpret some of those standards that have been published. Another factor that is not always appreciated is that a number of the new standards require a business to project forward what they believe will happen, for example, in amortizing upfront fees over the expected lifetime of a product. To the extent that what actually happens differs from the assumptions, we will see a greater degree of volatility in reported numbers.

There are mixed views on some of the principles underlying some of the standards. For example, the fair value approach inherent in IAS 39 – for financial instruments and hedging – may be appropriate in certain circumstances. It may be helpful, for example, in valuing a bank's trading book, where assets are being bought and sold within a relatively short period of time. However, there are instances where this market, or fair value, approach doesn't really represent the economic reality and where a longer-term perspective is more relevant – for instance, when a bank is hedging a long-term mortgage book with interest rate swaps.

Take another example – the insurance industry – half of insurance products are accounted for on the previous embedded value basis (discounted future cash flow), and the other half on the new fair value accounting basis. I don't necessarily favor one accounting approach or the other, but to have two similar products treated in a different way doesn't seem to make sense. I tend to believe that accounting standards should lead to the presentation of numbers in a way that is intuitive.

There are a number of aspects of IAS that will lead to additional volatility – whether as a result of the use of assumptions that turn out to be incorrect over time, or whether through the increased impact of market movements. Underlying trends in business performance will be harder to spot as a result. It remains to be seen how the investor community will respond to the potential swings in profitability that could result.

Inevitably when you have a change as big as the move to IAS there will be unintended consequences that will need to be ironed out over time. This is understandable – however, it does mean that rather than a single "Big Bang" introduction over a year, we are entering a transition period where we will see changes and refinements of the standards over a period of time. While it makes the lives of both those prepar-

ing and those using company accounts more difficult, it is an inevitable price of a most worthwhile objective – a single, consistent set of accounting standards used the world over!

Sarbanes-Oxley

Generally the intent of SOX is laudable – however, sometimes the reality doesn't live up to the aspiration. From a positive viewpoint SOX 404 really makes businesses think about their controls, how effective they are, and which ones are important. The more negative aspects are the low level and detailed prescription on the documentation of processes and controls required. If not managed carefully there can be too much form, not enough substance! I think the SEC has recognized this and has revisited the requirements, putting more emphasis on the controls that really matter.

One of my original concerns regarding SOX was the short timeframe for implementation – there was only enough time to document what already existed rather than making improvements where they were identified. The extra year for foreign registrants has given us the opportunity to step back and to make improvements in our controls – a real benefit in reducing the number of unnecessary controls and a focus on improving the key ones. It has also meant that we have been able to learn from the US experience.

SOX 302 certifications and accountabilities have helped too. It has re-emphasized to managers across the business that they are accountable for a robust control environment – and caused them to revisit the effectiveness of controls throughout the business. This is particularly important for those organizations which, like Lloyds TSB, have a relatively de-centralized business model. The CEO and Finance Director of any large organization can only sign-off on the Group financial results if they are comfortable that the appropriate controls are understood and followed within each business unit.

Basel II and risk

This banking-specific regulation is also taking us in the right direction, although it requires a lot of work to get there. Again, the amount of time available for implementation is short; the detailed requirements are only now becoming clear – quite late in the timetable. However, the thinking and discipline behind the initiative is "spot-on."

By ensuring the banks have adequate capital on their balance sheet to support the risks they take, Basel II encourages the necessary disciplines – for calculating regulatory costs of capital based on a rigorous analysis of operational risk, as well as market and credit risk. But in some ways Basel II does not go far enough – the economic capital that we use for making management decisions on where and how to invest is even better. More convergence between regulatory and economic capital would help here as well.

Implementation overlaps

While we have separate teams working on SOX and on Basel II, increasingly we are finding that their work overlaps – particularly in the area of operational risk. At Lloyds TSB, we treat risk management not just as a specialist competence but as something which is the responsibility of management throughout the Group. The implementation of initiatives such as Basel II and SOX has required the finance and risk disciplines to work very closely together using our respective experience and specialist skills to implement all this relatively new and complex regulation. Elsewhere and in the future? I can see the potential for further convergence between our two disciplines.

We're running specific training sessions in risk management for our finance executives – there is generally a presumption that if you're financially qualified you know all about risk, but that's not the case. Integrated risk management is the way forward, not only in banking, but in other business sectors as well.

Bringing together all our experience on regulation so far – what are the learning points? Really strong and truly professional project management is essential to ensure that the implementation stays on track and is consistent across the business. Don't overcomplicate things, keep it simple!

As international financial markets expand, concerns over the soundness of banking practices are driving stringent new requirements for financial institutions. These focus on management practice, regulatory control, and market disclosure. In particular, Helen Weir of Lloyds TSB, mentions the new Basel Capital Accord (Basel II). This mandates a more risk-sensitive framework – increasing both the extent of risk management and the level of disclosure. These risks are divided into three categories: market risk, credit risk, and operational risk.

Basel II should be a catalyst for financial services organizations to review their processes and infrastructure – and to build a foundation for flexible and profitable business growth.

For banks like Lloyds TSB, Basel II represents a huge project. There is a significant requirement for detailed data on customers, products, and profitability going back over a number of years in order to assess future risks. The data and methodology required for market and credit risk are relatively straightforward and well defined. But operational risk, and its *quantification*, is a relatively new field. As learning evolves it is being shared across the banking industry.

However, there are overlaps in the various regulations – for example, between the operational risk aspects of Basel II and the SOX 404 processes for internal controls. The workload impact is substantial – requiring fresh investment in outside expertise, data collection, operational processes and systems.

There is criticism of Basel II by some banks that it does not go far enough. They consider their own internal processes for capital allocation to be a lot more useful.

Over the past decade or so, financial institutions themselves have adopted the practice of allocating economic capital internally to assess the performance of their different business units. These measures, commonly referred to as "risk adjusted return on capital" (RAROC), assess the profitability of the institution given the level of risk taken. *This has led to the development of parallel capital management practices: one calculated and reported to the regulators, and one by which to manage the business.*

There are other examples, apart from Basel II, IFRS, and SOX, of situations where regulation has led to duplication, conflict, and the potential for confusion – especially for investors.

THE CASE FOR DUAL ACCOUNTING

Insurance is a good example of an industry in which traditional accounting principles don't provide investors with a broad enough view of how companies are performing. Publicly listed companies in the industry wrestle with different methods of accounting and valuation, and are heavily affected by the latest rounds of regulation.

Prudential is the largest listed pure life insurance company in the UK, with a reputation built up over 150 years. As a leading savings provider, with a strong mix of businesses around the world, its aim is to build lasting relationships through products and services that offer customers and policyholders value for money and security. Philip Broadley, Prudential's Group Finance Director, explains how he is coping with regulatory and accounting complexities.

 ## REALISTIC REPORTING
Philip Broadley, Group Finance Director, Prudential PLC

The role of the CFO is ever changing and that's always been the case – but investors today are more questioning than they've been in the past. Despite the fact that corporate governance has been strengthened over the last few years – those of us in Europe with US listings are still implementing US regulation – investors actually question more, and accept less.

Limitations of statutory accounting
Statutory accounting in the insurance industry generally, and in the UK in particular, has grown up around the need to protect policyholders. So the statutory basis, modified for our industry, is ultra-conservative in taking the view that policyholders will need to be paid out no matter what the circumstances. This leads to extreme caution in the way, for example, likely future investment performance is represented.

Nevertheless, Prudential has been required to account for its long-term insurance business on the "modified statutory basis" (MSB) of reporting under UK accounting rules. The results on this basis broadly reflect UK and overseas solvency requirements adjusted for local and US GAAP. Some aspects of MSB results are indicative of cash-flow generation and, to a limited extent, do resemble traditional accounting deferral and matching methods. However, MSB results do not provide a measure of the value that is generated each year for shareholders. This is because the Prudential writes long-term insurance business, the statutory profits from which may arise over many years.

If shareholders relied on the statutory information alone then, because it is so pessimistic, they would be investing based on long-past performance, rather than current activity. So it's important that we provide information that we believe is meaningful to both investors and policyholders alike.

Supplementary results

Accordingly, in common with other listed UK life assurers, Prudential also reports supplementary results for its long-term operations on what we call "the achieved profits basis." In the directors' opinion, the achieved profits basis provides a more realistic reflection of current performance than the MSB basis. This is because it better reflects the business performance during the accounting period under review.

I have been one of a number of CFOs of European insurers who have sought to harmonize the approach to supplementary reporting. All the large insurers are adopting European Embedded Value. This takes achieved profits on to its next stage of development and will improve comparability across Europe.

The supplementary – achieved profits basis – information shows the net present value (NPV) of our portfolio of policies: the NPV of cash flows that they generate into the future and over their lifetime. It reflects our expenses, the tendency of customers to stay with us (persistency), mortality rates and investment returns. In Figure 9.4, we illustrate the "achieved profits basis" methodology.

We are trying to present to shareholders the best estimate of our present value of the insurance business that we've already written – and have under contract – for a significant period into the future, say from 10 to 40 years.

I believe the achieved profits method not only provides a good indicator of the value being added by today's management in a given accounting period, but it also demonstrates whether shareholder capital is being deployed to best effect. Indeed,

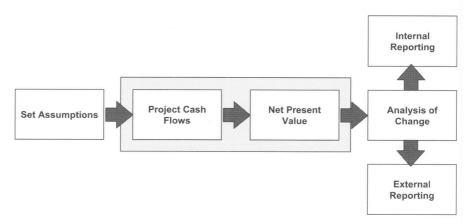

Figure 9.4 *Achieved profits basis methodology*

insurance companies in many countries use a comparable basis of accounting for management purposes.

It is important to understand, however, that achieved profits does require management to make assumptions about the future, and it is important to understand the sensitivity of those assumptions.

This is a value-based method of reporting, reflecting the changing value of the business. The value of shareholder funds on an achieved profits basis is the value of future cash flows plus the net worth of the company. The changing value from one year to another is illustrated in an extract from a recent Prudential annual report in Figure 9.5.

The changing value reflects the following components: the value added from new business sold during the year; the change in value from existing business (in-force profits) already in place at the start of the year; short-term fluctuations in investment returns; and other items such as dividends.

The value added from new business is a key metric used by management. Another good measure of management performance is how well the existing book is managed to generate in-force profits. Together, these two measures provide management and shareholders with valuable information on the underlying development of the business and the relative success of management.

The regulators' concern, however, is to know: what's the worst that can happen? What happens if investment markets are particularly poor over a long time period? What happens if customers die earlier, or live longer than was assumed when the policy was taken out? What if expenses go out of control?

So what we end up with in statutory accounting is a more prudent assessment of what's likely to happen, and no real anticipation of future cash flow.

Reconciling two accounting methods

The two accounting bases end up with the same profit figures in the end, but the timing of those profits differs. Profits emerge earlier under the achieved profits basis. Figure 9.6 illustrates the relative profit profile between the two accounting bases over a ten-year term for a typical insurance "with-profits" product.

The pattern of actual profit emergence varies by product. Generally, under the statutory basis, business is loss-making to start with, makes gradual profits over time, and there's a profit release at the end of the contract. Under the achieved prof-

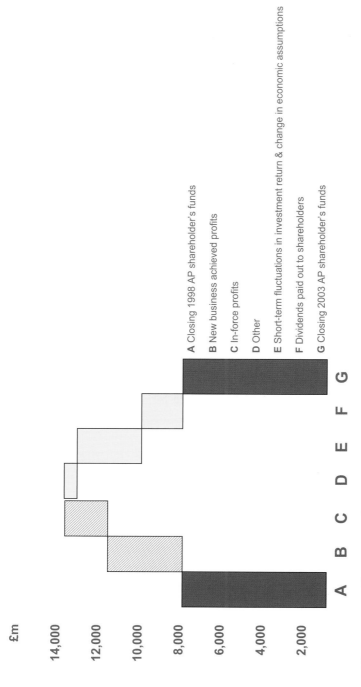

Figure 9.5 *Changing value of shareholders' funds 1998–2003*

A Closing 1998 AP shareholder's funds

B New business achieved profits

C In-force profits

D Other

E Short-term fluctuations in investment return & change in economic assumptions

F Dividends paid out to shareholders

G Closing 2003 AP shareholder's funds

£m

14,000

12,000

10,000

8,000

6,000

4,000

2,000

A B C D E F G

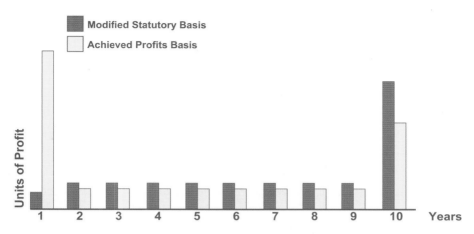

Figure 9.6 *Product profit profile: MSB vs. achieved profits*

its basis, the profit release is more immediate – but is also spread evenly throughout the life of the policy contract.

Each accounting basis has its use. I prefer the achieved profits approach for informing shareholders on how we're doing in terms of performance. Nevertheless, the statutory approach does provide the basis for deciding the level of dividend – you can't pay dividend out of future cash flow!

Internally, we use the achieved profits basis as an incentive. The majority of external analysts use the achieved profits basis for assessing the Prudential's franchise value – the potential to grow sales and the profitability of future business – and to validate our level of prudence.

Regulation in insurance
IFRS has not really arrived yet for us in the insurance sector. The IASB has not yet produced a standard specifically for our industry. It does accept, however, that conventional standards for revenue recognition don't lend themselves easily to our long-term cash flows. So the IFRS4 insurance standard makes only slight modifications to MSB accounting described earlier. It is likely to be near the end of the decade before we see a comprehensive IASB standard on insurance accounting.

Insurance companies, like the banks with their Basel II, are going to be subject to regulation for capital adequacy. This is known in insurance as Solvency II. But it's slow in development and is also unlikely to arrive for us until 2010. This makes longer-term planning, and external communication on the topic, extremely difficult. All of us in the sector dislike this uncertainty, but we have to live with it.

New role: CRO

We've just created the new post of chief risk officer (CRO) and separated many of the responsibilities – such as chairmanship of the asset and liability management (ALM) committee – which hitherto were part of my CFO role.

I believe this reflects best practice and was the right step for us to take. The risk function was getting too broad, ever more specialized and benefits from independence in our management structure. Nevertheless, there are overlaps between risk and finance. The CRO, our treasurer, and I work very closely together in managing the balance sheet, the risks, and finance.

Conclusion

The key challenge for us over the short term will be to improve the quality of what I call "narrative reporting." With all of our reporting, whether it is modifying statutory accounts for IFRS, improving our supplementary disclosures with the introduction of EEV, or our separate Corporate Responsibility Report, nothing is static.

I have seen a great deal of change, and I anticipate more to come. We will never reach a steady state – one where we are content that what we produce cannot be improved, or where we are not reacting to external change.

As Philip Broadley points out, risk, regulation, and reporting are all heavily intertwined. The banking industry, in many respects, leads the way in terms of best risk practices.

Generally, whatever the industry sector, there has been a compelling need for an enterprise risk management framework – one that provides key principles and concepts, a common language, and clear direction.

The COSO framework[1] (Committee of Sponsoring Organizations), which integrates risk and control, fills this need. It's subsequently been incorporated into policy, rule, and regulation – and has been used by thousands of enterprises to better control their activities.

ENTERPRISE-WIDE RISK MANAGEMENT

Enterprise risk is much broader than just finance and operational risk. It takes into account how all of a company's strategies, and all of its departments, are affected by risk. Enterprise Risk Management (ERM) is a relatively new concept that enables management to identify, assess, and manage risks in the face of uncertainty.

A successful ERM program starts with aligning risk appetite and strategy – evaluating strategic alternatives, setting objectives, and developing mechanisms to manage related risks. Risk appetite is the amount of risk an entity is willing to accept in pursuit of value. It reflects an enterprise's risk management philosophy, culture, and operating style. Figure 9.7 shows how an organization can chart its individual risks in terms of potential impact and their probability.

Using this approach to risk appetite, a line can be drawn for the organization – between what is an acceptable level of risk, within its risk appetite, and what is unacceptable.

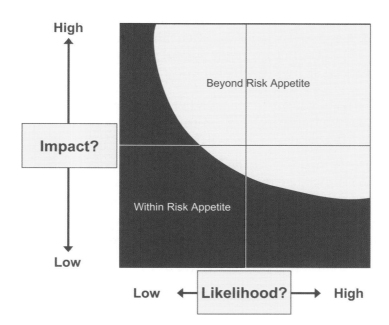

Figure 9.7 *Forming risk appetite*

Traditionally, risk management has had very negative connotations. It has been focused on compliance and box-ticking – unhelpful when it comes to driving the business forward! To quote the CFO of a major engineering company:

> "Risk gives rise to group and corporate strategy. Risk management is key to the whole process – it starts it off. Risk management is about getting the business strategy right. A company will go on a major acquisition spree, for example, but misunderstand the business and end up overpaying.

> "We categorize risks in terms of the likelihood of occurrence and the potential financial impact – and then prioritize the top five risks. Each quarter, we have a financial and business review to find out what we're doing to mitigate those risks. At the end of the day, strategic risk is where businesses succeed or fail."

Risks to a company can range from general strategic ones, such as the impact of low-cost competition from China, to more specific risk factors – such as the high risk of litigation in a particular subsidiary.

As shown in Figure 9.8, the ERM process consists of eight interrelated components.

The eight ERM components are derived from the way management runs an enterprise and, with the attendant information flows, the need for them to be integrated with the normal process of management. These components are defined briefly below:

- *Internal environment* – including risk management philosophy and risk appetite, integrity, and ethical values, and the environment in which they operate.

- *Objective setting* – ensuring that management has in place a process to set objectives and that the chosen objectives support and align with the corporate mission and are consistent with its risk appetite.

- *Event identification* – distinguishing between risks and opportunities; ensuring that opportunities are aligned with management's strategy.

- *Risk assessment* – analyzing risk on an inherent and a residual basis and evaluating their likelihood and impact, as a basis for determining how they should be managed.

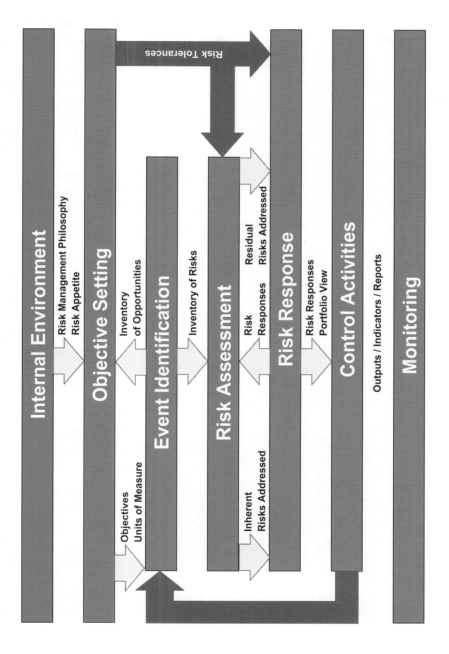

Figure 9.8 *Enterprise risk management components*

- *Risk response* – avoiding, accepting, reducing, or sharing risk – developing a set of actions to align risks with the entity's risk tolerances and appetite.

- *Control activities* – establishing policies and procedures to help ensure that risk responses are effectively carried out.

- *Information and communication* – identifying, capturing, and communicating relevant information in a form and timeframe that enable people – up and down, and across the enterprise – to carry out their risk responsibilities.

- *Monitoring* – a multidirectional, iterative process in which almost any component can and does influence another.

There is a direct relationship between objectives and the ERM components, which represent what is needed to achieve them. The organizational model for implementing ERM in an integrated way is depicted in Figure 9.9.

Each component of enterprise risk, *from objective setting to monitoring,* needs to be implemented for the enterprise as a whole – its divisions,

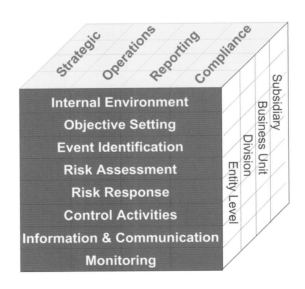

Figure 9.9 *Inter-relationships: ERM, processes & organization*

business units and subsidiaries – and throughout all business processes, *from strategy through to operations, reporting and compliance.*

Various stakeholders, such as investors, customers, and business partners, are all interested in an organization's risk appetite and want to reassure themselves that a company has its risk management processes under control.

Furthermore, there is an established link between the quality of a company's risk management and its performance in terms of value creation.

Consider next how New York Life (NYL), as a mutual organization, approaches risk. Although the current industry trend for mutual insurers is demutualization, NYL has resisted this move. Its contrarian strategy has played out very well, as described in an interview with its CFO, Michael Sproule.

MANAGING RISK IN A MUTUAL
By Michael Sproule, CFO, New York Life

We continue to focus exclusively on our policyholders – and on long-term sustainability. Living up to our promises for the future! We do not have to address the conflict between shareholder and policyholder interests that affects public companies. And we don't need to get bigger to be viable – we've had the largest individual share of the life insurance market for new business for three years in a row.

The company has a strong focus on core values – financial strength, humanity, and integrity. Our primary objective is to be here when our obligations to policyholders are due – and often that can take 30 or 40 years or more. The policies we design and sell represent a promise to pay – and we manage everything around that proposition. We maintain a conservative balance sheet and income statement and believe in providing financial transparency.

Our credibility is very important – and we have a wonderful story to tell! Despite being a mutual, we still publish unabridged GAAP financials, complete with footnotes. This enables the analysts to understand our performance.

Our CEO, Sy Sternberg, is the primary architect of the company's strategy. He provides strong leadership and vision and has built an outstanding management team. Within NYL, we have a very open management dialogue and the operating style that Sy has set involves everyone in the details. Executive influence percolates directly down through the organization via operational reviews.

Understanding and managing risk is central to our business. NYL has recently expanded the role of its Chief Risk Officer – beyond financial risk management to a more holistic set of risk management responsibilities.

We monitor risk based on a multi-dimensional matrix and we're implementing this approach using our decentralized model. This reflects our belief that the business units own the responsibility for risk management for their businesses. However, it's also important to understand and manage risks at the enterprise level. So we do prescribe corporate risk assessment templates for all to use. This is not a "complete every box" kind of bureaucratic exercise; it is up to each business unit to determine what risks are important to them.

Nevertheless, our financial risk management processes are becoming more and more complex. The financial approaches are increasingly grounded in stochastic-based models that are used to assess economic capital, product pricing, risk management, and the valuation of reserve liabilities.

These models must be used judiciously. Sensitivity testing to understand the critical modeling parameters is essential. And it's very important to recognize where these models may begin to deviate from reality: it is dangerous to blindly follow model outputs as if they are precise to ten decimal places.

It's important to have a healthy respect for what can go wrong – especially when you are modeling policyholder behavior under different scenarios. However, one of my concerns is that these models be used for their intended purpose – increasing our understanding of possible outcomes and managing risk exposures. They should not be used to create a false sense of security that, unknowingly, could actually increase risk rather than reduce it.

So risk management is a highly skilled discipline. In many industries it's the CFO who takes the risk management lead. In other sectors, such as financial institutions and in the case of NYL, there is an individual specially designated to do the job – the Chief Risk Officer (CRO).

THE ROLE OF CHIEF RISK OFFICER (CRO)

A global survey found that 45% of responding companies had appointed a CRO or equivalent. Although the majority of these were concentrated in the financial services sector, a further 24% of companies planned to appoint a CRO within two years and the role is set to become more common in other sectors.

CROs are being asked to shoulder the full ERM responsibility. Working closely with the CFO, there has been a radical change in their influence. The risk profession is developing standards and the CRO, rather than just being a perfunctory appointment or knee-jerk response to regulation, is now seen as part of the organization's strategic management team.

CROs are most effective when they provide the board of directors with a clear vision of where enterprise risks lie, help define a policy for off-setting those risks, and work to communicate that vision so that individual managers understand and support it. A typical job description for the CRO of a financial services company would include the following responsibilities:

- Establish corporate-wide risk limits.

- Approve risk-taking authority, capital allocation, and limit setting, based on a business unit's:

    –absolute and risk-adjusted performance;
    –risk profile and strategy;
    –earnings quality/consistency;
    –efficiency of capital usage;
    –diversification benefits or disadvantages;
    –management of reliability and competence.

- Establish and maintain corporate-wide risk management standards, such as:

    –business-unit policies and limit frameworks;
    –corporate risk data requirements;
    –reporting requirements for business managers, senior management and the board;
    –valuation and risk measurement methodology.

- Establish an enterprise-wide risk-reporting framework, including risk analysis and decision-making tools for:

    –aggregating and analyzing common risk factors across business lines (e.g. stress testing/scenario analysis);
    –conducting macro risk profile assessments, evaluating the impact of change drivers;

–reviewing and approving policy exceptions;
–managing stakeholder relations.

As in the case of NYL, the primary focus of a CRO is not on acquiring a minute knowledge of all areas of potential risk, but on the broader business perspective. A CRO who is presented as the ultimate expert on risk in every business unit, and the final arbiter of how managers operate, is likely to alienate other managers and make them defensive.

Despite the special responsibilities for risk of both the CRO and the CFO, it should not be forgotten that the responsibility for evaluating and monitoring risks within a large company should ultimately come from the trenches – *from front-line managers and department heads!*

STRAIGHT FROM THE CFO

- **Leverage Sarbanes-Oxley**

  Are your accounting policies, practices, and procedures adequately documented, communicated, and understood throughout your company? Identify the control gaps – then fix them, permanently! A well-designed and executed SOX compliance program should pay for itself, many times over! Ensure processes and controls support operational, as well as financial, objectives. Build ongoing value from initial SOX momentum. Consider process improvement opportunities for collecting additional revenue.

- **Convert to IFRS**

  Change the numbers – produce IFRS statements, compare to and eventually replace current reports. See how IFRS affects perceptions of business performance. Change the business – anticipate and plan for the necessary financial policies, procedures, and systems. Communicate the impact effectively to everyone who has an interest.

- **Avoid implementation overload**

  When implementing new regulation – don't overcomplicate things, keep it simple! Identify potential mistakes early and

---

test regulatory impact with pilot, pathfinder implementations before roll out. Look outside at what others are doing. "Fast-follower" is a good strategy.

- **Consider dual accounting**

  Would supplementary information help your shareholders better understand company performance? As in the insurance sector, consider publishing indicators that demonstrate the value being added by management and how shareholder capital is being deployed.

- **Establish enterprise-wide risk management**

  Integrate ERM in business planning and strategy setting, and deploy across all business units. Follow the COSO-inspired framework for linking company objectives with risks, controls, and regulations. Prevent surprises through earlier risk identification. Link ERM explicitly to business performance improvements.

- **Assess *your* risk appetite**

  Clearly articulate your organization's risk appetite. Communicate – develop a common risk language, be transparent, and promote a better understanding of key risks and their root causes. Monitor risk management and continuously improve your risk capability.

- **Appoint a CRO**

  The CRO should serve as an advisor and partner of the CEO and CFO. Integrity and credibility is necessary to communicate with business leaders, regulators and other stakeholders. Remember: everyone has some responsibility for enterprise risk management!

REFERENCES

1 COSO and PwC (2004) *Enterprise Risk Management – Integrated Framework*, Committee of Sponsoring Organizations of the Treadway Commission.

CHAPTER 10

Becoming a Sustainable Corporation

This chapter covers the relatively new issues of *sustainability, ethics,* and *corporate social responsibility* (CSR). What do these issues mean for the CFO – for corporate reporting and shareholder value?

Is CSR all just good public relations and "hot air," or it is real? Chairmen and CEOs of leading companies believe that it is real and that there are direct links between having high standards, a code of conduct, and shareholder value. Many CFOs, but not all, corroborate this view.

Nevertheless, one thing is certain: companies in many industries are taking the issues of ethics and social responsibility very seriously. This is particularly true for those companies that are especially sensitive to external perceptions of their corporate reputations. For example:

- *Companies in the pharmaceutical industry* are concerned with ensuring the efficacy and safety of their products; that they're putting something back into society; and that they maintain good relations with their customers.

- *Companies in the energy and chemicals sector* are concerned with the environment, pollution, and the impact of non-governmental organizations (NGOs). They're investing in renewable energy and striving to sustain the best possible relationships with the governments of the countries in which they operate.

- *Companies in financial services and consumer goods sectors* are concerned with ever-increasing demands by industry regulators and with their corporate reputations. For example, banks have to meet high standards of professional conduct in dealings with customers; food and beverage companies have to be seen by consumers as responsible in the way they respond to highly contentious issues, such as obesity and alcohol abuse.

This chapter broadens the reporting envelope by accepting that traditional financial reporting models are limited while recognizing that companies are responsible to a wider group of stakeholders, not just shareholders. It covers the views of investors, the trends in best-practice corporate reporting, and the potential for integration of the financials with the non-financials – the *"triple bottom line."* The chapter concludes by examining what companies are doing in relation to integrity and ethics, and what it means to be a *good* corporation.

For the CFO, the burden of reporting – what's going on in this much broader context – seems to grow heavier by the day. Surely *less* is *more*. Reporting regulations seems to be going in the direction of transparency: clear, comprehensible, and complete. Support is growing for the idea that externally reported performance information should be consistent with internal management reporting.

But as CFO, how far should you go? Are investors really interested in the broader picture? If so, is there a standard information set against which all companies should report? Do investors *really* reward companies with a good track record of sustainability, social responsibility, and ethics?

CASE FOR CORPORATE RESPONSIBILITY

We start with the realities for a CFO in pharmaceuticals, Angus Russell of Shire, a rapidly growing pharmaceutical company in the FTSE 100. Angus chairs the Corporate Responsibility (CR) committee, which is not just concerned with social aspects, but has a much broader agenda.

CORPORATE RESPONSIBILITY
Angus Russell, CFO, Shire Pharmaceuticals

We're in the business of making people's lives healthier and longer. Our aim is to build a successful, long-lasting specialty pharmaceuticals business that generates financial returns for our employees, makes a positive contribution to the environments in which we operate, and serves the needs of our primary customers – the doctors who prescribe our medicines and, most importantly, the patients whose lives are affected by them.

At Shire, we've deliberately avoided calling CR a "social" initiative. We don't see CR as "airy-fairy." Sustainability is about more than just meeting financial targets, it's a holistic approach to long-term growth. It's not just about charitable donations or good works in the local community. It's about corporate responsibility. It's about all the business – strategy, planning, execution, and even controlling – as well as building shareholder value!

A continued focus on the short term has to be wrong. The investment community tells us what information they need and why. These issues seem to boil down to risk and reputation.

The case for change

Government is putting pressure on compliance with CR best-practice codes through investment institutions – and there is a growing fear that this will be enshrined in future legislation, for example, the current UK company law review.

Investors are waking up to the importance of CR. They're scrutinizing not only environmental considerations – "going green" – but also corporate integrity, and the impact of human rights violations and unethical conduct. After all, there have been some spectacular corporate collapses recently.

The scope of a company's ethical and legal responsibilities – and the overlap between them – is shown in Figure 10.1.

As Figure 10.1 shows, certain legal requirements may be deemed "unjust" or "misconceived." Ethical concerns may not be covered by the law at all, and it is in this area that corporate focus is growing. Most companies, including Shire, are going way beyond minimum legal requirements. Even though we contract out 95% of our manufacturing, for example, we want to ensure that we do so in an environmentally proper and socially responsible way.

There's growing interest among companies on CR reporting – 132 of the top 250 companies in the UK now produce CR reports. We're also listed in the USA and there is increasing concern there too.

Consider the following:

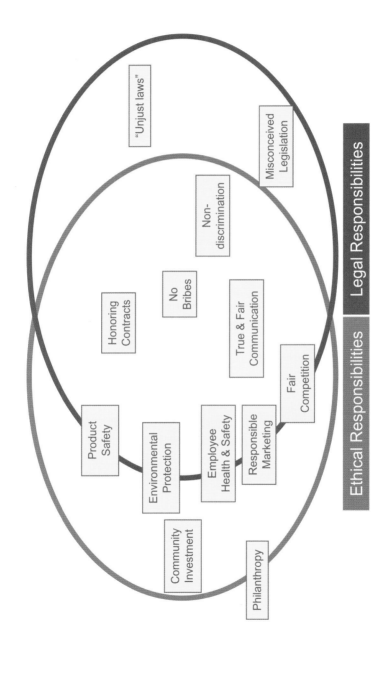

Figure 10.1 *Corporate responsibility & self-regulation*

- *86% of institutional investors across Europe believe that social and environmental risk management will have a significantly positive impact on a company's long-term market value.*
- *Dow Jones Sustainability Index companies outperformed the mainstream market by 23% in a recent 12-month period.*
- *A study by the Institute of Business Ethics of FTSE250 companies found that those with an ethical code of conduct outperformed the average on economic and market value-added indicators.*

There is still more news: £336 billion is being invested in the Social Responsibility Investor (SRI) institutional market. In another survey, 78% of senior business leaders across Europe voiced the view that fully integrating "responsible" business practice will make them more competitive. And nearly 70% of CEOs say that CR is vital to profitability. All this concern is understandable, since much of a corporation's shareholder value today is tied up in the value of intangibles, such as reputation and brand.

Shire is proud to be in the "FTSE-4-Good" index, which enables investors to ensure that companies meet stringent corporate responsibility criteria. It's great to be in this index – and essential not to fall out of it!

Link to shareholder value

The costs and potential downside to earnings of corporate "irresponsibility" are substantial. Of course, there are always ethically "grey" areas.

Figure 10.2 offers an illustrative example of the financial impact of CR. In this example, a company spots an opportunity to increase profits, but doing so raises ethical issues. The figure shows the potential impact of three different courses of action.

> **Scenario 1:** *The company makes the wrong choice and investors are aware from the beginning that it's a disaster!*
> **Scenario 2:** *For some time, investors are unaware of the company's unethical behavior – for example, that it uses child labor in a third-world country. Profits rise initially, but then plummet.*
> **Scenario 3:** *The company makes the ethically correct decision; earnings may be lower to start with, but they are sustainable over the longer term.*

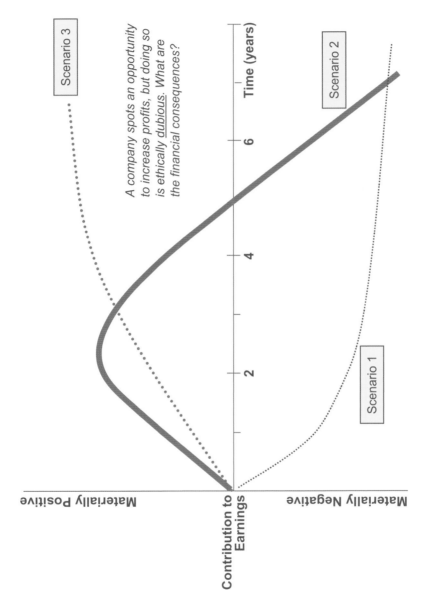

Figure 10.2 *The costs and benefits of corporate responsibility*

In our annual CR report, we have aligned our information with the guidelines issued by the Association of British Insurers (ABI), and the Global Reporting Initiative (GRI). We provide data on our drug development pipeline, our major products on the market, and our organizational changes. Our core values:

- *Integrity and respect – relationships are the foundation of our business; they are based on unwavering ethics and respect for individuals.*
- *Customer focus – we are customer driven; we focus on the needs of both internal and external customers.*
- *Global teamwork – the entire company is focused on growing our business and executing our strategy as a team.*
- *Openness and innovation – we believe that anything is possible and that prudent risks are worth taking.*

Integrating CR and risks

CR highlights reputation issues and the risks. We have a CR Committee, led by myself as CFO, comprised of line managers and EVPs. It reports to a non-executive committee. The directors set the tone from the top, and we have a small number of employees in corporate communications who assist us in this work. Our non-executive committee ensures that CR is "built-in" to the business, not "bolted-on"! We encourage the involvement of all employees in our approach. We recently hired 500 new US employees, who said they had read our CR report, were motivated by it, and were keen to join us as a result.

CR naturally aligns with, and is an extension of, our risk agenda. There is a natural fit with the work of the Audit Committee and we're currently identifying and mapping risks associated with CR. We now have scorecards on matters of reputation, risk, financial, and market performance.

The CR agenda will not go away; it continues to escalate in importance to business executives. It is fast becoming an umbrella management philosophy that underpins shareholder value and risk management.

In Shire, we're pleased that our approach to CR is leading to improved rigor in our management processes and an enhanced external reputation. We aim to continually improve our performance in this important developing area.

INVESTOR PERSPECTIVE

Investors do have expectations in relation to good business ethics. In recent investor surveys, for example:

- 73% of more than 190 investment managers throughout the world expect business ethics indicators to be mainstream within ten years.

- 80% of private equity investors indicate that they will sell their shares of companies with poor ethical profiles.

- 35 of the world-leading financial institutions have adopted the Equator principles for social and environmental screening of their global project financing.

- International investors, managing a total of more than €360 billion, have formed the Enhanced Analytics Initiative (EAI). This encourages analysts to assess corporate handling of business ethics.

When putting money into a company, investors want to be ensured of one thing: that their money is in safe hands.

A company's reports and accounts therefore have to extend beyond just the financials. Directors have to provide a review of operations, along with remuneration reports and other governance data. And for many companies, the mandatory elements of the report and accounts are just part of a broader set of routine publications that often include social and environmental impact.

The following are excerpts from narrative reporting requirements and guidance issued by a number of regulatory bodies and standard setters worldwide:

- In the United States, the SEC provides interpretation of the guidance for Management Discussion and Analysis (MD&A):

"MD&A requirements are intended to satisfy three principal objectives:

1 To provide a narrative explanation of the company's financial statements that enables investors to see the company through the eyes of management;
2 To enhance overall financial disclosure and provide the context within which financial information should be analyzed; and

3 To provide information about the quality of, and potential variability of, a company's earnings and cash flow, so that investors can ascertain the likelihood that past performance is indicative of future performance.

Companies should identify and discuss the KPIs, including non-financial performance indicators, that management uses and that are material to investors."

- In Europe, to quote from the European Parliament's Modernization Directive:

"To the extent necessary for an understanding of the company's development, performance, and position, the analysis should include both financial and, where appropriate, non-financial key performance indicators relevant to the particular business, including information relating to environmental and employee matters."

In its broadest sense, transparency refers to an organization's willingness to communicate openly and fully all the corporate performance information that every stakeholder group needs. As the demand for greater transparency has increased, narrative reporting has emerged as one of the solutions of choice for improving corporate transparency.

Companies that fail to embrace transparency risk significant damage to management credibility and shareholder confidence. More damaging still, these companies could face declines in market capitalization and corresponding reductions in credit and liquidity.

More than ever, investors are demanding a complete and accurate picture of a company's current health and future prospects. They want more than the historic financial performance information that traditional corporate reporting provides. They want the whole story in language they can understand and in formats they can use for analysis.

Despite the importance of having contextual information when evaluating the quality and sustainability of financial performance, investors in a research survey said that the information they receive:

- was not consistent from company to company;

- was not integrated with information on a company's overall strategy;

- lacked balance in the opinions expressed.

To quote one investor: "What's the earnings number? Anything I want it to be." And another: "Management can be economical with the amount of information that they do and do not provide to the fixed-income investment community." It is clear that investors are struggling to extract sufficient information from reports and accounts in order to answer some of their most basic questions about corporate performance.

Most investor needs could be met by a relatively simple evolution in the current financial reporting model. Any individual company can decide to go beyond GAAP to ensure that investors can evaluate the organic growth rate of their business and assess potential liabilities. Indeed, as we've seen, a number of leading companies are actively trying to do this today.

ETHICS AND VALUE CREATION

There is general acceptance of the view that good business ethics are a prerequisite of sustainable quality earnings and high shareholder value. But do companies and investors agree about what is *good*?

In Denmark, for example, the Danish Financial Statements Act requires that large enterprises report on non-financial issues in their management reviews. Unfortunately, there are no instructions for the reporting! So, a voluntary member-based network of some 54 investors and enterprises, called the Danish Network for Good Business Ethics and Non-financial Reporting[1] (NVIR), was formed with the objectives of:

1 Creating a framework for discussions between *investors and enterprises* on their interaction and issues of critical importance to corporate value creation.

2 Preparing recommendations about good business ethics and non-financial reporting.

The fundamental question raised by the NVIR group: Can and should enterprises report non-financials to improve share price, reputation, and competitive advantage? The simple answer was: Yes! 84% of indicators deemed important to an enterprise's *future* value were non-financial, or "contextual" indicators.

Ethical behavior is perhaps the non-financial indicator that is most difficult to quantify and value. It is also the most difficult one for the external environment to understand.

So the NVIR recommended a process for identifying which ethical issues are important to a company's ability to implement its strategy and create value in the future. This process is summarized as:

1 **Defining the fundamental prerequisites of good business ethics:** Does management contribute actively to creating a corporate culture that lives up to its obligations to its stakeholders? Does management ensure that everybody in the organization understands the reasons for and the importance of complying with these obligations? Is the handling of ethics integrated into management systems?

2 **Identifying and prioritizing relevant business ethics issues:** Does management ensure that ethical issues are identified, prioritized, and mapped in a structured manner? Does management ensure consistency between the priorities assigned to ethics and the values, policies, strategies, and objectives of the enterprise?

3 **Handling of prioritized issues and implementation:** Has management decided how ethics should be handled, and does it have action plans? Are there sufficient resources to implement those action plans? Are there incentive systems to support implementation?

4 **Follow-up and internal reporting:** Is there a program in place to monitor that ethics issues are handled as planned? Does follow-up take place through management reporting internally, and is it communicated externally to relevant stakeholders?

5 **External reporting:** Does management take a stand on business ethics and report on the process – as well as on the issues considered relevant and material to the value creation of the enterprise?

The increased focus on ethics issues has contributed to redefining ethical boundaries. What was universally accepted a few years ago is no longer perceived as being ethically sound. For companies and investors, increasing interest in ethical dilemmas will influence the pricing of shares.

Clearly, concern with business ethics and social responsibility is not a new phenomenon. Historically, enterprises with high ethical standards have enjoyed a better reputation and have generally performed better on the stock market. The value creation of an enterprise can be affected both positively and negatively by the requirements and expectations of its stakeholders. For example:

- **Consumers** will make buying decisions based on the social/ethical profile of companies providing goods or services.

- **Suppliers** have to comply with standards required by the companies they service – for example, with ethical guidelines for supply chains laid down by their customers.

- **Employees** are less likely to be loyal to employers that do not support social initiatives.

- **Non-governmental organizations (NGOs)** can impact corporate reputation.

- **Government agencies** influence corporate cost, taxes, and business risks through legislation.

BP, for example, annually reviews all its businesses in relation to ethical business principles – specifically, in relation to the activities of suppliers as well as employees. In its annual responsibility report, Nike describes its compliance with international conventions and guidelines.

Figure 10.3 illustrates the linkage between stakeholder expectations in relation to handling business ethics and the drivers of shareholder value.

Issues concerning business ethics will affect one or more of the cash-flow drivers contributing to shareholder value. The ethics issues affecting long-term value creation vary from one company to another – depending on industry, geographical location, business model, and stakeholder wishes and concerns.

CFOs should identify the ethics issues relevant to their companies and map them to their specific value drivers. Emphasis should be placed both on the *negative* implications – the potential losses arising from risks – as well as the *positive* implications – the opportunities for developing business.

Figure 10.4 shows how a company can classify ethical issues, across the enterprise value chain, in relation to various stakeholders.

Next in the chapter we continue exploring the approach to these issues in an interview with the chairman of Novo Nordisk, a company based in Denmark where much progress has been made on ethics, sustainability, and social and environmental reporting.

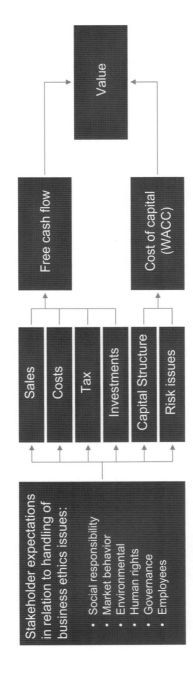

Figure 10.3 *Linking shareholder expectations to stakeholder value*
Source: *The Danish Network for Good Business Ethics and Non-financial Reporting (NVIR)*

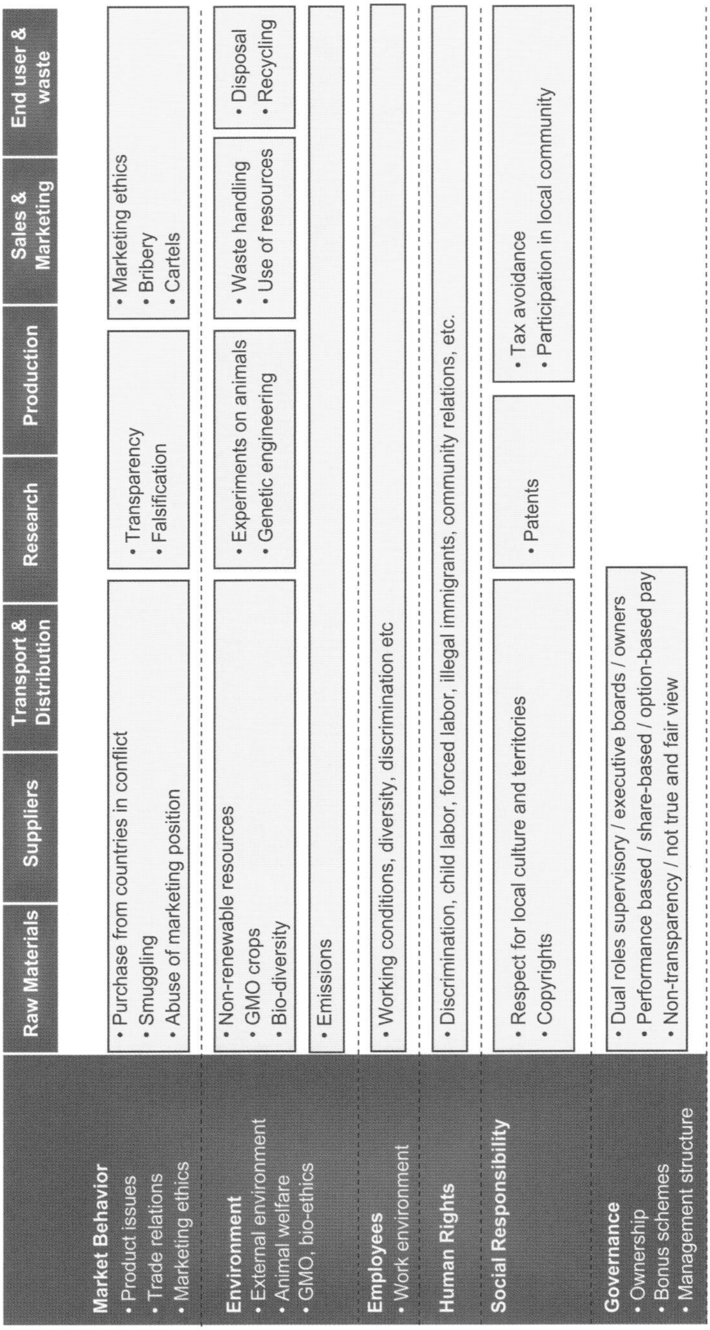

	Raw Materials	Suppliers	Transport & Distribution	Research	Production	Sales & Marketing	End user & waste
Market Behavior • Product issues • Trade relations • Marketing ethics	• Purchase from countries in conflict • Smuggling • Abuse of marketing position			• Transparency • Falsification		• Marketing ethics • Bribery • Cartels	
Environment • External environment • Animal welfare • GMO, bio-ethics	• Non-renewable resources • GMO crops • Bio-diversity • Emissions			• Experiments on animals • Genetic engineering		• Waste handling • Use of resources	• Disposal • Recycling
Employees • Work environment	• Working conditions, diversity, discrimination etc						
Human Rights	• Discrimination, child labor, forced labor, illegal immigrants, community relations, etc.						
Social Responsibility	• Respect for local culture and territories • Copyrights			• Patents	• Tax avoidance • Participation in local community		
Governance • Ownership • Bonus schemes • Management structure	• Dual roles supervisory / executive boards / owners • Performance based / share-based / option-based pay • Non-transparency / not true and fair view						

Figure 10.4 *Ethical risks across the value chain*
Source: *The Danish Network for Good Business Ethics and Non-financial Reporting (NVIR)*

A MULTI-STAKEHOLDER APPROACH

Novo Nordisk is a biotech-based healthcare company with 21,000 employees, operating in 78 countries, and marketing its products all over the world. Its vision is to be the world's leading diabetes-care company and its aspiration is to defeat diabetes by finding better methods of prevention, detection, and treatment.

Mads Ovlisen, the Chairman of Novo Nordisk (previously CEO) and also Chairman of Lego, provides advice on how to "take your people with you" in implementing sustainability, CSR, and non-financial reporting.

LIVING UP TO OUR VALUES
Mads Ovlisen, Chairman, Novo Nordisk

I believe for a company to be financially successful, it must have a broader perspective. As chairman of two of the leading companies in Denmark, I certainly subscribe to a very broad agenda. I don't think you can make people, who are your company, contribute the best of their mental energies by merely focusing on the bottom line. You have to provide them with a sense of meaning, a higher purpose. You need to work together towards a broader rationale than just making profit.

I don't think we need to make much change to the world of financial reporting. The constraints may be more illusory than real. Certainly, there is much that can be done to increase awareness about key aspects of doing business.

What sustainability means
From a global point of view, companies are being affected by issues of sustainability – the environment, social fairness, justice, and human dignity. When operating as a company in locations where these issues arise, we take a stand and enter into a dialogue before we proceed.

Only when business takes the initiative do governments get the courage and resources to act, according to Kofi Annan. So we need to be the ones to drive forward with partnerships, governments, and local interest groups.

There are limits to how much we can exploit the physical resources of this planet. Geophysical limits, for example, in the ozone layer, greenhouse gas emissions, and over-fishing. At the same time, there are limits in our social sustainability: for example, the deteriorating health situation in Africa. Such situations can create social

unrest and conflict. In developing countries, in India as another example, the population explosion and urbanization can lead to a breakdown in core family values and
social stability. As a business leader you have to act on these issues and be ready to
discuss them with your stakeholders.

Taking your people with you

*So how do you take your corporation with you? The answer is: developing a company
that works toward a "triple bottom line" agenda – (1) financial, (2) environmental
quality, and (3) social responsibility. This is a major undertaking. You need to make
certain that things get done – that you're not just responding through a reporting scheme. As a company, we have evolved to a stage where these concepts must
become integrated in the way we do business.*

*How do you make the business case for social responsibility and sustainability?
Simply by deciding "this is the way we conduct our business." And then making sure
that you properly document your company values before you start claiming that
you're living up to them! You don't want to be "selling hot air in little brown bags"!*

*Recently, we assembled 60 of our people from around the organization and asked
them to consider whether we were living up to our values or not. For example, we
asked: as a manufacturer based on biotechnology, can we really be certain that we
are open and honest in disclosing the experiments we've conducted and the methods
we've used? And how do we meet our stakeholder expectations in this regard? We
wanted to know where we needed some "moral adjustment" based on new insights,
and where we needed to take action.*

*Across Novo Nordisk, people are taking socially responsible action. These range
from raising money for charity through recycling from Copenhagen to Tanzania,
where employees set up robust but primitive IT systems to serve local diabetes clin-
ics, which they help establish in ship cargo containers. Making sure that every individual in our company feels responsible for sustainable development is what it's all
about. We've also teamed up with other manufacturers to conserve energy – utilizing their excess energy to minimize our consumption.*

*On the social side, we've helped create an initiative called DAWN (Diabetes Aware-
ness, Wishes, And Needs). This is a diabetes awareness program carried out by our
company in collaboration with the International Diabetes Foundation. It's launched
the first comprehensive socio-psychological studies of people with diabetes.*

Link to shareholder value

Is there a connection between sustainability and shareholder value? I'm certain there is. We will have to localize around the globe. For example, we are making a major investment in Brazil, and further investments in China. We are not only moving blue-collar jobs from Western Europe, but also high value-added intellectual capital. These moves are not just about who pays the lowest wages, it's about getting access to knowledge around the world. Of course, we always try to put Novo Nordisk employees first when we can. However, whatever the outcome, management involves them fully.

What's the role of the C-level in all this? It's very important for the CEO and the CFO to have a strong partnership. As chairman, I look for a special relationship with the CFO in order to ensure openness and transparency. A high level of trust between the Chairman and the Executive Team is critical. Good lines of communication are vital. Information must be digestible. Bad news must be shared immediately.

The management team must be able to communicate openly and honestly with shareholders. Sharing the vision of what you want the company to be is also important and we need to train the board – both non-executive and executive – in the area of sustainability. And the CFO has to be proactive in all this.

Sustainability is not owned as an issue just by top management. There is tremendous pressure from our own people inside the company to set the agenda and to improve our standards. Often I find management responding to the desires from within. How fortunate can you be?

In today's complex society, Novo Nordisk's view of how to engage with stakeholders is based on a reflective understanding of the positions and motives of others. Relations with stakeholders are not static, but change depending on the nature of the relationship.

There is much to be done in reporting on sustainability and CSR. Across industries, more convergence is needed on general reporting standards. This is also needed within industries for comparative purposes.

The development of reporting and suitable measures is a never-ending journey. Chairmen like Mads Ovlisen do not see it as a *below-the-line* philanthropic distribution of profits, but an *above-the-line* approach to managing their companies in a socially and environmentally responsible way.

The multi-stakeholder approach helps companies align different views and focus on the issues that are central to their earning the "societal license" to operate and innovate. The benefits to a company are obvious – staying tuned to stakeholders' concerns, aligning multiple agendas, prioritizing issues for action; and above all in recruiting and retention – *in attracting the best possible talent to the organization.*

BEST PRACTICES: CORPORATE REPORTING

In interviews for this book, CFOs around the world say: Yes, information on sustainability and a broader set of metrics is useful. No, a single information set does not exist that can specify precisely what all companies should report on. And yes, there is a strong perception that companies that practice transparency will be rewarded.

So, what can CFOs learn from companies that are among the leaders in terms of best practice in reporting? Best-practice company reports:

- Clearly discuss and visually illustrate corporate governance structures for sustainable development. These show the relationship between long-term strategic positioning and shorter-term incremental goal setting.

- Articulate vision and board/governing committee responsibilities for implementation.

- Communicate targets set, and progress made. KPIs are defined with supporting data, targets, and contextual impact summaries.

- Demonstrate and communicate organizational sustainability and the embedding of supporting processes.

- Include detailed information on key stakeholders and engagement practices, supplemented by criteria for success and perceptions of benefits to company/society.

- Provide information and candid coverage of the company's response to controversial industry issues, such as access to essential medicines in developing countries.

- Demonstrate an innovative approach to the societal effects of company products and services.

Coloplast, another Danish company, goes further in identifying, and where possible quantifying, the key activities critical to its strategy. It then goes on to link these activities to expected operating and financial outcomes. The information the company presents far exceeds regulatory reporting requirements.

REPORTING: CUSTOMERS, INNOVATION, PEOPLE
Case study: Coloplast

Since financial information is historical, it's important for Coloplast to report the values on the books correctly to shareholders. However, with the non-financial information that it reports, the company has the opportunity to look at the future – and identify value drivers, which are generally of more interest to shareholders and stakeholders.

Coloplast's customers don't really change from one year to the next – they're extremely loyal. The company manufactures and sells specialized, personal medical devices for health conditions. The company prides itself on being a good corporate citizen. It reports on sustainability and on progress in accordance with the Global Compact initiative.

As part of this process, Coloplast has reported on:

- *Customers – showing excellence in meeting customer expectations. Not only must its products make life easier for the individual user, but the company wants customers to be aware that products were made responsibly in every respect. In the past, it has published graphics on customer care using statistics on complaints, delivery performance, and customer satisfaction.*
- *Employees – demonstrating its ability to attract and develop people who like to work in an active environment where personal commitment is decisive. It publishes information on employee satisfaction, staff turnover, and management deployment.*
- *Innovation – pursuing an offensive patent strategy to protect the company's inventions. Coloplast reports on both patent rights and on new patent applications. Its goal is to have at least 20% of revenues generated by new products – those less than four years old.*

Although the company has for many years published non-financial information, it reviews each year the relevance and value of such information to stakeholders – and makes minor changes in what it reports from one year to the next.

Coloplast uses KPIs throughout the year to manage its business – they're not just published at the end of the year. Of course; reporting in itself doesn't achieve anything; it's what the company actually does that matters! Coloplast realizes that to create shareholder value, it must have a strategy for all stakeholders – how to treat them and how to follow up with action.

This case study refers to Coloplast's adherence to the Global Compact – the world's largest corporate citizenship initiative. The Compact is endorsed by the United Nations and by more than 2,000 participants from over 80 countries – including every industry sector, and organizations ranging from large multinationals in the developed world to small enterprises in the developing world.

The Compact recommends ten principles for companies to adopt in the areas of human rights, labor, the environment, and anti-corruption. Each participant makes a commitment when joining to communicate progress on its implementation of the ten principles – including internal policies it has in place, and impacts or outcomes.

Communication on progress should include a statement of the practical actions taken to show that the participants are living up to their commitment. For example, Paul Skinner, Chairman of Rio Tinto, reported on its social and environmental review:

"As a signatory of the UN Global Compact, we report on our web-based review on the ways in which we conduct our activities and carry out programs to support the principles, including protection of human rights, freedom of association in the workplace, and environmental responsibility."

TRIPLE BOTTOM LINE

Companies that produce an integrated report focus on three areas of impact: (1) financial, (2) environmental, (3) social. This is called the triple bottom line.

The decision to bring everything together in one report is a natural consequence of business performance and sustainability moving ever closer together – and of various stakeholders asking for a wider overview of the business.

Novozymes, the biotech-based world leader in enzymes and micro-organisms, uses nature's own technologies to improve industrial perform-ance and quality. At the same time, the company saves water, energy, raw materials, and waste. Its CFO, Per Mansson, leads the way in integrated corporate reporting and talks about the company's approach.

INTEGRATING ENVIRONMENTAL AND SOCIAL WITH ANNUAL FINANCIALS
Per Mansson, CFO, Novozymes

In the past, the issue of stakeholder relationships used to be about balancing dif-ferent interests – balancing all the different demands, be they from the local com-munity, the government (tax), shareholders, and employees. They all had to "eat" from the same cake.

This notion of stakeholder relationships has subsequently evolved. With the grow-ing influence of non-governmental organizations (NGOs) – such as Greenpeace and Friends of the Earth – and our growth as a company, it's now more about environ-mental issues. The type of technology that we promote involves genetic engineering, and although it is sustainable biologically, it attracts the attention of a wide variety of environmental interests.

Move to formal CSR reporting
It was a natural progression for us to move from providing scientific evidence to NGOs that we are performing satisfactorily in the environmental field to more for-malized reporting. Today, environmental impact is an integral part of our financial reporting. We set stretching external financial targets for the company – similarly, we provide information on both our environmental and social targets.

These non-financial targets are challenging and we take them very seriously. Our management incentives are geared to our meeting environmental and social, as well as financial, targets. In fact, 40% of management's annual bonus is based on non-financial measures!

If anything, I think we at Novozymes are too hard on ourselves when it comes to setting goals. Our productivity indices are now quite difficult to achieve since we have already honed our process efficiency over very many years – for example, in the area of energy consumption.

Every year, we take our improvement gains and reset the marker to zero. This means that achieving our environmental and social targets becomes increasingly tougher too!

Our eco-productivity index accumulates improvement benefits; it can be quite difficult communicating performance on this index to stakeholders. Just because we can't always meet our own annual self-imposed target doesn't mean that we're not doing well over the longer term. Communication on the non-financials is open to greater interpretation than the better understood financials.

Communicating environmental performance

We do 300 investor calls a year to communicate how we're doing. We do not experience a lot of questions on our social and environmental performance. Investors are mainly preoccupied with the financials. When we do get questions on environmental issues, they are mainly from specialized investment fund managers – for example, sustainability or "green" funds. However, investors have made it clear that they regard sustainability, and our performance in this area, as underpinning our "license" to operate.

Investors look at environmental performance as one aspect of risk. Environmental accidents, if they happen as a result of a company's mistake – for example, the pollution of a river leading to killing of fish – are typically reported quickly by the media. If this is a symptom of a much larger problem, it can rapidly escalate and hit a company's share price.

There are huge national differences regarding what is acceptable or not. For example, in little Denmark, we have more than 4 million inhabitants but the food industry slaughters more than 14 million pigs every year! Slaughtering on such a scale creates nitrate pollution, which in turn sets the country's benchmark for what is acceptable in this area. The US has quite a different population, acreage, and benchmarks. What is acceptable, for example, in terms of nitrate pollution will differ.

Integrating the non-financials

We integrate our reporting – we do not, like so many companies, parallel report our financials and non-financials. The driver of this integration is primarily cost. We also avoid the need for unnecessary coordination between what would otherwise be two sets of processes for data collection and reporting. It's also good discipline to have just one source of numbers.

In Denmark, your non-financials must be independently assured. However, the rules for this do vary from one country to another. With integrated reporting, we benefit as a corporate from having just one audit. We call this "one slot" auditing. The external auditors only come in one time slot during a year to do both the financial and non-financial audits.

It's important that the numbers relating to sustainability, be they environmental or social, are subjected to the same "checks and balances" as the accounting numbers. Of course, all this is rather new and there is very little precedent on which to build the necessary controls and assurance processes. So we're really developing these as we go.

There are some company and industry specific sustainability reporting standards – for example, some quite sophisticated guidelines in the chemical industry – but these are not yet universal or generic in application. As the GRI (Global Reporting Initiative) and Global Compact[2] rules evolve, in conjunction with what the auditing firms are doing, we should increasingly have much clearer reporting guidelines and a more consistent basis for inter-company comparison.

Rigor in non-financials

What I am looking for as a CFO in sustainability reporting is the same degree of discipline and rigor in relation to the preparation of the non-financials as we have in our financials. In our headquarters finance function, we consolidate financial and non-financial information in "one go" as part of our highly disciplined and timetabled monthly closing process.

As CFO, I make managers accountable for the quality of their non-financial data and supporting processes. I insist on proper data definitions and standards to ensure that non-financial information is consistent for comparing long-term trends. As with our accounting policies, if changes need to be made in our sustainability policies and definitions, we have a formal change control procedure.

We do have a specialized sustainability and stakeholder department. It provides coordination, ongoing training, and new developments.

We now feel we have greater visibility and focus on the drivers for business improvement. It really does make a difference to our performance. Are we at the end *of a journey? No, we are continuously trying to learn from others – companies like BASF, DSM, and Norske Hydro – and to improve.*

Novozymes believes that corporate governance is about saying what you want to do, keeping your promises, and documenting that you do so. Good corporate governance is also about openness and transparency – providing stakeholders with relevant and valuable insights for their assessment of a business.

The company goes as far as measuring whether it has the best possible management and whether the business is appropriately organized using the following tools:

- Organizational audit – measuring to what degree staffing, and organization overall and in individual units, corresponds to current and future demands.

- Facilitations – measuring to what degree business units live up to stated values, management principles, and basic rules for doing business.

- Triple bottom line reporting – measuring to what degree business units locally, and Novozymes globally, comply with stated economic, environmental, and social targets.

REALITY CHECK

A one-size-fits-all approach to corporate reporting doesn't work for everybody in today's diverse corporate landscape. Corporate reporting needs be realistic in reflecting the dynamics of each industry – and indeed the unique strategies of the individual organizations within and across industries.

Research for this book has led us to recognize the need for a three-tiered model[3] of corporate reporting, as proposed in Figure 10.5.

The proposed model for corporate transparency is on three levels:

- **Tier one**: A set of global generally accepted accounting principles (Global GAAP).

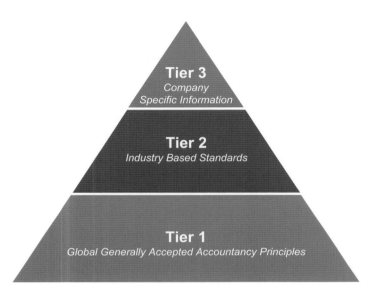

Figure 10.5 *Proposed three-tier model of corporate transparency*
Source: *Building Public Trust – The Future of Corporate Reporting – PricewaterhouseCoopers*

- **Tier two:** Industry-specific standards for measuring and reporting performance, consistently applied and developed by the industries themselves.

- **Tier three**: Company-specific information, including strategy, plans, risk management practices, compensation policies, corporate governance, and performance measures.

TDC is the leading provider of communication solutions in Denmark. It has more than 13 million customers – including landline, mobile, internet, and cable TV. Over the past ten years, the company has developed in an increasingly deregulated and competitive market.

Thorleif Krarup is Chairman of TDC – and an experienced veteran from the banking world. Here, he provides a reality check on this dash to a more "holistic" form of reporting.

ONE SIZE DOES NOT FIT ALL
Thorleif Krarup, Chairman, TDC Group

TDC is in a unique position in Denmark – we're a former monopoly and the incumbent player in telecommunications in the country. A little over half our profits come from Denmark, the rest from outside the country. When we were privatized, we retained a large customer base and our infrastructure.

In Denmark, the way we run our company receives a lot of attention from politicians, the public, and our competitors. We are therefore very interested in TDC's image and the perceptions of employees and customers in our domestic market. Our reporting inside Denmark is holistic: it covers both non-financial and financial information.

Dynamic CSR reporting
TDC executes its social responsibilities first and foremost by providing new technology and innovative services as the basis for the information society in Denmark. We want to pioneer environmental initiatives – for example, waste minimization and recovery – and create an inspiring and stimulating working environment.

Corporate citizenship means a lot to me, but I don't believe you should go over the top on the reporting. It's what you do that counts, not how much you write about it! We do discuss our social policies and responsibilities once a year with our board. These discussions do play a role in how we run the company but they have to be placed in perspective.

We recently incorporated CSR data in our annual report. But it's easy to lose sight of what's essential. The financial community now requires very focused reporting. "One size" does not fit all!

We now keep our annual report focused on financial performance and release our CSR reports separately on the Internet. CSR initiatives move so quickly that we feel that the web is the right communications medium.

The investment community is now global. The multiplicity of standards we have today has to be confusing for both investors and companies alike. The US voice will probably prevail, but if you want international investment, you have to comply with international regulation.

I believe investors will call for greater global accounting standards integration and also for more non-financial information. From my banking experience, I know that customers are the source of value and risk management is key. Together, they are of vital importance to investors. This is no different in the telecommunications industry.

In summary, I would encourage the drive by regulators to ensure that companies include non-financial information and commentary on strategic performance in their external reporting. The companies that do this most effectively should get the best share price!

There has been extensive research to identify practical and effective solutions for navigating the proliferation of new standards and stakeholder expectations – and to do so in a way that supports performance objectives, sustains value, and protects a corporation's reputation.

Increasingly, companies like TDC are saying that assessing the impact of business integrity, ethics, and values does not detract from performance but, in fact, enhances business performance when appropriately integrated throughout an organization.

In the past, most companies have viewed governance, risk, and compliance as discrete activities managed as separate functions. More often than not, they have tucked them away in a variety of pockets across their organizations. This approach has resulted in accountability and communication gaps, as well as redundancies and confusion. As stakeholder demands for increased integrity climb, these gaps can sharply affect business value.

To attain a level of *integrity-driven performance*, organizations need to address four fundamental enablers:

1 The change to a *culture* of business integrity and ethical values.

2 Integrating into *core business processes* their approaches to governance, risk, and compliance.

3 The capability to measure performance and calculate value through the right *metrics and dashboards*.

4 The use of *technology* to leverage overall effectiveness and improve efficiency.

A model for integrating governance, risk, and compliance is offered in Figure 10.6.

The CFO should consider formalizing relevant aspects of governance, risk, and compliance activities into a corporate *code of conduct* for enterprise-wide implementation – a reality check on company behavior. Typically, a comprehensive "code of conduct," such as that developed by BP, would include:

- The company's commitment to integrity – personal commitment from the top to the bottom of the organization, and the duties of those who supervise others.

- The company's group compliance and ethics program.

- Health, safety, security, and environmental policies.

- Employees – fair treatment, equal opportunity, respect, and confidentiality.

Figure 10.6   *Effective integration of governance, risk, and compliance*

- Business partners – gifts and entertainment, conflicts of interest, competition and anti-trust, trade restrictions, money laundering.

- Governments and communities – bribery and corruption, political activity, and the process of engagement.

- Company assets and financial integrity.

The success of implementing a code of conduct, *and making it stick*, depends on the right tone from the top, embedding the code into business processes at all levels, and the quality of the monitoring – ensuring that consequences for violation are enforced!

Some companies are beginning to publish combined reports on how they're doing in relation to these sensitive areas, including the number of cases of violations of their codes of conduct.

BECOMING THE GOOD CORPORATION!

Finally, we bring together the various themes – of sustainability, stakeholders, ethics, corporate reporting, and the *triple bottom line* – into one overarching theme: "the good corporation!"

GoodCorporation Ltd[5] is a company that has developed a Standard for responsible business practice in conjunction with the Institute of Business Ethics. Performance against the Standard can be independently assessed to systematically measure and improve corporate responsibility practices.

The Standard covers six areas of "good practice" – affecting employees, customers, suppliers, shareholders, the environment, and the community. Within each of these areas is a core set of business principles underpinned by day-to-day management practices that can be used to assess how well the organization works in reality. Examples of good business principles within the six stakeholder groups are:

1 Employees – *"the organization encourages employees to develop skills and progress in their careers."*

2 Customers – *"the organization does not offer or accept bribes or substantial favors."*

3 Suppliers and contractors – "*the organization pays suppliers and sub-contractors in accordance with agreed terms.*"

4 Community and environment – "*the organization aims to be sensitive to local community cultural, social, and economic needs.*"

5 Shareholders and financiers – "*the organization aims to protect shareholders' funds, manage risks, and ensure that funds are used as agreed.*"

GoodCorporation uses an independent assessment process that looks at four levels of evidence for each individual practice that supports the business principles. An independent assessor checks that:

1 A policy exists (policy documents are reviewed).

2 A system is in place to implement the policy (systems are examined).

3 Records exist that show that the systems works in practice (sample of records is reviewed).

4 Stakeholders, when asked, agree that the system works and is fair (interviews are held with employees, customers, suppliers, shareholders, community and environmental groups).

By measuring stakeholder feedback confidentially and systematically, assessors gather useful information for the company to help it improve stakeholder relationships in a controlled way. Using the evidence, the assessor awards grades against a five-point scale:

1 **Fail** – there is no policy or system, or it has largely broken down.

2 **Minor non-compliance** – there is a policy and system, but they do not always work.

3 **Observation** – there is a policy and system that works, but potential improvements have been identified.

4 **Merit** – the policy and system work well.

5 **Commendation** – the policy and system are examples of best practice.

The assessor will comment on the policies and practices where they meet the standard, or where potential improvements can be made. The company being assessed receives a report measuring its performance against previous years and current benchmarks. These ratings provide powerful management information used as a basis for action.

An illustrative extract of the summarized results of an assessment, by stakeholder group, is provided in Figure 10.7.

The results are confidential. It is up to the organization to decide whether or not it wants to publish the results in both internal and external communications.

Says Leo Martin, Director of GoodCorporation Ltd:

"This is not about social conduct, this is about all aspects of business behavior. GoodCorporation is about measuring what had previously been considered the 'fluffy stuff' and turning it into concrete business behaviors.

"The market has become saturated with non-financial reports, and they don't mean very much. The glossy reports on CSR will die away and what will be left will be the serious communications. More finance people are getting involved in corporate responsibility. The CFO is often seen as the change agent. Company law can't always be backward looking; it's starting to encompass the broader context – the wider relationship with employees and customers, and the company's future positioning."

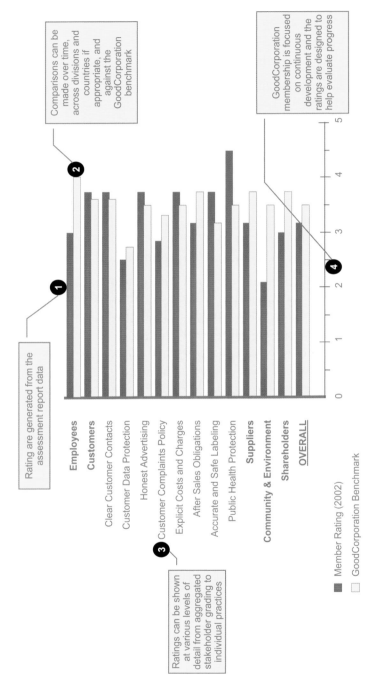

Figure 10.7 *GoodCorporation: illustrative assessment summary*

STRAIGHT FROM THE CFO

- **Lead with corporate responsibility**

  As CFO, do you lead your company's corporate responsibility initiative? Consider the costs and potential downside to earnings of corporate "irresponsibility." Make the business case: link CR with shareholder value.

- **Ask stakeholders what *they* want**

  Give stakeholders the information they need. Set out the principal drivers of company performance both in the past *and in the future*. Investors want to see the broader aspects of corporate performance through "management's eyes."

- **Broaden your corporate reporting**

  Determine the environmental and social context when evaluating the quality and sustainability of financial performance information. Test your key indicators against industry benchmarks. Communicate targets set and progress made. Provide candid coverage of the company's response to controversial industry issues.

- **Consider the triple bottom line**

  Evaluate the benefits of combining environmental, social, and profit information in one report. Are there incentives for achieving the non-financials? Take a corporate reporting reality check – a "one-size-fits-all" integration approach is not for everyone!

- **Link ethics and shareholder value**

  Define your fundamental prerequisites for *good* business ethics. Identify and prioritize relevant business ethics issues. Have you integrated governance, risk, and compliance? Implement a culture for *integrity-driven* performance. Follow up: report on ethics internally and externally.

- **Become a "good corporation"**

> Benchmark your organization against "good practices." Interview stakeholders: employees, customers, and suppliers. Are your policies clear? Do records exist? Do stakeholders agree that your practices work and are fair?

ACKNOWLEDGMENTS

PricewaterhouseCoopers Trends (2005) *Good Practices in Corporate Reporting.*

REFERENCES

1 Helle Bank Jorgensen (2005) *Good Business Ethics and Non-Financial Reporting*, NVIR.

2 Mark Brownlie (2005) *A Practical Guide to Communication on Progress*, The Global Compact.

3 Samuel A. DiPiazza Jnr, Robert G. Eccles (2002) *Building Public Trust, The Future of Corporate Reporting*, Wiley.

4 Leo Martin, GoodCorporation Ltd (2004) *Corporate Social Responsibility, From Principles to Profit*, BBC Worldwide Learning.

Index